Praise for Peter Coviello

For *Vineland Reread*

"Coviello—nearly alone among contemporary literary critics—joins in the project of his objects, making of them something more wonderful than they would be without his attention. We should be so lucky to be read by him."

JORDY ROSENBERG, author of *Confessions of the Fox*

"There's no smarter or more generous guide than Peter Coviello to the experience of loving and living together with books and music."

MATTHEW HART, author of *Extraterritorial*

"Coviello writes with a generous spirit and vibrant clarity. . . . *Vineland Reread* is also a primer on how one can be both judicious and joyful in the act of criticism; rigorous on the one hand, but brave enough to double down on your affections, too. It shows us how to love a work of art honestly, communally. We need readers and thinkers like Peter Coviello now more than ever."

SAM LIPSYTE, author of *Hark* and *The Ask*

"A penetrating and nuanced work of literary criticism . . . Coviello's astute and passionate analysis is a pleasure to read."

Publishers Weekly

"An account of literary experience that is as ethically and politically urgent as it is sparkling, vital, and fun to read."

GLORIA FISK, author of *Orhan Pamuk and the Good of World Literature*

Is There God after Prince?

PETER COVIELLO

Is There God after Prince?

DISPATCHES FROM
AN AGE OF LAST THINGS

The University of Chicago Press
Chicago and London

The University of Chicago Press, Chicago 60637
The University of Chicago Press, Ltd., London
© 2023 by Peter Coviello
Published 2023
Printed in the United States of America

32 31 30 29 28 27v26 25 24 23   1 2 3 4 5

ISBN-13: 978-0-226-82807-7 (cloth)
ISBN-13: 978-0-226-82808-4 (paper)
ISBN-13: 978-0-226-82809-1 (e-book)
DOI: https://doi.org/10.7208/chicago/9780226828091.001.0001

Library of Congress Cataloging-in-Publication Data

Names: Coviello, Peter, author.
Title: Is there God after Prince? : dispatches from an age of last
things / Peter Coviello.
Description: Chicago : The University of Chicago Press, 2023. |
Includes bibliographical references and index.
Identifiers: LCCN 2023002894 | ISBN 9780226828077 (cloth) |
ISBN 9780226828084 (paperback) | ISBN 9780226828091 (ebook)
Subjects: LCSH: Popular culture—United States. | Popular music—
United States—History and criticism.
Classification: LCC E169.12 .C66 2023 | DDC 306.0973—dc23/
eng/20230127
LC record available at https://lccn.loc.gov/2023002894

♾ This paper meets the requirements of ANSI/NISO Z39.48-1992
(Permanence of Paper).

. . . as Voltaire said, incantations will destroy a flock of sheep if administered with a certain quantity of arsenic.

GEORGE ELIOT, *Middlemarch*

Contents

Praisesongs and Descants

Say you're staring at a screen. Say that there you drowsily lie, phone-entranced, a glassy vacancy settling in behind your eyes. Say a fogged numbness of spirit has come creeping over you, coiled itself into your vertebrae, your lungs. And say this is how, one dim shut-in night, you run hard into a video of a band playing a new song of theirs, live in the studio of a West Coast radio station.

It all unfolds in the familiar way. The singer steps to the mic, delivers a few verses—*Do you remember the moment you finally did something about it?* is how she starts—and there it is: that small inward flutter. Guitars, a few silvery chords, and something prickles along the surface of your skin. A synapse or two misfires. There's a hitch, an infinitesimal jump in your blood, and would you look at that? Now you're awake.

* * *

So there's a very great Cincinnati band called Wussy, and they have a very great song called "Teenage Wasteland" which on a summer day in 2014 they performed at KEXP radio in Seattle, and dear god you should watch that video right now. I mean it, truly. You may be like, *Yeah, that is really not my kind of thing*, which, you know, fair enough—who am I to tell you that's wrong? But listen: it maybe just might be.

"Teenage Wasteland," as you might surmise from its winking title, is a song about growing up marooned in the pale and lonely expanses of the American middlewest and finding that, through the blessings of FM radio, you have fallen into sudden catapulted love with, that's right, the Who. I could say a lot more about that— about the forthright dorkiness of stanning, in the extremely post-punk year of our Lord 2014, an outfit as boomerish and rock-radio musty as the Who. Or how it's less a song about being *rescued* by rock-n-roll than it is about the glory of discovering, in some con-cussive burst of distortion and frazzled noise, an answering reso-nance to your own dreary teenaged misery. Believe me, I could go on. But none of that really matters.

What matters happens in the space of about forty-five sec-onds, and these are the moments I want you to see. The singer of this song is Lisa Walker—native of Muncie, Indiana, transplant to Cincinnati—and because this is an in-studio video we are po-sitioned right there beside her, in medium close-up, throughout. She looks more or less like the rest of the band, except not a dude: unfussy, a little unkempt, a punk but not insisting on it. She wears a frayed T-shirt you might wake up in, guitar slung across it.

But a few moments into the track and Lisa Walker, of Muncie, Indiana, is, you would have to say, transformed.

One minute they're just a band. But in the next we see that a sort of concentrated transport has gathered in Lisa Walker, that she has begun to address us as if from some neighboring di-mension, alive with extraworldly frequencies. The song car-ries on around her, swells toward another chorus, and there's a quick cut to the drummer (who, with stolid drummer chill, looks *entirely unbothered*), and when we look back she, Lisa Walker, has shrugged off her studio headphones, so that they come to rest pinning her hair to her shoulders, which we see her shaking free.

It's hard to imagine a smaller, more incidental gesture. *A woman shakes out her hair, sings into a microphone.* Here, though? Here it feels detonating, *volcanic*, like a new-turned page in the great glossary of rock-n-roll euphoria. Because what now comes shining straight through the person of Lisa Walker, of Muncie, Indiana, is something the religious-minded among us might just call exaltation. She goes on singing about misery, loneliness, the radio, yes. But it's all undergone a fantastic alchemical transformation, so that what we behold is something else again. Noted punk progenitor Jane Austen has another name for what transpires here—*joy*, she calls it, *senseless joy*[1]—and so entirely does this possess unkempt, unfussy Lisa Walker that the room, the song, everything that presents itself to your senses absolutely shimmers with it: an invincible radiance.

You should watch it.

For my part, I would go on to watch Wussy playing "Teenage Wasteland" with the obligatory juvenile repetitiveness, my desire for this scene of low-budget rapture each time satisfied but not fulfilled—posting it, reposting it, sending it off in texts and emails with temperate headings like "Five-Minute Argument for Being Alive" and "As Miraculous as the Backstage Stevie Nicks Video." Cheapjack confections like songs and records should not hold this much, you'd think. That they so routinely do is surely one of the persisting graces of mortal life.

But those enchanted seconds—they're not even the whole of it. Because before the song drifts out to its ending Lisa Walker says the strangest thing, something you would maybe not expect to hear from a person in the midst of such shuddering triumph.

For one short breath, she says, *it sounds like the world is ending*, and goddamn it if she isn't right.

*   *   *

Encounters such as this stand at the soft, pierceable heart of the essays assembled here. They pivot, in their differing ways, around matters of love, sorrow, and what such things might come to when it sounds so much like the world is ending. Each, after its fashion, wonders what it can mean to love trifling things like books and records, and to do so even now, in the midst of worlds so glutted with calamity—wreckage that keeps scaling, with vertiginous rapidity, from the sadly personal out to the political, the *planetary*, then abruptly back again. Each, after its fashion, tries to get some hold on just what it is that transpires in the charged space between our wearied workaday selves and the beguiling little objects that, on the better days, keep us attached to life.

An attachment to life: One uncheerful presumption in what follows is that precisely that quantity is perhaps more faltering, more inconstant, than we like to admit. But another is that things like books and records, even when they cannot fortify that attachment, are for many of us a way of taking its measure, of calibrating it out to the last fluctuating decimal. And that—as you will find me saying a lot here, often in the key of a startled, semibewildered joyousness not at all far from Lisa Walker's own—is a long human way from nothing.

I think of it like this: There are the worlds that make us, full of malignity and avarice, exploitation and struggle and halting moments of reprieve. And alongside these, there are the worlds we try to make, patched together out of scraps of this and that—texts and playlists, sex and talk, ardor and sorrow tracing their tight circuits around our lives. A sustained implicit proposition of this book is that one thing criticism might do—or try to do—is chart the ways certain cherished things (songs, poems, movies, etc.) fold these worlds together and, for a blazing instant or two, make them sensible to one another. That dizzying folding-together, you could say, is the secret subject of these essays, as much as any heartbreak ballad, radiant passage of prose, or Joni song.

*   *   *

Which is to say these essays form, cumulatively, their own quiet brief on behalf of "criticism." Or, at least, of criticism in a certain mode: promiscuous in attention, prone to overheating, in the agitated vernacular, and wrought round with the interwoven dilemmas of worldly grief, local sorrow, ordinary blindsiding joy. These are pieces that approach a jumbled array of objects chiefly by setting them back into the scenes in which they were found—these range hectically from the private (a kid's graduation, a divorce) to the exceedingly not-private (an election, a pandemic)—and speaking about them in the offhand idioms that circulated there. You will accordingly find a lot of room in here for immoderate devotion, lachrymose receptiveness, laughter unto illness, all sorts of sputtering wonder—as well as some boredom, some irritation, the lesser varieties of outrage, disbelief, disaffection. That, give or take, is the prevailing mode.

What follow, in other words, are *essays*: shortish bursts of ardor and appraisal, intertwining with life.

It perhaps goes without saying that this is not the only conceivable approach to the world of culture. (Having *feelings* about art, the polemicists among us might insist, is possibly the least interesting thing you can do with it.) Where, you might ask, is the levelheaded objectivity, the measured lucidity of detachment? To which I can only reply: *not here*. I pursue these different, rather more unplacid clarities not because they make for some absolute standard. As a person who also writes criticism in a more professionally academic mode, I can readily attest: they do not. Writing of this sort can claim for itself, it's true, a whole host of authorizing antecedents. For me, these involve everything from scholarly fare like Eve Sedgwick's *Tendencies* and Hortense Spillers's *Black, White, and in Color*, Seamus Heaney's *Preoccupations*, and Adam Phillips's *On Flirtation* to galvanizing works like *Flyboy in the Buttermilk* by Greg Tate, *Air Guitar* by Dave Hickey, *H Is for Hawk* by Helen MacDonald, newer writing by Jessica Hopper, Hanif Abdurraqib, Anne Boyer, and Teju Cole, and many, many another excursion into essayistic criticism. All these writers mean a lot to me, as thinkers and stylists both, and you'll find their mixed impress throughout the work that follows.

For all that, though, I suspect the nearer truth may be that such preferences as these essays display—their refusals to pretend not to know what heartbreak is, say, or bliss—have their roots elsewhere. You could think of it, I suppose, as a kind of faith-keeping: just one small way of staying true to those noisy, voluble, homegrown scenes of appraisal and dispute where—perhaps like some of you—I first learned what it might mean to care about books and records with a prodigal, a lifewide devotion. Such scenes take up a good deal of airtime in the pieces gathered here, though I can tell you right now this is not because they weren't in many respects preposterous, because of course they were, prolifically so. But then that's so much of what love does, isn't it? High up among its metamorphic endowments, *it makes us preposterous.*

If I'm loyal even still to those bygone passages, it can only be because they solidified in me the dim intuition that there might yet be a great, great many understudied things for "criticism" to grapple with, no matter their ill-suitedness to scholarly dispassion, the chilly rigor of abstraction. I can list them off, by now, like a kind of catechism: the weird and devout fidelities our objects brew up in us, say; the jolting ways they adhere to the world—or, with uncanny precision, diagnose our stuckness within it; the talk-drunk intimacies we build up around them, made of praise and invective, shock and delight, all the substrates of pain and grief and vaulting untempered love.

No sensible person would say these are the *only* human things worth caring about, in art or otherwise. Fair warning: in what follows, they are a lot of what I care about.

*   *   *

I should be clear, though. All this jangled susceptibility and amateurish besottedness: none of it means to suggest that things we love in this hyped-up way are therefore, in any especially large-spirited sense, *good* for us. I am not much interested, I mean, in producing a vision of art or of culture as some sort of, I don't know, heartening moral analgesic, a saving bounty to our lives, the social order, the cold and calculating hypercapitalized world. I will say a lot of overheated and low-key indefensible things in the pages ahead about pop songs, sentences, flickering pixelated images. I will not say that.

I hope you can see why. I get the reasons we are sometimes seduced into making a sort of false-positive case for the planetarily redemptive virtues of the things we love, I do. (In a world ready to dismiss out of hand any but the most instrumentally, instantaneously profitable modes of thought and imagination, it can be hard not to.) And yet. Having spent a number of years teaching the children of the enormously and bookishly wealthy, I can tell you with some authority that there are few things the winning classes are readier to believe in than the broad, vague uplifting-ness of culture—of poetry, story, song, what Vladimir Nabokov (or rather, his furiously ironized mouthpiece, *Lolita*'s Humbert Humbert) calls "the melancholy and very local palliative of artic-ulate art."[2] Nobody, I think, needs to have that particular object of secular faith burnished into greater gleaming brightness. Not in this world, not in *our* world, which daily brokers such unstrain-ing peace between an incomprehensible vastness of human harm and, among the ranks of the less-harmed, an eager presumption of the general giving goodness of art. The torturer's horse, in Auden's great poem, may yet scratch his innocent behind against the tree. The torturer himself is by now as likely as not listening to Wilco or, I don't know, Lana Del Ray. Maybe Drake.

The point of which is not that one is therefore obliged to be somehow *against* art or culture or their many-spangled artifacts, which at any rate is not a position you're likely to imagine me tak-ing as you read through the pieces gathered here. When I make this killjoy case to my students, I will sometimes put it like this: *We do not always love what is good for us.* Grown-ups, I think, know this, or should. Have you ever embarked upon a consuming, ludi-crous, extremely ill-advised love affair? Then you do not need me to spell it out for you. Desire, as you'll have learned, is not a uni-formly improving aspect of the world—and would be a meaner, pettier, less cyclonic thing if it were. Pretending that this is not so, pretending that what we love not only makes us better but makes *the world* better, seems a bit of after-school-specialish prevarica-tion I'd like to do without.

The things we love may be startling, rapture-making, unravel-ing; their bare existence may at times feel to us like a living mir-acle, as much of grace as we are likely to encounter in our broken mortal span. I believe more or less all of this, as these essays gregariously attest. But none of it means these things do much for the world as such, beyond the small, small, small virtue of arming us with unaccustomed ways to think about it. This, I will continually insist, is not nothing. But it is awfully, awfully, awfully close.

*   *   *

And, as it turns out, closer every day. It's here that we come to the preoccupation that threads meanderingly through these essays, growing less and less implicit as we go. *Is There God after Prince?* is a book about loving things in the shadow of a felt, looming disaster—in the grain of an *endstrickenness* that every twenty-first-century day has made harder and harder to ignore. A pulsing undercurrent of these pieces accords, I think, with a pulsing undercurrent of this past decade, and it is to do principally with an impending, ever less imaginary series of comings-to-an-end. "Twenty thousand years of this," the TV comedian sings in a ballad about the despoiled human world, "*seven more to go.*" That's a usefully compact formulation, but you needn't take his word for it. In cultures high and low, across art, theory, commerce, you name it, a fascination with the terminal has found its quavering voice. How could it not? Just look around, look up. A West Coast friend texted me last year. "My outdoor pandemic haircut got canceled," he wrote, "because of the fires." Uh, what? "Yeah, it was too dark to see." We have all gotten texts like this.

People, you will have noticed, have lots of ways of getting into relation to this environing collapsingness, of feeling out its contours, assessing its shifting atmospheric pressures in the weather of everyday life. Maybe your angle is news-based, Twitter-enhanced; maybe you think a lot about the post-2008 contraction of life into the clarified ranks of the obscenely secure on one side and, on the other, everybody else, clawing their way through their apportioned quantity of desperation, half-glimpsed futurelessness, proximity to disaster. Maybe you spend a lot of time worrying about the queasy listing, there in the orchestration of markets quaintly referred to as "global governance," toward democracy-flavored versions of what, not that long ago, you'd have just called fascism. ("These are the hallmarks of security-state dystopias, yes, but have you considered our robust streaming platforms?") Or maybe you live your life near kids—whose ceaseless new beginnings cannot help but feel like endings, some of them quite entirely heartbreaking, to the grown-ups around them—and this has scrambled all your signals, made an end to any clarity you once might have had about the matter of ends. Maybe you smell smoke in the air.

And yet here you are—still reading, still dropping the needle, still telling your friends about this one great thing you saw and *are you fucking kidding me you haven't seen it yet?* Like I say, this reading, and listening, and watching, this clamorous needy attachment—none of it is nothing. These essays are surpassingly interested in the thing that, however barely, it is. And in what can be made from it.

*   *   *

One final note: Laced in here are the lineaments of a capsule autobiography. You'll find a person for whom the 1990s—his twenties—were important; a person who came to be invested in things like novels and poems, as well as literary criticism and even literary theory, with the same derailing intensity of devotion he had first found in the vicinity of songs and records, and who (like many another in his aging-white-dude demographic) came to think of them in mixed-up, combinatory, densely cross-wired terms. You'll find, too, a person whose grown-up life some time ago ran quite suddenly aground—spectacularly, if unexceptionally—in ways that involved home, children, "parenthood" in fractured conjugations. (Kids, you'll discover, take up a great deal of consideration in what follows.) You will find a person who then stumbled his way into a wider arena of happiness than, at one sad time, he would've said was at all likely.

All of this is true, or true enough. *I am the man; I snuffled; I was there.*

What you'll also find, though, in essays that zigzag across the cultural landscape of the last decade-plus, is a person engaged in a different sort of project, one adjacent but not identical to the humdrum turnings of his life. I just mean that you'll find someone working out, phrase by phrase, how to sound like himself—to make a voice, translated to the page, that speaks like he speaks, and not just when he's standing behind a lectern. *Is There God after Prince?* pursues a conjoined interest in ardor and endstrickenness into a multitude of corners and cul-de-sacs: into songs by the Jackson 5 and SZA and Pavement, Phoebe Bridgers and Gladys Knight, writings by Sam Lipsyte and Paula Fox and Paul Beatty, movies like *The Shining*, shows like *The Sopranos*, as well as videos, poems, pop artifacts of more or less every kind. It hopes to test out some of what criticism might be—how much battered sorrow and radiant delight it can get into one place—in a time of frightful slow-moving collapse, an era of Last Things.

That's it. You couldn't call it a "method," I don't think, and certainly not a program. More like an unforesworn weakness for praisesongs, descants, whatever gets you through the night.

Talk, Talk

You know how it begins. You're out to dinner or on the subway. Maybe you're on the phone. Most probably, you're in a bar. And out of the loose talk and ambient sociability there emerges a sharper drift, or just a frontal assertion: "The new Los Campesinos! record is absolutely their best." Or, "If you don't love 'Elvis Presley Blues' with all your human soul I'm not sure we should be friends." Or, "Maybe Vanessa Beecroft needs to fucking stop."

You know the rest. What happens then, if you're lucky, is something between a bar fight and a love song—an aria, sung in multiple voices, of disproportion, implacability, and devotion. Thomas Pynchon gets the texture of this kind of talk exactly right in recalling an exchange between a teenaged punk-rocker and his girlfriend's dad:

> "Hey, so, Mr. Wheeler," Isaiah said at last, "how you doing?"
>
> "What's this 'Mr. Wheeler,' what happened to 'You lunch meat, 'sucker'?" this line having climaxed their last get-together, when, from a temperate discussion of musical differences, feelings had escalated into the rejection, on a quite broad scale, of most of one another's values.[1]

On a quite broad scale. What's right here perhaps above anything else is the sense that what is up for grabs when we fight about what we love, and why we love it, is *value*: the terms through which we appraise the world, and do our best to render it habitable. Dave Hickey, a writer at his best when tracking "the way people talk about loving things, which things, and why," calls this the "street-level negotiation of value," and the ardor, inventiveness, and real-time agility of these negotiations are only a few of the reasons to love them.[2] (We might love them too because such talk is also, often, a way of actually sustaining our most cherished intimacies in and through conditions—temporal, geographic—that tend to erode them, and of turning those loves, their totems and their histories, into shareable language. But that's another story.)

So is what happens there—the hyped-up talk, the denunciation, the only half-unmeaning hyperbole—something we can recognize as criticism? Here is all that I have to say: we should.

There are, after all, right now, a number of ways of dismissing this kind of talk. It does not cure cancer. It is not rocket science. It makes claims no more verifiable than unverifiable and does indeed partake of the kinds of self-indulgence and self-delightedness for which the bourgeois classes are known. But charges of pretension and complacency are not the worst of it. To the degree that we understand fighting about bands, or artists, or authors to savor of a kind of in-group clannishness—a disciplinary policing of what is hip—then to just that degree does a now curiously modish critical vocabulary inherited largely from Pierre Bourdieu come to seem, in a twinkling, apposite. It is Bourdieu, on this reading, who reminds us that in certain precincts of the mercilessly capitalized world the choice of objects on which to bestow one's devotion, particularly aesthetic objects, is in essence a strategy of distinction, a way to insist upon one's own exalted place in a social hierarchy whose material ungroundedness—whose evanescence and immateriality—does nothing to diminish its viciousness. Many a contemporary arraignment of the hipster, and of the urban plague of his skinny-jeaned brethren, falls out in exactly these terms.

And yet and yet. I'm ready to concede at least part of the point about the debilitating snark of so much object-love. ("You don't like tUnE-yArDs? Peasant.") We all know people like this, people who expend great quantities of capital in these economies of cool and who use their enthusiasms, or the performance of them, like a carving knife. The art world, it is fair to say, is no stranger to the species. (Nor for that matter is the academy. Or Brooklyn. Or Shoreditch. Etc.) But in truth I have no real heart for this kind of quasi-sociological hipster-hate. When I see kids bedecked in the accoutrements of one emerging microtrend or other, I do not, I confess, experience so immediate and blinding an access of rage that I am forced to reach, gunslingerlike, for my copy of *Distinction*. Perhaps indefensibly, what I see are kids who love things, and who are using what languages are at their disposal (sartorial, affective, sometimes steeply monetized and sometimes not) to give that love some kind of heft and shape and articulacy. Those languages aren't my languages—like most of my friends I prefer complex syntax and bar-fighting: this is why we are friends—but I don't dismiss out of hand the latent acuities of their love, whatever its object and whatever its mode.

Those affectations and my preferred kind of talk share, after all, a submerged and, I think, wholly estimable premise. This is simply that loving things, loving them articulately and combatively, is itself a style of engagement not a lot less rich for being as informal, uncredentialed, and overheated as it is. You come to that scene of talk not to push people away—not unless you're an *asshole*—but to *collaborate*, and to collaborate particularly in a project I regard as a kind of world-making: of converting the bursts of joy you experience in the presence of certain objects into usable terms, a vocabulary made of parsings and principles you might then use to grapple with a difficult, broken world. (To know why you prefer the Minutemen's "Doctor Wu" to Steely Dan's, or Sam Cooke's "Bring It On Home to Me" to Van Morrison's, might be to know a lot about the kind of world you want to make.) We invest ourselves in those scenes because they're places where we learn how to contest first-order questions of value, yes. But they are also where we get to insist, with the cyclonic force of all that enthusiasm and invective, that despite the vast mediating machinery of new-millennial capital and multiplying systems of instantaneous commodification, what we love *matters*, and matters in ways that, because they are unstable and unpredetermined, must be fought over, and over, and over.

I suspect everyone who cherishes slight, useless things enough to devote such disproportionate quantities of life to them can recall the experience of falling hopelessly in love with a song (or sculpture, or book, or whathaveyou), and knows without having to be reminded what that inflooding sense of captivation is like. I don't mean to imply that criticism needs to be rooted in some account of that sensation, or that engagement with any object must always return to, say, the sense of raw exhilarated wonder before the fact that so inexhaustible and singular a thing *actually exists in the world*—however transforming that feeling has been for many of us. Nor am I louche enough to suggest that criticism ought to end up there, determined to give words to those bright intensities. But I do think work that severs itself too utterly from these wellsprings of responsiveness runs the risk of devolving, pretty swiftly, into what Hickey calls "term papers and advertising."[3] And so, like Joni says, if you want me I'll be in the bar.

PART I

Sounds

Ask someone who is truly obsessed why *they feel that way. They will sputter, they will feel you are interrogating their private world, they may spout a list of reasons, but ultimately they can't fully explain it. Obsession has an irrational or subrational heart. It is a bit like falling in love, I imagine.*

DANA SPIOTTA, *Stone Arabia*

Is There God after Prince?

It's the Maine midwinter, hardfrozen and dark.

I'm trying to live through it as best I can, but it is not going entirely well. I am, in the first place, a newish arrival, which means that I am considerably less fluent in the protocols of madness-deflection than I might be. But I am also, in my newness, another kind of unsteadied. I have been actually employed, as an actual professor at an actual college, for about six months, and not for a moment have I been free of the sense of an imminent, disastrous *exposure*. Perhaps feeling an obvious fraud is a function of being in your first job. Whatever the case (and whatever my crosscutting elation at having any kind of job at all), adult professional life is for me a precarious sort of performance, brittle and unconvincing.

I am twenty-seven years old. It is, inevitably, 1999.

But then, from deep in some yet-unfrozen reservoir of optimism, a decision comes to me, a fateful decision. I decide that I will have a party. I decide that I will have a *dance* party. I decide to send a mass email to every person I've met and to many others I haven't.

It reads, "Please come to my apartment on Cleaveland Street for a party celebrating the 15th ANNIVERSARY OF PURPLE RAIN. Any and all non-minors welcome."

And so, on a February night at the back end of the Clinton era, a bunch of souls wintering out in a sleepy New England college town conspire to beguile an evening with whiskey, low-key drugs, and many hours of in-house dancing, in an underfurnished and rapidly overheating living room, books piled in listing towers, boots and coats stacked in a jumble in the corners. I remember looking around me, seeing even the starchiest of my daylight colleagues and fledgling friends now sweat-soaked and giddy, teetering toward a Prince-induced euphoria, and thinking, *Oh, I can live here.*

Among the semi-acquaintances to show that night, one makes a special impression. She is the friend of friends and has come, decked and ready to dance, despite the fact that she is, I know, in the latter days of what has been a hard, slow-moving divorce. Her ex must have the kids for the night. I tell her I'm glad she came.

Later I will say, *You walked in. I woke up.*

For years and years afterward, every midwinter, we'd throw dance parties, though these were a few blocks away, in the home she and I and her girls made for ourselves after we were married. Our friends knew these as Purple Rain Nights or, more simply, Prince Parties.

*   *   *

A friend in England scored tickets a few summers ago to one of those impromptu solo gigs Prince had taken to performing. Despite what was for me a near fatal onset of envy, or perhaps in order to express it, I wrote her a series of badgering emails. Tell me about the show! I said. *What was it like?*

Her response was memorable.

"It was unlanguageable," she said.

"Also, I think I might be pregnant."

In a similar, sadder way, this too—yesterday's awful, blindsiding tear in the fabric of things—is unlanguageable.

There is of course the routinely undoing power of grief, in response to deaths no matter how mediated—it is, god knows, an impressive quantity. And there is, too, the familiar drift of our metaphors, in sorrow, out toward the terrain of measure and measurelessness: the too-huge influence, the too-many songs, the too-proliferating memories, the too vast territories of joy.

I am with you, fellow-grievers, in all this. I found out in a coffeeshop, texting with a friend. I stood for about ten minutes on the corner of Clark and Foster, weepy and paralyzed, unable to imagine what to do next.

Was there eating lunch, after Prince? After Prince, would we talk on phones? Take trains?

Was there sex after Prince?

*   *   *

I want to say a small word about this, our newest burden of the unassimilabile.

I want to say that Prince is hard to grieve because he is, in an only barely not literal sense, divine.

I want to say that the categories that most attend him, and that the light of his person illuminates, are not those made by the hands of men.

I want to say that for nearly forty years Prince has served as perhaps our greatest explicitly religious visionary, the one most devoted not only to God but to heterodoxy, heresy, blasphemy—to all that, in these latter days of privatized belief and well-bred "spirituality," lends to the realm of religion whatever ongoing vitality it has.

I want to say that Prince is the least secular rockstar we have ever known.

*   *   *

The greatest sentence I ever heard spoken about Prince was spoken by my friend Gus, who was on a panel discussing Prince's soul-blinding cover of Joni Mitchell's "Case of You." To get the at the magic of the song, Gus suggested, you had to understand—and the song would instruct you in this—that so much of the shivery erotic power of Prince depends upon a kind of *inconceivability*, a sense of Prince as not so much a being apart but as a being at once here with us and inhabiting in simultaneity some world unfathomably other to ourselves. "Prince's spare version," he said, "is so perfect, so airtight, that its sexiness comes from a wholly different place, a place no one has ever been except while listening to Prince's music."[1]

God did I love this. (He would go on, "What do you think Prince wore while he was recording this? If I were his girlfriend, would he let me dress him? . . . I, at least, don't believe such questions have answers.") I remember hearing it and thinking that nothing else I knew had put a finger so deftly upon the way so much about Prince could shade off toward, or rather ascend into, a sublime otherworldliness. It could be flaky, this otherworldliness, or funny, or bewildering, or—as loving burlesques like Dave Chappelle's made vivid—just wonderfully weird.

You were silly, like us, I'd think.

But then, as in "Case of You," it could seem like a bottled-up dose of enchantment itself, a thing beamed in from a dimension barely imaginable, adjacent to the world, where a different sort of gravity and physics prevailed.

You have listened to Prince. You know the wondering hiccup of thought—the mind-sputtering joy—I mean.

All of this makes him kin to Bowie, of course, with his shifting intergalactic personae, as well as to cosmically minded Afrofuturists like Sun Ra and Grace Jones and George Clinton and also, in his way, Hendrix. But Prince isn't *cosmic*, exactly, or not in the same way as Bowie, as Jones. His otherworldliness is not that of an alien, a sci-fi visitant. It is rather the otherworldliness of someone very much of this world but the whole of whose being seems italicized by, given substance through, a set of animating principles quite entirely apart from those of ordinary mortal life.

You can see this inner attunement, this call of an organizing otherwise, everywhere in the archive of Prince. Think of the zone of impermeable privacy he creates around himself, on stage but also in song. (There has never, ever been a male singer who's made more of *coyness*—a flirtatious recessiveness and withholding. *I said, Cool—but I'm keeping my pants on*, he says while getting into the bath with Dorothy Parker. It *kills*.) Think, sweet jesus just think, of the unrivaled power of his HOTNESS. Everybody knows that Prince is a miracle of transitivity, invoking then bewildering all the nearest idioms of race, sex, gender, *time*. (Think of his hotly feminized masculinity, his queer Blackness that is *also* straightness, though one that remains, indelibly, queer as fuck.) His Blackness and his maleness and his straightness and his queerness: all these roles, like the sexiest fucking Emersonian in the history of the world, he endeavors to embody after a new and unprecedented way.

Stop whatever you are doing and, right now, look up the video of Prince performing at the goddamn *halftime show* of the goddamn *Super Bowl*, back in the winter of 2007. Watch him stride the stage, a five-foot-something colossus in turquoise and peach. Watch the rain caress and exalt him. Look, truly, look at the comportment of this man, as he struts and leers. Look at that knowingness, that *grin*. It is the inward smile of someone watching with serene indulgence as an entire world tries to imagine a set of terms capacious enough to hold him, to grasp the atomic-scale detonation of swagger and style and sex that is his person, and fails to do so.

Look upon my works, ye mighty, that smile says. *Now let's fuck.*

This, friends, is the otherworldliness—let's just say it: the *divinity*—of Prince. Without contempt, without pity, with louche bemusement and flirty solicitousness, he stands apart from the creaky organizing edifices, the aspiring little taxonomies, of the merely human. They address him, but they do not adhere to him. He speaks in, and as, something otherwise, but also, deliciously, near.

Put on his songs, any of them. Here, they say. Do you need a reminder of the exhilarating limitlessness of the world apart from the knowable and known? Here you go.

*   *   *

Of course, for many of us the nearest name for the possibility of that luminous otherwise, unfolding here within the gardens and groves of this-worldly life, is sex.

This is what it means to call Prince the high priest of carnal life. No one—I want to say, *no one in the history of sound or creation*—better understands the way sex is a passage to a world fantastically apart from ourselves. That is, also, us. He calls us to it.

*   *   *

"The praying hands of humans," the religious historian John Modern writes, in a sentence that has meant a lot to me, "pray to no man, which is strange indeed in a world in which modeling the human is the key for knowing the human and much else besides."[2] He is thinking about what it is to live, as the phrase goes, in a secular age. And he is noting that it is a hallmark of secularism to mistrust any measure of Man that is not, as it were, man-made. The secular endeavors to make the human the measure of all that is.

Prince, to this impulse, is pure radiant confoundment.

And if this makes him a wonder—the prophet of the holy fuck, flooding the world with these bright shards of unconverted divinity—it also makes him hard to grieve. His death is unassimilable because it partakes of the unassimilability that he always, in that splendid otherwordliness, carried around with him.

He is hard for us to grieve because grief, too, is a thing, a tool, made of and for this world.

It's a sad thought: nothing—nothing in the world—can console us in this.

*   *   *

We are not, however, resourceless.

An old friend contacted me yesterday—the sweetest of men, middle-aged now like me, but with whom I had done a good deal of growing up, after a fashion, back in Maine. He'd been at that long-ago midwinter party. He had danced into, and well past, insobriety.

We traded the news. We condoled. And then he said something that, in a day of little implosions of heart, unraveled me.

It's unassimilable, I said, isn't it?

"I know," he wrote. "Not prepared for it. Prince brought me so much joy and, oddly, courage. He made me less shy."

If you knew him, this dear and tenderhearted man, and could

imagine him in some dim corner of his adolescence, heartened by a man in purple scarves and wearing makeup and talking about Jesus while playing a fucking *shredding* guitar, you too might find your heart breaking a little, in happiness and sudden bereavement.

"I will read thousands of tributes," I told him. "None will be better."

Because it is hard, truly it is hard, to encounter the otherwise inside the human. (Sex is only one of its forms, though as Prince reminds us it is among the most compelling.) It requires fortitude, solidity, a devotional patience. And it's frightening. To move toward it—not to hide yourself away—takes courage.

But there are these songs. *The world beyond the world?* they say. *Baby, that is* life. And then, with a generosity not much in this broken world can match, they invite you into it, in these little passages of turbulent grace. Here it is, they say—*electric word!* You'll find it in the rhythm and the harmony. You'll find it in the lewd beauty of the funk, in the delirious inconceivabilities of sex. You'll find it on the two and the four, the one and the three, in the groove so funky it's on the run. The guitar that gently weeps. The voice of the man who only, only, only wants to see you, laughing.

The Last Psychedelic Band

Not long ago, when I taught at a college with a gold-green quad and undergraduates with inheritances to squander, kids in Sufjan Stevens T-shirts would roll up to me, faces bright and quizzical, a question trembling on their lips. "But, I mean," they'd say, "what were the '90s *like?*"

They weren't being satirical, I don't think. (They had been class-bred, most of them, into a rigid politeness.) They were just curious—earnest children with their noses pressed to the diorama-glass, on a field trip to the Museum of Back Then.

"What, actually, *were* the '90s?"

For those of us of a certain age—and really, I think, for anybody enjoying another of the periodic vogues of lumberjack flannel—the question carries with it a certain queasy gravity.

There are some good reasons for this. If, for instance, you are not now and cannot be the bygone person you were (goateed, choker-clad, summarily ridiculous), neither can you pretend that the sweet and benighted pre-Zuckerbergian soul you were then has vanished, traceless, like a winked-out star or, I don't know, public education. I'm no great believer in "generations." (All generation-talk, I have grown fond of saying, is marketing, and not a thing else—with the slender possible exception of reference to boomers, who, let's agree, are human history's wholesale fucking Worst.) And yet I also know, with a seasick certainty, that who and what you spent your youth falling in love with is, in its way, indelible.

Maybe this is not how you greet the news that a record called *Crooked Rain, Crooked Rain*, by a band called Pavement, came out a windpipe-closing twenty-five years ago this month. Good for you, child. Maybe you recall the '90s through different media, a Nas record, a club-drug flashback, Enya, "Friends in Low Places," *Friends*. Fair. But for me? To tell the somewhat sorry truth of it, there's possibly nothing else that so condenses the decade as that goddamn record. It's not that I love it, exactly—or maybe I do, or did? I've come to think of it rather as something like the wallpaper of a certain, ultimately supersmall, slice of '90s consciousness: nothing you'd die for, or even necessarily cherish. Just something you've lived in long enough to have absorbed, with strange entireness, into your sensorium.

I hear it now and it rearranges something in my viscera, though what, and why, isn't easy to say.

*   *   *

Here are two propositions. The first is the most obvious: songs, as everyone knows, are the very greatest of archives. They are the containers, the modes of aesthetic technology, where many of us store away those passages of bygone time that are most precious to us, and most resistant to preservation in any other form. They carry inside them not only places and persons, dates and names, but entire scenes, atmospheres, drifts of mood and spirit insusceptible to conservation in the glitching, halting media of words. And so we keep them there, many of us, in these flimsy pop products, as if for safekeeping, like seeds in an underground vault, guarded against deterioration, loss, apocalypse. Again, everybody knows this, or at least everybody who has ever fallen in love with a three- or four-minute jolt of pop intoxication. Only one consequence is that in among the many things you might hear in songs—old joys restored to the present tense; the cruel passage of time; your own heart's history—is the flourishing of what we might call counter-possibilities: all the desires and aspirations and inflections of political will, all the reaches of the thinkable, that have since become mute, inaccessible, inoperative. (Or, at least, that *seem* to have done so, since history, as we are forever finding and forgetting, is significantly weirder than most of our models suggest.)

And so, a second proposition: If we're being somewhat grotesquely provincial, we might think of the '90s as marking the blip of planetary time between the fall of the Berlin Wall, in the autumn of 1989, and the events of September 11, 2001—between, that is, the alleged "end of history" and the end of the end of history. Of course the conventionality of this demarcation masks many, many other trajectories that might be worth our attention. There's the bubble-inducing plummeting of interest rates, say. Or the ramping up of a Reagan-Thatcherite gutting of public services, now under the liberalish guise of public-private *partnerships* ("ending welfare as we know it" and so forth)—or, in tandem with this, the harvesting of vaster and vaster swaths of the racialized poor into the maw of incarceration. We might think, that is, of all the attempted technocratic fixes to what writers with names like Piketty and Arrighi have taught us to recognize as the steep post-'73 contraction of global capital. It's those many patchwork fixes, and their synthesis and operative cogency, that we have long taken to naming (if sometimes a bit lazily) "neoliberalism." Easy enough, now, to say the '90s accordingly marked a moment awash in a liberal triumphalism that, for all its fulsomeness, never quite covered over the rot.

But don't listen to the economists. This is how Paul Beatty puts it, in a miraculous novel from 2008 called *Slumberland*. (Have you read *Slumberland*? If you have not, let me assure you that nothing in your life is so important that you can't, right now, be reading *Slumberland*.) Our narrator is a Black Angelino who finds himself in Berlin in the fateful fall of 1989. On the day itself, he encounters a man who proves to be an East German spy. This man has much to tell him. "No doubt," the man says,

> your president will take credit for the fall of the Wall as signaling the end of Communism, but it's all part of the master plan. It's a misdirection maneuver somewhat analogous to your trick plays in American football, a geopolitical Statue of Liberty or fumblerooski, if you will. Soon, my dense Afro-American friend, you'll be casting invisible digital votes in the name of democracy. Enslaving the vast majority of your workforce with a negligible minimum wage in the name of liberty. Charging mobile-phone users to *make* and *receive* calls in the name of free enterprise. Training the very same religious zealots of the desert who'll . . ."
>
> The robust revving of the eight-cylinder engine drowned out the rest of his prognostication and my question about what in hell was a mobile phone.
>
> "Come," he said, patting the passenger seat. "Come see the breach in the wall through which the four horsemen of the American apocalypse will ride."[1]

When I say this novel is miraculous, part of what I mean is that it appeared in the just-marginally-precrash spring of 2008. Think of it! Think of all that hadn't happened. Think of all we didn't quite know. Or managed to imagine we didn't quite know.

*   *   *

Some four years after the imagined interview from Beatty's novel—precisely my collegiate years, incidentally—five white Californian twentysomething dudes made a record, which would appear in February 1994 under the title *Crooked Rain, Crooked Rain*.

Here's what I'll say about it: it's fine.

No, it is! I mean, it's great actually, if you're the sort who likes that sort of thing: punkish, slack, clever, noisy, and meandering, cut with flights of genuine melodic loveliness, in-jokes, jams. A sort of unforesworn guitar-rock grandeur, lurching and woozy, suffuses much of it. If I remember right, Rob Sheffield called it "a concept album about turning twenty-eight," which is evocative while telling you next to nothing, and in that sense an extraordinarily good description of the record. It is, paradigmatically, the thing that will eventually be called "indie rock," and there you have it. It's easily my favorite Pavement record and I like it even unto loving it—sometimes, when caught in the right backward-looking mood—but I wouldn't pick a fight with you about it, not like I might about Belly, say, or Jawbreaker, or every sound Mary Timony ever made.

"Friend," I'd say. "Comrade. Let's agree: it's a totally very fine record. Another IPA?"

But why pretend? The nearer truth is that, however I may have resisted Pavement's demi-deification, however I may have disparaged the record with studied indifference, it's never quite released me. Or some of it has not. Take, for example, the one song that's kept me in its decade-spanning grip, and that still pricks and prods me whenever it spins up on shuffle. It's not "Silence Kid" or "Cut Your Hair," those alterna-microhits. The song is called "Unfair."

Now, listen: you don't have to persuade me of the foolhardiness of leaning too earnestly into the elliptical undergraduate-Ashberian lyrical misdirections of Stephen Malkmus, the band's movie-star handsome singer and chief songwriter. But let's indulge ourselves, just this once. For "Unfair" is, quite unambiguously, a song *about* something: it's a song about California. Or rather (like the song "Two States" from Pavement's previous record), "Unfair" is a song about the maldistribution of California's resources across the north-south axis. *Manmade deltas and concrete rivers*, Malkmus says (though he drawls it Dylanishly into "riv-ahhs"). *The south takes what the north delivers.* And that's "Unfair": *Chinatown*, basically, as two-plus-minute punk rock diatribe.

But the punkishness, it turns out, is what matters most. Because if I continue to adore this song—and I will not lie to you: I really do—it is not least because it marks the moment in the whole decade-plus career of this band where the impress of punk rock is, I think, the least mitigated and the least diffused. About punk rock I always thought Greg Tate got it most right, in a review he wrote about DC hardcore pioneers Bad Brains, back in 1982. "But listening to the Sex Pistols," he wrote, "is like listening to a threat against your child, your wife, your whole way of life. You either take it very seriously or you don't take it at all."[2] Indie-rockers, we might not unjustly say, tried hard to hedge exactly these bets: to borrow some of the propulsive window-breaking exhilaration of punk rock while, if not dismissing the threat that lay within it, ironizing it, carving out room for the recognition that their own bougie-kid anger, whatever its acuities, might also be, in some real ways, unjustifiable.

There is irony enough in "Unfair," sure. *Wave your credit card in the air*, the singer says. *Swing your nunchuks like you just don't care!* And yet and yet. What's captivating to me even now about "Unfair" is that, for those few suspended moments, *exactly these polarities are reversed*, and it's ironic disavowal that is undermined—or, I don't know, swamped—by a quality of venomous and un-self-canceling anger you will struggle to find elsewhere in the Pavement archive. And, yes, maybe it's just the second guitar making those slashing pentatonic dives down to the root. Maybe it's just the lunatic release of Malkmus's voice, in full vengeful caterwaul. But then again maybe it's the sound of that frequently mannered voice encountering, at last and if only here, a sort of in-the-world shittiness it doesn't much feel like passing over in stoner drollery. What you get at any rate is something in a different, differently violent, key.

So when the song ascends into its sweet swift delirium of anger and invective—when Malkmus starts shouting about how he's *lost in the foothills on my bike / Trek Enduro—say goodnight / to the last psychedelic band / from Sacto Northern Cal*—what exactly do we think is transpiring? What *is* this song, anyway? Why bring together '60s psychedelia and '70s punk as a bulwark against the ascent of some still-embryonic '90s yuppiedom? Why this exercise in manic, jubilant polemicism from a now hypercanonical band whose politics not one person, ever, has mistaken for particularly incisive or particularly interesting? Why, oh why, the Trek Enduro?

I'll tell you what I hear, or what I want to hear, in "Unfair." I hear those greatest of punk rock virtues: negation and refusal. I hear a refusal of easy-to-hand triumphalism, such as the '90s were positively glutted with. I hear too, in that harkening-back to bygone countercultures and defunct forms—that *last psychedelic band*—a sharp reminder that liberal progress, so-called, is always someone else's catastrophe, someone else's extirpation, happening typically far off, somewhere else. (Like, say, Sacramento.) And then, in that concluding feral yowl, wherein the singer warpingly elongates the phrase *I'm not your neighbor*, I hear the point-blank rebuke of any imagining of politics that would disavow conflict, pretend away antagonism, or imagine even for a moment that these might be overcome with goodwill, consensus-directed optimism, technocratic hacks. "*The south takes*": that's the blank unyielding fact the song chooses to stand on, and that it refuses to see mystified.

That's what I hear. And I want to hear all this because what I also hear in "Unfair" is an altogether comprehensive evocation of the twenty-two-year-old I was when first it found me. He comes back to me, that ordinary and not evil-hearted and *plungingly stupid* young man, all in a glow. He is a person who, riding the waves of '90s boom and bust, and keenly mistrustful though indeed he was of pallid Clintonite optimism, could nevertheless have said remarkably little about the real antagonism of the political, or about the real scale of the toll of resource extraction under the guise of market-integrated enfranchisement, or about any of the four horsemen of the American apocalypse riding through the new-fallen Wall. He did not yet know that an ironizing ambivalence about the empires of liberal dominion was in fact internal to their governing operations, and not some sort of critical outside. (His bleak liberalism, you could say, was scarcely bleak enough.) He could have done better, this person, and did not. Despite a great deal of help—from friends, lovers, teachers, books, the death-shattered world, and even from the inconsequential fluff of the motherfucking *indie-rock songs* to which he devoted yawning chasms of concentrated energy and imagination—his unlearning of the horizoning presumptions of a basically liberal ethos would take a long, long while. Today, I'm not sure there's much of anything else to hear.

Karaoke for the People

(Instructions: find a copy of "Harnessed in Slums" by North Carolina's Archers of Loaf; of "Midnight Train to Georgia," by Gladys Knight and the Pips; of Chrissie Hynde, of the Pretenders, performing an acoustic cover of Radiohead's "Creep." Each track should play out in about the time it takes to read the accompanying essay.)

1. Thugs and Scum

The algorithm, I have grown fond of declaiming, is as much of the inapprehensible hand of God as we are likely to know in this sorrowing mortal world. I'm thinking of whatever abstruse sequence of code it is that operates the "shuffle" function on your phone, iPod, whathaveyou. It is a thing of mercy and of grace. In grief, it delivers unto you bright shafts of unforeseen solace. In delight, it amplifies. On car trips, or bus rides, or standing benumbed in one of the many interminable queues of modern life, it condoles and distracts, sending out sparking little flares of memory, imagination, desire. I confess I am never less a critic of technomodernity than when held in the altogether voluptuous embrace of the shuffle algorithm, convinced once again of its benevolent clairvoyance.

God knows we've had need enough lately for fantasies, however delusional, of benign enveloping powers. Like everyone I've taken my solace where I can find it: in the classroom not a little, in old movies, in the delicious absurdity of Run the Jewels gigging at NPR, or in the genuinely inexhaustible pleasure of watching Nazis get punched, again and again and again, in sync with a range of pop gems. I've disappeared myself into novels newish and old.

Following the wise counsels of the internet I watched *Call My Agent* with a devouring intensity, as though if I stared at it hard enough I would be transported, Star Trek–like, directly onto the stony streets of Paris.

I've been going to bars a lot too. I don't know if I mentioned that.

But the best solace by far, the greatest of these, has been the algorithm. How could it be otherwise? What's more warming than reencountering a track long-buried in your playlists, some mislaid gem that opens up, the instant it declares itself to you, such a richness of thought and sensation? It offers so many of the things you might want right now, in this giddy season of political retrogression: a reminder of the possibilities for beauty, say, or for brilliance. A spectacle of sorrows made radiant, or of paralytic rage leaping into form. And it can remind you too, the way songs are forever doing, of the closeness to you of people from whom you might just then be separated, by work, or the day, or geography, age, life. Here comes a track from *Hejira*, or a Scissor Sisters song, and all at once, in a swift inflooding rush—*there they are*, those distant comrades and loves. Restored to you.

If you have an unmanageable quantity of heartsick rage or stupefied despair on your hands, let me recommend a protracted descent into the errant generosities of the shuffle. It makes nothing happen, of course. But it can be replenishing.

* * *

That, anyway, is how I reencountered one wholly demographically predictable song from my distant youth that, as soon as it got slotted into randomized rotation, lit such a fuse in me that I played it maybe eighty-seven times in the few days that followed. It's not the best song of all time, or even of the indie-rock '90s.

It's not even the best song by North Carolina's own Archers of Loaf. (Though I can recommend the whole record on which it appears, *Vee Vee*, as a great conduit for, and intensifier of, your underemployed fury.) It's fine. It's *fine*. But holy mother of god did it go instantaneously into my accumulating playlist, currently titled SONGS FOR YOUR ANTIFASCISM.

A couple of days into my renewed shuffle-sponsored obsession with the song in question, I was riding the train home from work to drop my stuff and then meet some friends and head out to the airport for a suddenly convened protest—yes: that queasy day—and as I did the chorus, the repeated barked-out chant, sang right the fuck through me. It's called "Harnessed in Slums"—the elderly among you may remember it from the Lounge Axes of your youth—and these are its anchoring phrases:

> *With thugs and scum and punks and freaks*
> *They're harnessed in slums but they wanna be free*

In a hoarse, strangled sort of yelp, that's how it goes: *thugs and scum and punks and freaks*, again and again, repeat till page is full, printer.

And listen, I know what it is: a '90s rocker amped up by velocity and bile and not a whole lot else. But it is also, I swear to you, *perfect*. Forget the anthemic righteousness of its opening phrases (*Snuff the leader with the badassed plan / Take what you want from the palm of his hand*). Forget the spazzy hyperkinesis of it. Just the chorus: that sequence, that Whitmanian litany! It's like the conjuring of a dreamed-of coalition. There's the faint note of racialization in *thugs*, that keyword of asshat racists nationwide. There's the snarling contempt for the poor and the downtrodden in *scum*. There's the explicitly sexual perversity nested in *punks*. And then there's the great democratizing breadth of *freaks*: freaks! The

racially despised, the impoverished, the queer, the joyously unrec-
onciled. It's a motherfucking *roll-call* is what it is, beamed from the
trough of the '90s to the glowing furious heart of Trump Times.

I know it's not for everyone, this aggro-ish whiteboy rocker,
truly I do. You may do better with the sharpened gorgeousness of
Solange, or the new-cut soul of Anderson Paak, or with a million
other things culled from your personal canon. But oh, oh the vivifying magic with which this one found me and lit me up.

Later that night, standing with maybe a thousand Chicagoans
mobilized on the spot against the fresh-sprung obscenity of the
Muslim ban, I felt the cadences of the song coursing through me
once more: a sprung compression in the shoulders, a surging in the
blood. I looked around me and it rattled in my ears and there and
then, for one long seizing moment, I knew a swift upwelling love
for *everybody there*, strangers and friends, punks and freaks, all of
us doing together the nearest thing we could think of to interrupt
the progression of awfulness.

And here's what's best about this little gift from the algorithm:
the feeling of that gorgeous cold night—of mobilized solidarity,
of massed opposition, of a communal turning in the direction of
refusal—burned itself right into the fucking sinews of that song,
that long-ago three-and-half-minute spasm of jumped-up rancor
and delight. It is there forever, and nothing can undo it. For the
rest of time, I'll hear it, and there it will be: the noise, the longed-
for reignition, and then the brief and certain and indestructible
sensation of grace.

2. Midnight Train

Not many years ago, at an academic cocktail party for which I was
asked to supply the soundtrack, a friend accosted me as the first

strains of "Midnight Train to Georgia" came drifting out over the gathered, its horn-ballasted groove settling around the chatter and tinkling flatware like pollen in the springtime air. She strode over, pointing skyward as if to the source of the enveloping sound, and said, if not these precise words, something like them: "Dude— why do you hate women?"

And here began one of the greatest music bar-fights I've been a part of in a long while, a thing of hyperbole, improvised invective, delight redoubling itself. For then and there, in sturdy and you'd have to say convincing detail, this friend unfolded before us an impromptu counterreading of "Midnight Train." "A tender ballad," as she had it, "about a successful career woman who gives up her vibrant working life to be with her fucking loser of a man." In its essence, she claimed, it's a purely reactionary pop song: an anthem of female devotion and self-sacrifice, especially palatable to a national audience that, by 1973, had grown wary of upheavals in the cultural life of gender wrought by years of increasingly unignorable feminist protest and ferment. (She brilliantly marshaled the Googleable fact that it was written by Jim Weatherly, who was inspired by—of all people—Farrah Fawcett, who it turns out at some point near the apex of her glam career had moved herself out of LA for no purpose other than to be with Lee Majors, after some non–*Bionic Man* project or other had flatlined.) What could an unpausing love for the song reveal in a person, she said in rousing conclusion, other than a poorly concealed, inveterate antifeminism?

This, comrades, is how you dispute with your friends about songs.

So NO! I said, no no no! Because listen, I said, to Gladys Knight's *voice*. Listen to that caressing and fine-grained expressiveness. What it expresses, above all else, is sorrow. But it is a sorrow that, in its astonishing composure—its regality, you almost want to say—stands on guard against anything that sounds even the least bit like pity, or contempt. Everything about her voice, I said, means to acknowledge the sorrow of the man in the song, and to hold open a place for it: to recognize what he has suffered, in failing, and to do so without so much as a trace of condescension or belittlement. (*Even sold his own car . . .* MMM.) I think it's most of all a song about trying to produce for that man an account of failure that does not read it as shameful, and that does not make it incompatible with dignity.

Now on *this* account, I said, "Midnight Train" takes its place among a roster of other earlyish post–Civil Rights songs. (Think of it, perhaps, as a companion piece to "Livin' for the City," also from 1973, but transplanted to LA.) So much of what the singer labors to realize for the man is what we might call the *historical contingency* of his failure—the fact that, in his world, the decks were always stacked, and anything other than failure was only ever going to be long, long odds. That such labor falls to her, that such labor in fact takes as its form conventional female self-sacrifice, that the song's name for all that labor and all that self-sacrifice is "love": this is what makes "Midnight Train"—listen to it, to her—so much a heartbreak.

Soon enough others got in on this fight, picked sides, staked out positions, extending them into digressions more and less esoteric. One great friend, in response to the question, "But what about the Pips?" asked us to consider how they seemed always to interrupt the narrative with caustic, undercutting ripostes. *Superstar!—but he didn't get far.* "Clearly," she observed, "they are Gladys Knight's unconscious." On it went, in tones of semiserious implacability and hyped-up devotion.

And that is what I mean when I say (as I am forever saying) that fights like this, about the objects we love, are themselves a kind of love song. What else could they be? Look around the scenes of our lives. You will find there far, far fewer habitable languages than you might wish for the expression of all those vital loves that travel between people who are not, say, coupled; who are not "family," at least as the census has it; who are something other and better than the corporatist idioms of "colleagues" allow or the neutered invocation of "friends." This talk, this making-together of a language of disparagement and joy: this is how people marooned from those commonplace languages of devotion—marriage, couplehood, etc.—contrive to build for their togetherness a habitable form. It is the language these errant modes of love devise for themselves, the preserve we make for a kind of conjoinedness that's oblique to more normative styles of attachment, stranger, denser, queerer. Call it bar-fighting, call it criticism, call it a kind of affective karaoke, or just call it joy. Whatever you call it, I am here to say that, like "Midnight Train," it is also, always, a love song.

3. Creep

We all know the pleasure of trading songs—especially, I think, cover songs—with new lovers. How they acquire in the exchange something of the bright atmosphere of romance's beginning. How, later, when you encounter them again, they can seem to shimmer with all that dreaminess and erotic captivation. It makes sense. If you're not sixteen, all your love affairs are covers—repetitions, with a difference. And this can make the inclusion of covers in those early mixes especially sweet. Some years ago, at the outset of a steep and sudden and unworkable love, my new friend and I passed back and forth versions of Joni Mitchell's "Case of You," and each iteration, from Joni to Prince to Lloyd Cole, seemed to entwine itself around one of those radiant new discoveries that, as they unfold, make the commencing of the affair so fitful and intoxicating. You know, before anybody's love gets lost.

But not all exchanges come from these radiant moments, these scenes of plenty. Sometimes you're given a song in the midst of a passage of great devastation. And sometimes it's a cover.

*   *   *

Listen, I can take or leave Radiohead, and I feel a like indifference to this early hit, from before they became the next Only Band That Matters. But if you *wanted* to hate Radiohead—which I do not, but I mean: go with god—this song can help you. "Creep" is song of overweening male narcissism pretending to be abjection. When the singer says, *You're so fucking special,* you can feel all the weight of his wounded contemptuousness, how much he resents the "you" in the song for having had the gracelessness to be hurt by whatever shitty thing he's done. Her hurt, her pain—it's made him feel *so bad.* The whole song is a fake mea culpa, behind which is an aria of extravagant male self-pity.

Chrissie Hynde's cover of "Creep," meanwhile, takes the original and fucking demolishes it. It does so by leeching out every least filament of self-pity, note by harrowing note, so that what you're left with is a pure and crystalline and almost unendurable self-contempt. This singer reinvests the song with the possibility that the lover she's hurt maybe was special, in some way or other, and with the gnawing suspicion that she has done genuine harm—that something raw and undermining and perhaps incurable in her own troubled self has once more turned love to ash. It's like Aimee Mann's "Wise Up," but in the first-person. Or Johnny Cash's cover of "Hurt" tuned to the note of an intimate self-made misery. Think of it as an inside narrative of the wretched life of a lonely heart: a song of sorrow and self-revulsion.

I only know this version because years ago it was sent to me by a person who, after some months of quite ordinary human wreckage—ruinous deceit, unmeaning cruelty, etc.—emailed it to me more or less out of the blue. For a while, over those initial dark days and shattered nights, I had suffered a lot from what I took to be this person's persisting inarticulacy, her stonewalling disinterest in (as the shrinks and middle managers say) *taking responsibility* in any genuine way for what aspects of this lifewide conflagration were hers to own. That brutal line from *Middlemarch* kept galloping back to me: *What place was there in her mind for a remonstrance to lodge in?*[1] It was, as such encounters can be, crazy-making. At least for a while. Eventually, I got over it, or got over it enough to tell myself I'd gotten over it.

But then from out of that blank wall of speechlessness came this song.

And I know—oh, I know—it might be nothing more than my own wounded male narcissism talking here, my own expansive and impressive capacities for self-pity. But believe me when I tell you: I think it was maybe the best *I'm sorry* I've ever received, or am likely to receive. Not curative, not some loss-smiting restoration. But something. It helped. It helps.

The Everyday Disaster

There is a prickly moment, jolting and a little haunting, that comes smack in the middle of a great book by Jennifer Doyle called *Campus Sex Campus Security*. In it, she's working through some of the complications of the language of trauma as it operates in how we talk, and how we think, about sexual violence. But then she takes an arresting turn. "What would it mean," she writes,

> to detraumatize the discourse of rape? What would it mean to reconcile the language of trauma (as a "fate worse than death") against the ordinariness of peoples' experiences with sexual coercion?[1]

The ordinariness of peoples' experiences with sexual coercion. You read it and your breath catches. It's the kind of sentence that makes the clocks in the room stop ticking.

For Doyle, the trouble with the language of trauma is not that it is without purchase or use, not that it doesn't get at something real in the gruesome ecology of sexual assault. It is rather to do with what she invites us to think of as a kind of media-ready spectacularization of "sexual coercion": a frictional mismatch between "trauma," with its maximalist intensities, and the more commonplace varieties of gendered duress and gendered harm. Under the hard glare of the language of trauma, Doyle suggests, something of the debilitating *ordinariness* of that harm—the grinding, exhausting, soul-dispiriting dailiness of it—gets harder to see. It becomes a thing at once ubiquitous and not easily attested to, difficult to describe in all its rich and shitty and everyday detail.

Only one way to think about #MeToo—the hugely unfinished project that was commenced more than a decade ago by Tarana Burke and that continues to unfold around us—is as a decentered, collective, polyvocal effort to bring just that ordinariness into livid relief. It is a project that means to do work on what you could call the multiscalar sexual violences of day-to-day patriarchy—to give us better purchase on just how much strain and sorrow and labor, how much fucking *life*, is chewed up by the effort to manage them. Doyle's incendiary little book offers an especially fine point of entry into that project, and I commend it to you in those terms. But it may be that you can discover something similar, some like alertness to the lower frequencies of workaday gender shittiness, in things still nearer to hand. You might hear it coming out of your speakers. You might listen, I mean, to the singers.

Two singers in particular, both of them American twenty-somethings, seem to me to be animating this terrain with special vibrancy. They come from very different pop galaxies—they are indie-folk chanteuse Phoebe Bridgers and hiphop and neosoul phenom SZA—but their records share more than the sharp divergences of sonic texture, style, or algorithmic niche might lead you to believe. The both of them absolutely excel, for instance, in that venerable and genre-transcending subcategory of pop artistry, *the ballad of fucked-up love.*

All praises to that centuries-deep reservoir of song and story, for sure. But part of what SZA and Bridgers share, too, and what's so beguiling and so vital about them, is a singular shrewdness about the whats and hows of the loves that might fuck a person up—a canniness, I mean, about hurt, about the shifting violences of desire, and above all about the running-together of the ordinary and the terrible in a world formed so entirely by the astonishing presumption of men. They don't make songs about trauma, these singers, or not exactly. They make songs about a certain kind of on-the-regular gendered awfulness, which are also songs about the labors of spirit required to live a life in relation to it. About that presiding awfulness—call it, if you want, Disaster Heterosexuality—they have a lot to say.

* * *

A few songs on Phoebe Bridgers's debut record from 2017, *Stranger in the Alps*, take up, in the post-Joni style, the aftereffects of a bad breakup. Sometimes ruminative and wounded and sometimes anecdotal and offhand, these songs are less the rancorous fuck-yous they might be than they are rueful, semisad, alive with mordant wit. But something else transpires as well. Take "Motion Sickness," about the slickest pop production on the record, in which you can hear a Lilith Fairish condensation of everyone from Sheryl Crow to Paula Cole to Shawn Colvin to Liz Phair. It begins:

> *I hate you for what you did*
> *But I miss you like a little kid*
> *I faked it every time, but that's alright*
> *I can hardly feel anything, I hardly feel anything, at all*

As an announcement of arrival into the ranks of singer-songwriters, you could surely do worse—it's got meanness, self-deprecation, the hint of something more bruising, all laid out in tight balanced tension. That tension, in effect, is the song. Over the next few minutes, in shorter and longer circuits, the singer plays out an alternation between an angered sense of having been hurt by her ex, in a real and stunting way, and something else: a niggling residual tenderness. She won't give up on either, the hating or the achy longing, and that sustained irresolution charges the song with its nervy tensile energy.

Stick close, though. Because those genial notes, the friendlyish if barbed asides, corrode. In the final verse the singer finds herself contending with disquiet in a different register. "You said when you met me / you were bored," she says, repeating the line, and it's there—in the ex's willingness to *say* such a thing, *out loud*—that we come to our swift reminder that this person, whatever his attractions, was not the kind of man who held his lover's fragilities especially tenderly in hand. He is, to say it differently, an asshole, a person of haphazard cruelty. But then there's the kicker: "And you," she sings, giving up a bit on her own impulse to shield this ex from a more punitive kind of scrutiny, "You were in a band when I was born."

Now, for all that's delectable about the achieved icy contemptuousness packed into that line, it's not especially pleasant for the singer of this song, I don't think, to realize she had been made so easily a part of someone else's hyperfamiliar erotic trajectory. He's the shitty older man preying on the vulnerable young women in the scene: a type if ever there was one. And there she is, locked into this dreary, diminishing drama, and trying to conjure for herself some viable flight away from it.[2] The singer of this song has resources, absolutely: unblinkered clarity, cold wit, her spectacular burgeoning talent. You get the sense that these are—mostly, sometimes—almost enough. What you're left with, here and across the whole of *Stranger in the Alps*, is just that pained almostness. As much as anything else, that special calibration of pain is what gives shape to the world of this person coming of age—gathering her strengths, plotting a path—inside the quotidian disasters of heterosexuality.

*   *   *

Almost concurrently, but from a different aesthetic precinct, there came the record of another young woman riding out the rough seas of contemporary femininity. This was SZA's *Ctrl*, which has aptly been described as paradigmatically Frank Oceanish in its wedding of hiphop beats and neo-soul progressions to a breath-catching, outrageous melodic fluency. You find it most of all, that fluency, in the singer's rangy, liquid, preternaturally author-itative voice. SZA is that rare and wonderful thing: a belter with *tact*, an extraordinary delicacy. And here too, throughout *Ctrl*, is the record of a young woman not much interested in disavowing desire—it is not an album much involved in respectability politics, say—but in working through its dense entanglements. "Love Ga-lore," the record's second single, gets to this precisely.

A spare couple of chords and loose beats across which still an-other of the record's vaulting melodies is strung: this, it seems, is "Love Galore." It offers itself as a song of clear-eyed postbreakup anatomization, told from the side of the woman who has called it off: "I said farewell / You took it well / Promise I won't cry about spilt milk." There's a he-said, she-said quality to the track too, enhanced by Travis Scott's semiwounded answering verses and the swaggery boastfulness of SZA's voice in response. (She is a singer who knows how to exult: "You'll do what I want / Get what I want / Get what I need.") It's a song, you could say, about getting rid of a man, desiring him too much to quite let him go, and being sort of OK with that.

But not entirely. As it turns out, the song pivots on an invocation of violence—and not merely emotional violence—that it almost immediately drops. About that violence: this is not, say, a Whitney Houston song, where the submerged context of inflicted pain is a thing you notice mostly through its soaring virtuosic overcoming. There is virtuosity enough all over *Ctrl*, no question, but "Love Galore" is nearer Edith Piaf, or Billie Holiday, where the interplay of virtuosity and of violence, explicitly named, gives the thing so much of its painful vitality. For what are we to make of the vanishing rapidity with which the song offers up, among the other sorrows of entanglement with a troubling man, the line, *Why you hit me when you know you know better?* It's a small sort of thunderclap, and the offhandedness is so much of what makes it rumble—as though that were the only possible register in which you might catch hold of this pain's unspectacular ordinariness, how seamlessly it fits inside a world where the horizonless entitlement of men is the context for what the song, not bothering to fuck around, just goes ahead and calls "love."

That's maybe a lot for a pop song to hold, but this one absolutely does it. Truly, if you wanted to trace out the shape and heft of that lived-in masculine entitlement, the homely violence of it, you could do a lot worse than to pay attention to the timbre of SZA's voice here—to the way the singer's jolted woundedness walks itself out, straightens its shoulders, strides into the concluding line of the verse: "got me lookin' forward / to weekends with you." I could talk to you for an hour, for two, and still not exhaust the microshifts of intention, mood, and misgiving that dart and charge across these few seconds of sound. Here, too, is not a song that wants no part of heterosexuality, or that is interested in foreswearing desire, the turbulence of sex. But it is, down to its smallest movements, a reckoning with the scene of that desire, the pain-delivering worlds that give it shape.

*   *   *

It's easy to think that, in an Age of Disasters, all songs should be polemics. Or that, when looked at right, all songs will turn out to *have been*, however they landed in their moment. That's maybe not wrong. Still, I'm not sure you do well to think of SZA, or of Phoebe Bridgers, as topical polemicists—unless your sense of "topical" has been usefully expanded, elasticized, which may in the end be the point. What we have before us, I think, is something different: shutter-burst portraits of two young woman working to get in relation to a workaday environment of coerciveness—presumption, entitlement, violence at different scales—that is the solvent in which "desire," "sex," and "love" continue to appear for them. They have a lot to say about that environment, its contours, its changing weather. They have a lot to say, too, about the countervailing *resourcefulness* of the women who find themselves navigating it—each performance, as Hortense Spillers memorably puts it, "a precise demonstration of the subject turning in full conscious knowledge of her own resources toward her object."[3] Those resources are considerable, full of clarity and accumulated power, always there and almost enough. Polemics, not-polemics, whatever: testaments.

What We Fight about When We Fight about Doctor Wu

Fair warning: this is not to be a wading into the deeper waters of Steely Dan esoterica. I'm not going to parse the weird bleakness of "Charlie Freak," explain the boom on Mizar-5, unravel the time-signatures of "Your Gold Teeth," or take up your evening "speculating for hours on the meaning of a certain enigmatic question in the lyrics of 'Any Major Dude,'" to lift a phrase from Michael Chabon's *Wonder Boys*.[1] Nor do I have much of technical interest to share with you, about the harmonic intricacies of various hepcat solos, or about the Dylanishness of Donald Fagen's diction and phrasing, and even less about the impress of midcentury America be-bop on the early-'70s pop ambitions of this one band. *Sorry!* For any and all of this, I commend you to the outer moons of internet commentary.

Instead I'm going to tell you the story of a long fight I once had about Steely Dan—a fight that turned, then, into something else.

The mise-en-scene of this dispute will be, I think, familiar to many of you. It was significantly after midnight. You would not at this point have called us *wasted*, though technical sobriety had been forsaken some time earlier. My friend John and I were in the basement just then, foraging among the varieties of finger-food that had gone unconsumed at the party. And here at the tail-end of a day that began with a child home sick from school, and that somehow devolved into the project of playing, with this child, the complete discographies of a number of '70s bands in reverse chronological order—at the end of this day and this night, we were listening to records, and fighting about them. The question before us was simple: which is the greatest Steely Dan record? It was that kind of talking, the kind whose characterizing features and form you're likely to know: the cheerful counterfactuality, the ambulatory indirection, the easy shuttling between a style of largely absurdist speculation and sudden plummeting descents into *very serious assertion.*

John was the ideal coconspirator for this kind of fighting, for a multitude of reasons, only two of which I'll mention: he and I had by this time been talking this special kind of talk for better than twenty years, and there are few people in the world for whom I feel a love as comprehensive or as detailed. We'll come back to that conjunction—talking, love—in a moment.

But first: Steely Dan? *Steely Dan?* Listen: I know. If only because, to those disinclined to the band, such disinclination typically takes the form of an ardent and vocal dislike (rather than, say, indifference), I do not need to have explained to me the million-petalled flower of Steely Dan's uncoolness.[2] Here's what I say to the haters: fair enough. I do not need to be persuaded of the jazz-nerd preciousness of much of the affection for this band, of the tedium of some of their coke-binge obscurantism (or of its explication), and least of all of the irritatingness of the particularly male, particularly *boy* style of hyperappreciation that surrounds them: those exquisite parsings of the finery of technique, execution, and mastery, or of the academic nuances of influence and pedigree. (Like many of you, I have been that boy.) The phrase "yacht-rock" gets at the self-satisfaction and the pretense quite nicely, I think—and gestures, too, toward the almost total lack of propulsive, uncoiled fury in their catalog: of *rocking*—and so needs little elaboration. Preciousness, pretense, production value, and a certain rockless-ness: not much to wonder at in the absence of any real through line of Steely Dan's influence in the otherwise omnivorously cannibalizing world of postpunk and indie rock, where so many of my most ardent affections, and John's, would long reside. (I suppose postrock is a possible exception here? I don't know; does it go well with amphetamines and post-hippie ennui? Then maybe.)

In any case our fight, though undertaken with something other than high seriousness, was neither backhandedly dismissive nor premised on the covert coolness (what a friend calls the "double-reverse coolness") of appreciating something so banal. There was too much of something else—earnestness, you might say, or joyousness, or love—for either of these. And so it was that, while burning the fuel of these other affects, our fight that evening enlarged and expanded itself, and became a new thing.

Now, there are people in the world who find fights about questions with no possibility of a definitive answer to be pointless, and worse: wasteful (another word for this is "masturbatory") and maddening. I cannot claim to understand these people. For as the dispute grew more intricate, and its terms more porous and entangled, John and I experienced what I would like to call a revelation, such as is said to be commonplace among mystics, and philosophers, and other idle persons.

Many of you will know the 1977 song "Deacon Blues," which captures the sex-and-smoke-tinged sadness of Los Angeles as gorgeously as anything you could hope for. Like most great LA stories, it's a song about living a life inside the scene of so many misfired aspirations, so many best hopes both unrealized and yet, in a mostly gruesome way, unextinguished. (Los Angeles: Land of

Undead Dreams.) You know the quotable lines: "I cried when I wrote this song / Sue me if I play too long"; "They got a name for the winners in the world / I want a name when I lose." *I want a name when I lose.* To be on the losing side of the city, but to be distinguished in that losing by a name: that is the ambition of this singer, a man cynical and beaten but too languorous altogether to be called hard-bitten or hard-boiled, whatever the noirish echoes surrounding him.

But there in John's basement, as the talk ramped itself up into unsought dimensions of argument and invective, the ions in the air began to charge and reassemble. And so, like Keanu seeing the lines of code pouring down the walls, at last we understood: Deacon Blues is the name of this person, at this time. But he has other names *and he lives in other songs.* Other songs, from across the whole range of the Steely Dan catalog, feature the man who would become Deacon Blues—the same person, the same guy—but going by different names and frozen at different moments on the temporal curve of a life that bends, with sad inexorability, toward just this West Coast desolation.

Who else, we realized in a gasp of comprehension, who else is Lester the Nightfly, title character of Donald Fagen's first post–Steely Dan record (*I'm Lester the Nightfly, hello Baton Rouge / Won't you turn your radio down / Respect the seven second delay we use*), but a return to Deacon Blues at an earlier, infinitely brighter moment, when he's an early '60s late-night radio DJ pouring out "jazz and conversation / From the foot of Mt. Belzoni"? How much richer in poignancy do both songs become when they are understood to be narrated by the same person? "I've got plenty of java and Chesterfield Kings," Lester the Nightfly says, "But I feel like crying / I wish I had a heart of ice." Yeah yeah: but we know that in fifteen or twenty years he won't even bother with the crying.

"The Nightfly," under this dispensation, becomes a song about heartbreak, but *youthful* heartbreak—the kind that carries with it the secret thrill of entrée into the tumultuous world of adult romance—and "Deacon Blues" becomes a song about the desolate places you find when your heart just won't break anymore. Nor do you lose points for thinking this narrative tracks along the same arc that runs from Camelot optimism to late-'70s malaise.

"Donald Fagen," I remember saying to John, "historian for our time."

"Vico of North Jersey," he offered.

But there is more. A few months later I came back to Chicago and John picked me up at the airport. He didn't spring it on me at once. In the car, maybe twenty minutes into the drive, somewhere on the northwest side, he spoke these words: "I've been thinking about 'Doctor Wu.'" And he had. For there, in "Doctor Wu," is where the real corrosion happens, where we find a major crisis-point in the trajectory from Lester the Nightfly to Deacon Blues. In a way that had somehow always escaped me—maybe because of the lovely Phil Woods saxophone part, or because of the sweet silly comedy of its names and its queries (*Are you crazy? Are you high? Or just an ordinary guy?*), or because of its gradual overcoding in my mind by the Minutemen's eternally triumphant cover of it—"Doctor Wu" is an exceptionally rough little song, about a bad patch that gets, abruptly, worse.

"Katy lied," is how it begins. "I was half-way crucified / I was on the other side / of no tomorrow." Well, ok. But only after the second verse do you get really any of idea of what he is talking about here. It happens so offhandedly you can pretty easily miss it. (As I did, for about two dozen years.) "Don't seem right," the second verse begins, "I've been strung out here all night / I've been waiting for the taste you said you'd bring to me." Oh—strung out . . . the taste you said you'd bring to me—*oh wait*. The singer of this song is half-way crucified *because he's a junkie*. Doctor Wu is this song's Kid Charlemagne: he is the nicknamed dealer. But it's not just a song about being strung out in Biscayne Bay. It is instead a song about being strung out, trying to find your score, going to your girlfriend's house, and finding her fucking your dealer. "*Katy lies / You can see it in her eyes / But imagine my surprise / When I saw you . . .*" He knows from the first Katy lies—they're junkies: that she fucks someone else isn't what's shattering here—but the *dealer*? *Their* dealer? This, somehow, is what makes the scene radiant with abjection, the finding of the bottom beneath the bottom.

And this is what happens to Lester the Nightfly: he begins playing jazz radio, gets into a scene that goes bad and druggy (as jazz scenes do), finds himself strung out in Biscayne Bay—and then, in flight from this freeze-frame moment of maximal humiliation, wends his way to California, there to crawl like a viper through the suburban scenes. Twisting through a decade's worth of songs, in other words, is the orchestrated unfolding, across varied moods and seasons, of the story of one character's life.

I remember looking across at John as he drove, the mad and happy glitter in his eyes as he caressed some lyric or other, gesticulated for emphasis. I remember taking in, as if in dopey compressed montage, the ways he and I had unfolded as characters for one another over the fast-accumulating years. And I remember feeling an oceanic certainty that I would never, ever get tired of listening to Steely Dan.

*   *   *

I have said that John and I had been fighting about Steely Dan for twenty years, and that we loved one another. Better, perhaps, to say that fighting about Steely Dan is at once how we came to love one another and the form that love found for itself—one mode of its enactment, its nurturance, and its renewal. There is nothing unique in this. It is what you do when you are young, but not only (I think) when you are young: you love things (songs, records, books) and in the abundance of that enthusiasm you *talk*, you measure that love with and against others'. You mix your words and your delight up with that of another person, or of many people, and you feel out what's provoking, or disquieting, or otherwise pleasing about how those words and those enthusiasms rub up against one another. What you forge together is a kind of idiolect, a semi-private vernacular of appreciation and critique, ardor and invective. This is one of the things you do when you fall in love: you and your beloved make a language together—with words, theories, your bodies—that you then refine and refashion over many years, until it comes to carry within it much of the whole history of your love. William Faulkner somewhere calls this "the best of all talking" and let me say: he is not wrong.

My own fascination with the talk that gathers around the objects we love most in the world—books and songs and paintings and movies and such—runs right through John, and my love for him, but it doesn't terminate there. For a long time I thought that just one of the things criticism might do, or at least try to do, is be true to that talking. I don't mean to say it is not, in a host of ways, stupid—insular, self-pleased, inane—because of course it is. Indeed, there is by now a whole set of theory-inflected counterclaims that ask us not to forget how easily ardor, preference, discrimination can be translated into a sort of gladiatorial status-seeking, some vicious microcalibrated economy of Cool, Coolest, So-Not-Cool. I don't even know that that's wrong. I am a professor. Have you been to a visiting lecture, a seminar? I have known people like this, yes.

But none of this seems to me real discouragement from wanting to take seriously the joyousness, the inflooding sense of richness and abundance, by which we are sometimes surprised in the presence of an object—and, also, in the presence of the people with whom we want to talk about it. Criticism, in this scene, encompasses something other than exposure, deconstruction, or critique, and is not a thing you do in impatient response to some deficit, falsity, duplicity, undermining paradox, or elemental inadequacy in the object itself. It is not sustained by a sense of that joyousness as, at base, a species of false consciousness. (Which is not to say objects of our love cannot be or contain all these things.) Criticism might also be understood as the making of a language—and with it the making of a precious kind of sociality, fractious and lovestruck—whose roots are in ardor and captivation, something kindled by those moments of exhilaration that songs so offhandedly produce. Talking is not the cancellation of such passages of joy, not the mark of joy's consignment to the fallen realm of discourse. You can think of it instead as one mode of joy's enlargement, its enactment.

So when I hear people fighting about some new band I don't know, or what's awesome and why, or what's an abomination and why, I don't necessarily regard that clamorousness as the perseverance of some economy of cool that in its relentless hierarchy mirrors with eerie, sad precision the system of late-phase capitalism in which it is enmeshed. That fighting, this talking: these are also, often, love songs. In them are the residues of moments of exhilaration and delightedness so captivating that they want only to amplify and extend themselves. Listen right, and what you can hear there is the sound of people learning, or remembering, how to be in love: in love with the possibilities of objects, in love with the possibilities of other people, and in love with the possibilities of the scene of belonging that loving things in this garrulous way is always making and unmaking. Part of what's so exhilarating, too, is that in this scene of talk, there are no experts, only enthusiasts and coconspirators. There, where we're all frauds and hustlers, the world cracks open a bit, and even a band as precious and yacht-rocky as Steely Dan—*Steely Dan!*—can find a place at the table of joy.

PART II

Ceremonies

Love in the Ruins

On a late-spring day sometime in the mid-'90s, I found myself sitting with a friend on a stone bench overlooking a prospect of conventional, but nevertheless pretty estimable, pastoral loveliness: green valley and distant hills, cinematic cloudscapes, placid lake, etc. The friend with whom I sat was just then at the collapsing end of a love affair, and because she was a few years older than I, and much, much smarter, I experienced her distress with a kind of baffled shock. (She was, alternatingly, angry and sad, inhabiting each mode with some force.) I can remember looking at her and thinking: If that much articulacy and worldliness and fierce intelligence didn't insulate you from such vehement heartsickness then—jesus—what would?

I was young.

We looked at the scene spread out before us, and together took in its failure to be restorative in the ways much of our reading had suggested it ought to be. We talked, I am sure, about Elvis Costello. And so, unable to countenance this much sorrow in a person I found so comprehensively winning—keen-witted, generous, beautiful, so easily possessed of the mysterious knowledge of how to be brilliant *without being a dick about it*—I tried to say something I thought both consoling and true, something about sadness and happiness and the world. "It's hard to get too sad," I said, "because whatever else happens, you're never going to run out of books and bands and songs you love. I mean, nothing can happen to take those things out of the world, you know? They'll always be right there for you, always."

We'd not been friends for all that long. But she loved me enough, even then, to let it go.

* * *

I assume that if you're considering going to graduate school with any real seriousness you need not have recited to you the litany of reasons, from the Marxist to the karmic, not to do so. If you cannot say those reasons off to yourself like beads of a rosary then perhaps you have not, in fact, given the matter enough thought. But jeremiads like those of, say, William Pannapacker (in the *Chronicle*, in *Salon*) are prominent enough, and well-circulated enough, that they don't need to be rehearsed at length here. (Summary: DO NOT GO.) I have no real wish to dispute those accounts of the perils of a commitment to graduate school, and even less their appraisals of the exploitative machinery of institutional higher education, even though I do think such dire accounts can be a bit, you could say, monochromatic. No one, I think, has written a more thoughtful, subtle, or moving rebuttal to the Pannapackers of the contemporary scene than Jonathan Senchyne, in his exquisite piece "Working Classes," and I'll leave to you the pleasure of reading his account of why it was that, even in the frightening absence of any assurance of a tenure-track happy ending for his story, he found the pursuit of a PhD in the humanities greatly rewarding—at once self-solidifying and self-enlarging—in ways the JUST DON'T GO narratives persistently misapprehend.[1]

But if I don't quite have a dog in this fight (whether or not graduate school is good *for you* is likely to depend upon variables too numerous and case-specific to generalize about with much non-polemical efficacy), still I want to offer a small testament to at least one of the ways a graduate-school education might be of real human use to you. I'd put it, at its briefest, like this: one day, at some unanticipated juncture on the trajectory of your adult life, something cataclysmically bad is going to happen to you. It will be, in the ordinary way of things, shattering and unendurable. And when this happens you may be startled to find that you have an extraordinary resource in, of all improbable things, the years of your graduate education: in the people you loved there, of course, but also in the ways you learned to think there, and in the worlds that, by loving and thinking and talking and fighting in that same shared space, you learned to make together. That's not everything you might wish for, after many costly and laborious years, I know. But neither is it nothing.

In some ways this has, perhaps, little enough to do with graduate school as such. Live a vibrant, vital sort of life and the people to whom you are drawn in your twenties will, it is fair to hope, come forcefully to your aid in moments of need. Maybe this isn't true of law school or business school—which, god, is one sad fucking thought—but I'm ready to believe it is, just as I'm ready to believe it is no less true for those who pass their younger years outside the expensive confinements of institutional life. And yet I do feel inclined to make a case, however partial and biased, for the special sorts of provision made for you by years of graduate life. Keep that bias in mind, and keep in mind too that, in the cautionary words of late-night advertisements, your experience of the product may be different.

Unlike some wiser and more deliberate peers, I did not enter graduate school with overmuch in the way of a career trajectory in mind, or even an especially solidified sense of what it was, precisely, within my discipline that I wanted to study. (Modernism? Twentieth-century poetics? Nineteenth-century America? Shelley? They all beguiled.) To the degree that something as dignifying as a "rationale" could be retrospectively assembled, I'd say I was there chiefly because of a complex ardor I'd come to feel in the presence of certain kinds of objects, an ardor I could not then exhaust or explain to myself with anything that felt like adequacy, but in which I suspected, with dim wordless intuition, that something of a real and lasting and unpredetermined kind of value lay concealed. That such an impulse is alarmingly proximate to, say, an undergraduate's simultaneous belief in (a) the generalized coolness of, like, *books* and (b) the preciousness of his own insights—this is not lost on me now, and was probably not much lost on me then.

But listen: I went to graduate school and several very great things happened, and happened particularly to that quotidian object-love. Two of them seem to me in retrospect to have been the most sustaining, though they are so interwoven it's difficult to think of them in sequence or isolation. For the sake of clarity, we'll put them in order. First, that avidity for certain kinds of objects was forced to find for itself *languages*, analytic vocabularies that offered precision and conceptual density in the place of the inchoate enthusiasm with which I arrived. Here is the first remarkable transaction: they did not, those wrought and difficult conceptual languages, *cancel* that quality of delighted captivation by, in effect, professionalizing it, forcing it through the narrow channel of a trade-language, or disciplinary idiolect. (I had been assured, by more than a few probably well-meaning professionals, that the cumulative effect of graduate school, if not the actual point, was to smother all the sparks of untutored enthusiasm you might bring to the scene of your education.) But an idiolect, I came to know, is not the opposite of ardor, just as articulacy need not be the grave-yard of pleasure. The languages you begin to speak with more and more assurance and agility, and to make more completely your own: these, sometimes, are ardor's vehicle. They can give coherence to the complex delight you feel in relation to certain objects, as well as a versatile, usable form, by which that delight can, in turn, be sustained, elaborated, enlarged.

That's one way of thinking about what you're doing in graduate school, whatever field you're in: you are being trained to see the world in the grain of a spectacular, inexhaustible complexity. (Be warned: academic discourse prefers complexity in explanation even when—ethically, politically, affectively—simpler accounts may be more appropriate or effectual.) You are enjoined to develop an analytic vocabulary that equips you, first, actually to see the world unfolding around you as in fact possessed of a detailed, finely textured intricacy; and second, to describe that intricacy, and why it matters, with clarity and precision and grace. And one can see why the acquisition of such languages might be described as an arduous, solitary, joy-dampening sort of work, made no less so, now, by the often frankly exploitative conditions that mediate that labor.

All that's true. But it's also true that these are languages you are learning to inhabit *in concert with others*. And this is the second, similarly great thing that happened to me in graduate school: I found that what one might cherish with a sustained, lifewide devotion was not only objects—books, passages, arguments—but the scenes that kindled around them, scenes forged in the heat and friction of contestation and knit together by, precisely, language, the languages we were just then learning to inhabit. The almost inevitably collaborative quality of graduate life matters greatly—or it did to me—since talking about why you love what you love with other passionately interested parties, or why you find one idea generative and another hackneyed, or one book's political intervention clearly the superior of another, does more than give you improvised training in the use of critical languages you'll need later, in whatever kind of "professional" life you find for yourself. Making a language together is, after all, another way of describing what it is that happens, not only when you're enduring the often attritional sociability of institutional life, but *when you fall in love*, with friends, with lovers, with entire scenes. We all know how this happens. In your besotted ardor, you invent together a baroque terminology that carries within it your styles of apprehension, your delights and your disdains, the whole fabric of the scene that, by speaking this language back and forth over years and refining and reworking and reanimating it, you and those you love elaborate into being.

In this way, if you're lucky, the trade-languages of your discipline can get interfused with the heated, ambulatory, extravagant kinds of talk by which the intimate worlds you assemble in these years are sustained, worlds that are marked by frustration and fear, without question—it is graduate school—but also by great quantities of intellectual exhilaration, and hilarity, and care. Eventually, of course, years, and the demands of varying modes of life, will have their dispersive effects. But one of the things you may find you're left with in the aftermath of all that upheaval and displacement, along with your questionably valuable degree, is just that mixed and variegated language, that winning idiolect. Continuing to trade versions of it back and forth across windening distances, you may find, is one of the ways the best, most energizing aspects of those worlds can be nurtured, transformed, extended into unforeseen futures.

And then, one day, you encounter something that is outsized and terrible, that devours ardor at the root and will not be dislodged by even the most venerated of the objects that have for so long nourished you. Language itself, no matter how conceptually rich or steeped in the history of your dearest affections, will seem like the thinnest and most friable of scrims between you and horror. And I promise you, though you may not recognize it at the time, the voices of the people calling you back to a scene of language-making you once inhabited, and back to a self trained in patient discriminations and in the wringing of clarities from messy indistinction—they won't cure you, these voices, alas. But they will act as a testament and a reminder. You will need both.

Circumstance

Odds are there's not much I can tell you about graduations that you do not already know. If you've been only to one, you will know the basics: the mawkishness, the viral replication of platitudes, the speeches and encomiums and ill-advised flights of Latin—the sound of a dead language being killed, a friend once said—and the generally glacial pace at which things proceed and process.

But there is also, a little bewilderingly, the crossing of all this ritual tedium with bright-lit moments of genuine exultation, of accomplishment and pride and love overflowing.

The sharp conflict between these two things, the numbing and the suddenly radiant, might be one reason people so often cry at graduations.

But there are others.

If you're curious about these other reasons for tears, I know who can help you. Ask the plus-ones. Ask the standers-on-the-edge of commemorative photos, the queerer kin. Ask the step-parents. Ask the *ex*-stepparents.

*   *   *

Because of what I do—teach literature and theory and especially queer theory to college-age kids—I probably think about rites and ceremonies rather more than I'm made to attend them. This is not the worst thing about doing what I do. Along the way I've picked up a few benchmarks for that thinking, for wondering about how rituals make and unmake visions of kinship, family, and love.

For instance, in a beautiful book called *The Wedding Complex* from back in 2002, Elizabeth Freeman cracked open that great ritual of heterosexual consolidation and, reading the wedding's baroque arrangements of persons and relations with exquisite care, restored to view all the queernesses nested there within it. A wedding, she showed, ritualizes all the looser, lateral, errant forms of intimacy and attachment—think of groomsmen and bridesmaids, think of flower children, think of the wide array of communal invocations—that the legal act itself, the *marriage*, means to subordinate and deemphasize, as it sanctifies coupledom as the paramount social form. As Freeman presents it to us, the wedding is a ceremony haunted by queer ghosts: a ritual that can't help but broadcast all the expansive, extrafamilial forms of belonging from which the marriage itself seeks to remove the couple.[1]

I'd like to be able to say something similar works itself out in graduation ceremonies, those ponderous rites of ascent. But honestly—and here, maybe it's just the obliquity of my own experience talking—I incline to doubt it. For the graduate, there are teachers, mentors, friends, and fellow travelers, and this is all duly noted. Still, it can feel a bit rough, the culminating shout-out directed, inevitably, to Mom and Dad.

"Will the families stand up?"

This is a wholly unmalicious moment. But it also brings into swift relief the obvious fact that all the pageantry and speechifying might have encouraged you to mislay, which is simply that occasions such as these are as much about the concretization of a specific social fantasy—a vision of the good life, or at least the normal life—as they are about anything else at all.

Queer theory, by the way, has always known this, and has given us wonderful tools for anatomizing these microclimates of sociality. In an essay from better than two decades ago, which has lingered undissipatingly in the rooms of my thought since I first encountered it in grad school, Eve Kosofsky Sedgwick wrote of "the brutality of a society's big and tiny decisions, explicit and encoded ones, about which lives have or have not value."[2] What she says of *lives* is true, also, of forms of relation. So the closer you can get to the charmed circle of official family, the more rich you will be in these particular forms of recognition.

And the further afield you are? Well, from the perspective of those outerlands, you might find yourself asking, with urgency and with pain, a different set of questions: What makes my place here? What ballasts these unofficial attachments, these deinstitutionalized loves? Ongoing devotion? Responsibility and care?

Will the families stand up? What is it that makes for anybody's enfranchisement under the sign of family? On whose authority do you know to stand or stay seated?

A lot can occur to you inside the long moment of this hesitation.

And then, perhaps, it comes to you. You start to entertain the thought that what ties you to this moment is that other thing around which "family" is ever and always built. That thing, of course, is sorrow.

* * *

Here is what you do if you are someone like me, someone on the cusp of official family. On a rainy morning in the upstate countryside, inside an echoing gymnasium of exposed concrete and scant bunting, join the dozen or so supporters of a sweet kid about to graduate high school. What is your place among them? This is a question of high emotional resonance but also, in the moment, of a more practical sort of confusion: where to sit?

Accept the luck of things and take the seat that's offered to you.

This is how you find yourself seated immediately behind the woman with whom, for a while, you raised the child about to graduate, back when this child, her daughter, was in grade school and when the two of you were married. Take your seat behind this woman, whom you loved with a devouring and half-frantic ardor, and watch as she casually touches the forearm of the man for whom she left you, years ago now, those few weeks after you found out you and she were not, as you had thought, going to have a baby. Sit maybe a foot behind this man, his overstuffed camera bag, his rolled-up bluejean cuffs. Look for a long blinding time at the naked nape of his neck, as he whispers nothing consequential in the ear of the woman you were married to, and then, one day, weren't.

It's at this point that time will start to get gluey. And so, as your stomach begins to turn over on itself, as second by second you feel yourself coming wholly unstrung, tie yourself together like this: as intently as you can, think about the wonder of love you feel for this kid, this beautiful miraculous kid, sitting up there invisible to you among the crowd of girls. Not, as occasions like this are always reminding you, *your* daughter, maybe not even your stepdaughter anymore, but the girl to whose mother you are no longer married. And feel that love as, in this strange and unnerving way, it comes shivering through your body.

It will help, at this point, to try to recall what a friend once told you about "that familiar pairing," as she put it, of women and tears. Crying, she said, is for women often the expression of cyclonic sorts of feelings, like grief and especially rage, that can in the moment find for themselves no other acceptable outlet. And cry, and cry, and cry, and cry.

*   *   *

It's remarkable to consider the genuine impoverishment of our conceptual vocabularies when it comes to imagining forms of care and nurturance—of love—that fall even a little aslant of the normatively familial. We can throw a world of praise and Emmys at fare like *Modern Family*, we can cultivate the not-unuseful (if a bit therapeutically saccharine) languages of "blended families," we can in our more fulsome moments insist *love makes a family*. None of these things is malign. Neither do they do much, cumulatively, to dislodge the sign FAMILY, with all its unexpurgated narrowness of vision, from its place of singular prominence.

Graduations are far from the only time we see this. Another example: Years ago the little college where I taught made the altogether sensible decision to implement a uniform policy for parental leave, so that the newly pregnant would no longer be left to negotiate what terms they could for themselves in individual arrangements with supervisors, unbound by any strict policy or precedent. At the faculty meeting where this was being finalized some colleagues and I, many of us associated with queer work on campus, suggested that this was so welcome a development—but oughtn't it to be a policy that extends *not solely* to new parents? Oughtn't it to address anybody entailed in responsibilities of care that become, suddenly, outsized and unworkable: people with parents or siblings or friends who find themselves in dire need, with lovers or cohabitants who become sick, or with children not their own for whom they are abruptly required to tend?

Make the basis of the policy, we suggested, "intimate care," rather than parental leave. Wouldn't that be a form of distinction at least a little less invidious?

I won't say those suggestions were greeted with hostility, exactly—though there was some—so much as exasperation and a genuine bewilderment. Couldn't we see that this clear and elegant policy could only be muddled by these esoteric extensions? After all, as we were reminded *repeatedly*, people in such situations could surely work out private, individual arrangements for themselves. Or were we just antifeminist?

It was hardly a crushing blow, just another small reminder of the order of things. But I can remember thinking how neatly it tracked with the turn in national queer and progressive politics toward what would later be called "marriage equality." I don't mean that quite as dismissively as it might sound. Yes, there is an unhappy irony here, in the ways a complex ethic of intimate care, energized by the fraught and shifting alliances among feminists and queers of color and sex radicals and the sick and the dying, would give way to a national politics devoted to the re-enshrinement of the connubial couple. You can indeed feel pretty disheartened when you think even for a moment of the astonishing richness of theoretical legacy in queer scholarship for addressing precisely these questions—from Gloria Anzaldúa on the borderlands to Samuel Delany in Times Square all the way out to Sedgwick's wonderful remark about "the theoretical parsimony of the Oedipal scenario"[3]—and of how easily it was all made marginal in the rush toward that all-trumping freedom, the freedom to marry. If you came of intellectual age in a moment before "marriage equality" was the coin of the kingdom, you will know well of what I speak.

But it is understandable, more than understandable, that there should be politics mobilized around marriage. This is so much the case that even to be ambivalent about this political turn—as many of us are—can feel churlish and ungenerous. Nobody isn't happy for their friends who choose, because now they *can* choose, to be married. (Least of all divorced people like me.) It simply is the case that a multitude of forms of entitlement and social enfranchisement reside still in the normative family. And these forms of recognition—recognition in its most public as well as its most intimate senses—are a long human way from negligible.

*   *   *

I'll say this for graduation ceremonies: you are afforded the chance, in those tranced unmoving hours, to do a great deal of thinking.

As I sat there, feeling a desperate gratitude for my ex-wife's sister, who occasionally put a steadying arm around my shoulder and fed me a stream of tissues, I confess I thought not that much about the intellectual and political trajectories of theory from the '90s. Instead, I thought about exactly the sorts of things you're meant to think about at graduations.

I thought about the kid up front—now a poised, arch, rangy eighteen-year-old—going to kindergarten, wearing this huge beaming toothy smile. I thought about the singular ferocity of her six-year-old crying jags, many of which were about, disarmingly, *justice*. (There she is crying at swim lessons because she had been scolded for breaking a rule, though it was a rule that, with an outraged sorrow, she insisted she hadn't been told.) I thought of visiting her at this school far from home, to which she had determined, a little heartbreakingly, that she wanted to go; about how amazingly free from insolence she was in her desire to put distance between herself and the people who loved her, and whom she loved; about how I described her, and her laserlike focus, to friends in those years. "She's like an arrow speeding through the air," I said.

I had a quick clear vision of driving home from ballet in a winter snowstorm, and talking together about the awesomeness of "In Between Days," by the Cure.

And as the sound of it in my head drowned out for a happy moment or two the speaking of dignitaries and deans (*oh it couldn't be me and be her in between without you*) I thought about the grace, the splendid pop magic, with which songs just like that had sustained us, me and this kid, especially in those awful, queasy months after I'd left our house, when my contact with her daily routines became so abruptly attenuated. Since she was eight I'd been making her mixes on her birthday—I was and am very much that guy—and through the blessed gift of microprocessors I'd been able to keep them all, archived across a series of devices. For her eighteenth birthday I had in fact remade her the whole collection, some twelve hours of music, a great sheath of CDs.

But in the months and then the years after the divorce, I'd begun sending her music whether or not it was her birthday, for Valentine's Day or, once she'd gone away to school, for exams. I remembered a text she sent me once about a Santigold song: "Your mixes," she said, "are all that gets me through study hall." For weeks I'd hear it and feel a jolt of uncut happiness.

*   *   *

These were the better, the more manageable moments. As the ceremony's minutes slow-dripped along, there were others. For instance, I was reminded of how wastefully I'd passed a lot of the days since my removal from the immediate orbit of this child's life. So much stupid time was spent thinking—if you can call that short circuit of counterfactual obsessiveness *thought*—about the person seated now just in front of me, and of how she lived her days. There had been at the scene of our dissolution so much wreckage, so much haphazard cruelty, and I regret to say that I had, in my more broken moments, treasured up visions of some secret sorrowful reckoning. It is hard not to: you imagine this face, this once so-cherished face, and then you imagine it haunted by sadness, an inarticulable regret.

Sit where I sat for a few hours—though honestly a few minutes would have done just as well—and you will see that this is, in addition to pathetic, wishful and inane. There is no great mystery here. People live with what they have done, the griefs they have made, in the absolutely usual way, the way everybody does. It's simple: You build around yourself an ordinary, analgesic life, made up of accreting moments and small gestures. That whisper, that glance.

Everyone has a right to this. It is no crime. I will tell you this, though: to see it up close, in the fine grain of its details and in slow articulated time—this, I promise you, is edifying. You look away and look away until you can't.

It's probably true that, for just about everybody attending them, graduations make for a queasy seesawing of delight into sorrow and back. But for me, the intimacy of those two feelings had a different taste. It was as clear a reminder as any I've ever had that there is another name for that mix of joyousness and unexpended grief, and for their permanent adjacency. You might just call it *ex-stepparenthood*.

*　　*　　*

Like every other intellectual movement or strain of critical thought, queer theory is periodically pronounced dead. There's nothing particularly malign or wrongheaded about these cyclical bouts of derision, Oedipal though they may be. In a *Chronicle* piece from a few years back marking the end of the venerable Series Q from Duke, Michael Warner addressed the dialectics of queer theory's demise and ongoingness, and noted in particular a fruitful ambivalence in the strongest new queer work about its own organizing rubric. Taking as exemplary Jasbir Puar's pathclearing anatomization of the racist and imperializing logics at the heart of an increasingly hegemonic queer liberalism, Warner noted that Puar's *Terrorist Assemblages* works simultaneously as a brilliant critique of queer politics *and as queer critique*.[4]

I think he's right. Which is another way of pointing to something of the unexpired utility of queer theory, in at least one of its extensions. Whatever else one can say of it, this work offers us an intricate critical archive that, however beguiled we may be in the contemporary moment by the marriage plot, enriches our conceptual languages, and particularly our languages for imaging the fraught terrain of intimate life, inestimably. It is work that, with an imaginative force that has accumulated over decades, reminds us of all the sorts of love that are no less durable, ardent, or cherishable for being more or less nameless. Think of Lauren Berlant's great thumbnail description of queer scholarship as rooted in the effort "to focus on patterns of attachment we hadn't even yet known to notice, patterns in which sexuality and intimacy are enacted in a broad field of social relations that anchor us to life." She goes on, beautifully, "Being a friend, a regular, a neighbor, a part-time lover, an ex-lover, an intimate; being gender dysphoric, or just plain gay or straight—all of it is seen as an effect of many causes and a complex, intimate practice of world-building."[5]

Nothing about the world suggests to me we have less need, now, of just this impassioned articulacy, this expansion of the roster of attachments we can recognize as sustaining and valuable. And sometimes I think we need such language as badly as we do, such galvanizing inducement to recognition, not because loving people do not instinctively wish to employ and extend it. We need it because it is a thing the world encourages us, ritual by accumulating ritual, to forget.

*   *   *

At the end of all the pomp and photo-grabbing clamor, I sat with the new graduate for a few minutes in a room of rich, wood-paneled decor with rain-slanted light pouring through the latticed windows behind us. I gave her the gift I'd thought she might enjoy, and it plainly made her very happy, which was wonderful to see. She read the inscription, which said something simple, and then turned to me and said something simple, and this caused my voice to tighten and my eyes to well. And then, as the impulse to tearfulness strained at me yet again, she looked at me.

The look she gave me is all I want to keep from the day.

Like her, it was direct, and smiling. It was wordless. What it said was: *I know this was hard for you, but really everything is ok.*

So when I say that she is miraculous, this is what I mean. I mean the astonishment of a kid who smiles this smile while surrounded by what from so many angles looks like disaster—ex-husbands, new spouses, a dense cross-wiring of adult sorrow—and who, somehow, makes room for all of their love.

Minutes later the lot of us—cousins, exes, aunts, steps- in many forms—crowded around her for the obligatory portrait of this once-ever assembly, what Philip Larkin calls "this frail travelling coincidence."[6] Before I detached from the gathering and made my way to the parking lot, she kissed me goodbye and said, "I'll see you next week?" She would. And then, a little wearily, grinning at everyone around her and eyeing the sky smeared with clouds, "Are we done here?"

Joy Rounds First

I am not a sports fan.

It's true, I watch a little, and have some bits of gear—my Italia jersey that I wear when the World Cup comes around, my Yankee hat—and in a vague way I keep up. But having a stake in the fluctuating fortunes of the New York Yankees has never felt to me like, say, a devotional practice, in the way that listening to bands and reading books and fighting about them so plainly has been. I've liked the Yankees fine. But the truth is I have not loved Mariano Rivera with anything like the life-traversing ardor with which I've loved Emily Dickinson, or Carson McCullers, or Prince, or Mac and Laura from Superchunk.

So imagine my surprise as, in these last weeks, I found myself planted night after idle night on my couch here in Chicago, watching the last season of one of those Yankees unfold, one mediocre outing into the next. When people I know express surprise that I watch baseball at all—I evidently do not project the convincing vibe of someone who gives a lot of fucks about baseball—I have this stock line prepared for them: Some people meditate; some people do yoga; I watch baseball. And it's true. *It chills me out.*

But these weeks have been different, and not because it's now autumn, the season of high stakes play in baseball. Not so for the

Yankees, who have been all but mathematically out of it for some time. The drama, for me, has been elsewhere. You probably know by now that the Yankee captain, Derek Jeter, has for the whole of the year been taking a kind of victory lap around baseball. About this hypermediatized peacocking, as about Jeter himself, I have found it hard to care that much one way or another. It's tedious and sappy and hyperbolically commercialized, certainly, the sport's way of staging an elaborate season-long commercial for itself and its confected virtues.

Of course the mawkish spectacle has also been accompanied by an inevitable Jeter-hating backlash, much of it a kind of push-back against traditional sportswriting's gauzy appraisals of "character" and "respect" and, oh god, "grit." Fair enough.

But then a truly strange thing happened. Reading the backlash, cycling through still another account of how statistically *only just ok* Jeter is, about how idiotically distracted everyone's been allowing themselves to be by inessential extrafactual aspects of his twenty years of on-field performance, I discovered, a bit wonderingly, that I was agitated, *angry*. I got angry, I mean, in the way I might if someone had written a dumb account of a book I really cherished, or a singularly ungenerous record review.

This was a surprise.

*   *   *

How do we account for athletes? Are they simple collections of data? I'm not so sure, though neither I am much interested in turning them into stand-ins for our least imaginative values ("giving 110 percent" etc.). Still, being unduped by the dipshit invocations of *character* and the like has seemed to require a pretending-away of much that makes games watchable, and players compelling, and sports themselves intricately joyous, in ways that do not reduce to metrics. So, in the key of backlash, the otherwise capable Tom Scocca offered this paragraph of pure performed unknowing:

> Like most star athletes of his era, he kept his public persona intentionally blank and dull, but with none of the awkward self-consciousness of the similarly restrained Rodriguez. Depending on their allegiances, baseball fans could imagine him to be classy or imagine him to be pissy, and the limited evidence could support either conclusion.[1]

Honestly I read this and thought, Dude are you fucking joking me? Blank and dull? To come to that conclusion you have to ignore, effortfully, the whole rich trove of things that make the player who he is and has been. I'm thinking of all those accrued microgestures and tics of personality that as a kid you imitate and as an even casual observer you gather in in their assembled mass—*like the reader of a character in a novel*—until you have a character, real and fictional at once, over whom you can agree or disagree as your pleasure takes you. Roger Angell, in "The Interior Stadium"—an essay of such luminous beauty and stacked compounding perfections it ought to be studied forensically, liked a Bach chorale—gives name to this kind of fabulating pleasure-taking: "baseball in the mind," he calls it, and reminds us that it is a procedure that, from outside the diamond at least, defines the experience of the game as much as any metricized rank or tidy column of figures.[2]

So I mean: *Blank and dull?* This guy? That shrugs away the wry grin, the capacity for deadpan humor, the odd coldness he could sometimes show, the occasional arched eyebrow at some opposing player as they chatted around second. And this is not even to mention the right hand up to the umpire, the clapped hands rounding first, the downward lateral slash of the practice swing. All of that is blank and dull only if what you want is Mad Al Hrobosky.

And while none of that makes him the greatest Yankee of all time or even a good shortstop, still I'd say the pretense that none of it is even there is its own kind of bullshit, a kind of trying-too-hard to be over any but the hardest of hard facts. Again and again I thought: this is like appraising a novel in the conviction that the character of the sentences, their curl and bite, *does not matter*, not at least in relation to what happens to whom and how. Reading the backlash, I was reminded of nothing so much as certain kinds of technocratic boy-critics, determined in their critical austerity to be unseduced by the frivolous distractions of pleasure.

Another way of saying this is that I realized, dear reader, that I maybe loved Derek Jeter.

* * *

And so there I was Thursday night, in the familiar position: supine, beer in hand, enjoying a baseball-induced lateral drift away from my life—and enjoying too the warm embrace of my elegant new couch. Everything, I should say, was new, the couch, the table, the TV, the room, the city, everything. I was back in Chicago at all only because, after some sixteen adventurous years teaching at a small college in coastal Maine, in the spring I'd accepted a job out here, in this city to which I had over the years developed a habit of returning in moments of great exuberance or great need. I'd arrived in early July, right around the All-Star break.

And, a bit like the Yankees, I'd had a trying sort of summer, some wins scattered around what often felt, in a day-to-day way, like a lot of losses. As it turns out, it's *hard*, launching yourself into such lifewide upheaval, harder at least than it was when last I changed cities and jobs, as a buoyant and mostly witless twenty-seven-year-old. All of it had left me a bit glassy-eyed here in Chicago, feeling a weird combination of battered, faintly exhilarated, and, often, very, very scared. *Are you excited?* People would ask. And I'd say, Oh, I'm sure I'll go back to feeling excited, once these tides of panicky dread recede.

They did not, not immediately. Instead I walked around this city I had always delighted in and experienced a strange sort of dislocation. I had people here, in fact some very dear loves, and a small band of generous-hearted friends of friends who were willing to meet up for bourbon and sympathy. All of this was steadying. But I felt too, with sometimes terrible acuity, the difference between having some people and being part of a world—some dense and coherent collection of interwoven loves among whom you feel not just safe, and not just pleasingly legible, but enriched, enlivened, pushed out toward ampler versions of yourself. On the losing days (and I confess there were more of these than otherwise) it felt like desolation, this living at the center of a world grown, suddenly, pretty uncrowded. I'd wake up in this new place, blink myself into consciousness, and there'd come this quick hot burst of fear: of aloneness, of isolation without remedy, of a separateness from the heat and light of the turning human world.

*   *   *

All of this was alive in me as I sat there watching Jeter's final game unfold. But it wasn't just the spectacle of this forty-year-old gamely wheezing through his final days, though I confess that for much of the summer I'd enjoyed watching Jeter play in much the way you might enjoy a Medieval morality play entitled

MIDDLE AGE. (Jeter's final season was so much not that of Mariano Rivera, who'd retired the year before, and provided a daily fantasy of the possibility of time-smiting agelessness.) Maybe it was just the heightened focus of impending loss, that bright clarity of vision that comes to you when you know you're watching something as it takes place, in real time, unpredetermined, for the last time. And yet it didn't feel elegiac, exactly. Nothing about it wrought me up with a sense of diminishment or impending loss. Instead, the whole last game—the RBI double in the first, the fumbling throwing error the next inning, followed by that crooked self-deprecating grin—came to me steeped in a kind of pleasure I hadn't been looking for, and was surprised to find.

Inevitably, as the innings clicked along, the game was more and more attended by the specific delights of social media, its odd and warming proximities. Via email and text and Twitter, across Facebook posts and threads, there came the companionable satire and invective. "Will Jeter play old-timer games or go full Jay-Z and start hanging out with Marina Abramovic?" one friend inquired. And then another: "As an older and wiser Red Sox fan, one who has known many defeats but finally some triumphs, seen the ebb and the flow, one who has learned the humanity and frailty of opponents and heroes, I think I have the good grace to say, fuck every Yankee ever, and the horses they rode in on, twice." It was like that, which is to say: ordinary, familiar, and great.

But then the drama kicked in, the lead, the *loss* of the lead, the dawning realization that Jeter would, indeed, come to bat again. And there it was. You've seen it and, I hope, heard it. Go to your computer, google "Jeter's last at bat," and thereupon: behold.

Now, the idea that watching a player speed around first base could be like hearing the key change in a song you once fell in love to—this may not be news to you. But Derek Jeter, in his last at bat in the Bronx, smacked a B-grade fastball into right, and he rounded first in a state of half-shocked delight, and this lousy losing team gathered around him as if they were once more actually champions, and the huge new stadium, that wretched monument to the grossest neoliberal expropriation, shook on its soldered foundations, and my heart, my stupid counterfactual heart, leapt into my throat.

But you know, it was just Derek Jeter, middle-aged man in a costume, arresting time and holding it open, precisely the way a song does—the way he'd done for me in 2003, when I was watching the ACLS playoffs in New York and was newly married and imbecilically happy; or in 2009 when I'd last taken my broken-open life to Chicago for repair and renewal and he'd won still another World Series, the final game of which I watched in a corner bar while wearing a Mickey Mantle jersey my uncle had given to me only months before, as a way of saying what he did not quite have the words to say, which was, "It's awful that you're so sad, but listen, you have nothing to be ashamed of and I love you still"; or on some dull Maine night in the middle-aughts when one of his weak rally-killing double-play groundouts gave me and a bar full of Sox fans something to whine and joke and fight about.

Like about ten million other people, I'd had a lot of life transpire in the company of that quasi-virtual figure being mobbed on the infield in the Bronx. So seeing the undiluted joy of it, of the moment and its consummation and its instantaneous canonization . . . this rolled through me as an exhilaration just as silly and rapturous as it was statistically unsound. And it didn't even feel like *winning*—even I am not so counterfactual as that—but something much, much better: like a testament to pleasures shared and undiminishing, like the nearness of loves undispersed. It was

a moment of my enfranchisement as a fan, a fan in the saving way
I've long understand fandom to work, and I don't know about you,
or Keith Olbermann, or those fact-checking boys on the internet,
but I'm gonna keep it with me like a memorized sonnet, like a
heart-lifting last sentence, like a love song coming up on shuffle.

Loving John

My John story begins with the following minor epiphany, folded into one bright corner of John O'Hara's beautiful novella from 1960, *Imagine Kissing Pete*:

> After I became reconciled to middle age and the quieter life I made another discovery: that the sweetness of my early youth was a persistent and enduring thing, so long as I kept it at the distance of years. Moments would come back to me, of love and excitement and music and laughter, that filled me as they had thirty years earlier. It was not nostalgia, which only means homesickness, nor was it a wish to be living that excitement again. It was a splendid contentment with the knowledge that once I had felt those things so deeply and well that the throbbing urging of George Gershwin's "Do It Again" could evoke the original sensation and the pictures that went with it: a tea dance at the club and a girl in a long black satin dress and my furious jealously of a fellow who wore a yellow foulard tie. I wanted none of it ever again, but all I had I wanted to keep. . . . They were the things I knew before we knew everything, and, I suppose, before we began to learn. There was always a girl, and nearly always there was music; if

the Gershwin tune belonged to that girl, a Romberg tune belonged to another, and "When Hearts Are Young" became a personal anthem. . . . In middle age I was proud to have lived according to my emotions at the right time and content to live that way vicariously and at a distance. I had missed nothing, escaped very little. . . .[1]

"Nearly always," he writes, "there was music," presiding over a scene of vivid abundance—"of love and excitement and music and laughter"—that comes before the falling-off, the quiet life, the moment when we know, in an evidently deflating way, "everything."

A gorgeous turn, I always thought, given to an old point, which is just this: whatever else you can say for adolescents, they fucking know from desire. So much of the world is inaccessible to them, a thing transpiring on some misty far-off shore. But it is also un-fixed, unfated, yet to be locked into pattern or place. It makes for dreaminess. Add music into the mix—even George Gershwin will do for the purposes of *throbbing urgency*—and you get something reliably combustible.

This is at least part of why it's never seemed to me wrong to observe that there's something regressive, some trace juvenility, in loving records, radio, pop songs. *Regressiveness, juvenility,* I sometimes think—*you say that like it's a bad thing.* What do they do, these three- to four-minute interludes of captivation, if not connect us to prior states, half-buried versions of ourselves? Where better to turn for a reminder that certain alivenesses, to vulnerability and ache and exhilaration, are maybe not as foregone as a quieter life suggests? Honestly, you could love them just for that. A lot of us do.

*   *   *

Some years ago a writer named Laura Kipnis got a good deal of press for a piece she wrote about that favored diversion of disaffected grown-up life, adultery. "Adultery," it was called, and her basic, only partly ironized position was: strong-pro. As Kipnis sees it, the main utopianish thrust of adultery has to do with the way it "dares to stake out a small preserve for *wanting* something," even if it does so "largely through the always available idiom of sex." This is a complicated quasi-utopianism, though, not only of wanting things (fresh start, new flesh) but of wanting oneself—or, you could say, of wanting a self that gets to want things, to want what it desires without the cushioning overlay of preemptive disappointment. "Passionate love," Kipnis writes,

> is one of our few chances for self-reinvention, to shed our ties
> to quotidian personalities and their often badly tattered in-
> timacies, lashed as they are to histories of disappointment,
> anger, and other forms of personal failure. In other words . . .
> what keeps you glued to the phone till all hours of the night
> exchanging soul-searching, whispered intimacies is actually
> the courtship of another new object—*yourself*—and a new set
> of conditions for personhood. The beloved mirrors this new
> self back to you, and aren't you madly in love with both of
> them, with two idealized love-objects?[2]

Out of that mad love Kipnis builds her case for the enliveningness of adultery, and for the ways it can restore even to people grown overfluent with resignation the sharp sense that happiness, fulfillment, a life unsmothered by discontent, all are live possibilities.

I've made it seem a shade fanciful and professorish, but there's a lot to recommend the piece, which if nothing else is written with an alertness and an agility not common to exercises in contrari-

anism (that dreariest of genres, so cherished by professional assholes). Still, there's always seemed to me something off about the
argument, even beyond its desire to recode what is basically *the*
signature avocation of bourgeois indolence as some kind of insurrectionary training ground, a vanguard praxis of the furtive and
concupiscent. Adultery, after all, is hardly the only scene where
dreaminess and desire enjoy a reckless flourishing, or where you
might encounter *wanting* in its furthest-flung conjugations. I can't
be the only one who reads Kipnis's account of the exhilarations of
adulterous sex—"perhaps something new does enter the world . . .
for a minute, you had your perspective shifted, had a new emotion . . . change seemed possible"—and thinks, *Dude, maybe get
a turntable.* Nor can I be the only one who gathers up its terms
(something new? the possibility of change? a crushing sense of
dread shot through with spiky exhilarations?) and is like, *Prevailing awfulness notwithstanding, there was indeed a lot to being seventeen, yes.*

As *Imagine Kissing Pete* is there to tell you, these two things—
the turntable and the nervy vibrancy of youth—are often one, and
it makes sense. Think of it even for a minute. Recall how you *listened.* Remind yourself of the experience of playing some set of
songs literally hundreds of times, with an unwearying devotion, as
though buried somewhere within them were the encoded secrets
to a future happiness. Think of the eerie sense of being found, *seen,*
by a song. Think, dear god, of young trenchcoated Lloyd Dobbler
(né John Cusack), boombox aloft, standing undeterred in a misty
late-'80s dawn as Peter Gabriel's "In Your Eyes" ascends plead-
ingly to the ears to love-object Diane Cort (née Ione Skye), in the
deathless *Say Anything.* All these scenes of overvaluation, idolatry,
melodramatics in every key—they are part of the venerable folklore of adolescence. "There is color in their souls," the great early

theorist of adolescence G. Stanley Hall wrote more than a century ago, "brilliant, livid, loud."[3] Or as another critic has it, contending with the afterlives of a Blonde Redhead record: "These are the kinds of songs that can smash a person to pieces, because they somehow invariably zero in on the soft emotional centers that made our adolescences as turbulent as they were. They find feelings that we don't think about much because we like to imagine we've mastered them."[4]

That critic is a man called John Darnielle—whom you may know by the name of the band that he also is, the Mountain Goats—and allow me to say: he knows of what he speaks. He makes for the second part of my John story

*   *   *

The first time I saw the Mountain Goats perform it was on a counter at a tiny record store on Valencia Street in San Francisco, in what must have been the fall of 1996. You could say I was by then no longer an adolescent, though to believe that you'd have to credit the nonjuvenility of twenty-five-year-olds. He played a brief set sitting up beside the register, accompanied by a sometime collaborator, a violinist, who had I think just flown in across the Pacific, or was maybe about to depart? I remember there was an atmosphere of sociable affection brewed up between them, as of friends happy to have intercepted the other in his orbit, if only for this thrown-together half-hour.

I say this like I recall the performance in some detail, but the truth is I do not. My friend-from-forever Mark had seen a listing in some local paper, thought it might be worth checking out. I had moved out from the grim expanses of western New York only weeks before, and so what I most remember is the little plume of delightedness that erupted in me then, ignited by the plain fact of just goddamn being there, and not back east—inside a scene where music was happening, made by people I hadn't heard of, whom I could watch perform while standing shoulder-to-shoulder with maybe a dozen city-dwelling strangers, and Mark too. I hadn't even lived upstate that long. But some part of me had felt starved, marooned and desperate, out in the unpeopled wilds of Route 17. "We live four hours in every direction from most human culture," I liked to say then, with a dickish assurance that suggests the governing moods of adolescence were not in fact much behind me, no.

So to be part of the small ceremony of that in-store show, then and there? Believe me when I say it felt like nothing so much as the faltering ship of my life righting itself at last, or starting to. I remember I bought two CDs that day, Mark a few records, and off we wandered into the sunny Mission, transformed but not yet knowing it.

Smash-cut, then, to three or four years later, to the back corner of a Chicago venue called the Empty Bottle. I'm there with another forever-friend—this one called, in fact, John—and we've assembled to see the Mountain Goats, in whom we had come by then to take a steep, conjoining pleasure. What was not to love? For years Darnielle had been putting out these homebuilt, half-janky-sounding records—you could hear the turning gears of the cassette player he recorded the songs into—that were clever, a little weird, dorky, cerebral, tender. There were songs about breakups, Sweden, Thomas Hardy, Chaucer, the Cubs. Indie-rockish, book-smart, treasuring up our tendernesses, what were we to do, John and I, but surrender to those sweet rushes of infatuation?

Loitering in the back room with my preshow High Life, I find myself startled by a different sort of recognition. "Dude," I say to John, "I think that's him." In the near corner, unobtrusive, glass in hand, there stands a slenderish, mediumish, not especially noticeable figure who, turns out, is also among the most gifted songwriters of his generation. Nobody is talking to him. I watch, a little incredulous, as this companionlessness extends from one barloud moment into the next. And so unmenacing in aspect is he, so without the force field of self-regard thrown out even by the minor celebrities of this ultralocal demimonde, I nerve myself to go over, say hello.

I have real reservations about meeting heroes. It's embarrassing, when you're not nine, to *have* heroes—for you, for them. They maybe do not need the personalizing intrusiveness of your ardor. Then, too, they may be fucking awful. It has been known to happen. As I've gotten older and written more and traveled a bit I've had the chance to meet some of the people whose work I love, and my answer has almost always been, "Thank you—I'm good."

I'm happy I did this, though—happy then, and happy now— because John Darnielle turns out to be exactly, but exactly, the person you'd expect him to be: gracious, engaging, bubbling with an enthusiast's chatty receptiveness. Where his songs are recondite, delicate, and bittersweet, he is all friendliness and immediacy. We talk about Chicago, the Midwest. I mention I am a professor, and he allows that he has known some of those. We speak a bit about books, writers. We part with a handshake, off I go to my John, off he goes to the stage. There he will sit for a mesmerizing couple of hours, in front of a roomful of people as no-longer-teenaged as I and, to appearances, every bit as crushed out.

*   *   *

What makes for the special weather of adolescence? You know the textbook answers—that one experiences in adolescence the intensity of first things, like love and sex and freedom and betrayal, undulled by repetition or an overlay of nostalgia (this is the "strength and pain of being young" thesis we get in Phillip Larkin, for instance[5]); that the unfinished becoming of adolescence produces these feverish and never-to-be repeated dramas of anxious self-perception (see here, for a heartstopping expression of same, *The Member of the Wedding*, by Carson McCullers). All this is true enough. But I like to put it a bit differently. Adolescence, I think, is a moment defined by a great and terrible dual discovery. It is when you learn, first and with some astonishment, that the world is overfilled with people, beyond the closed circle of the family, who might love you. You discover extrafamilial love—better to say: you discover sex—in all its world-enlarging turbulence and exhilaration. *However.* In almost the same instant that you learn about the vast promise of extrafamilial love, you learn too that most, or indeed all, of those people in the world who might love you *will fail to do so.* Anyone *could* love you; no one, apparently, *wants* to. If you wanted to know about the dreaminess and laceration of adolescence, the frenzied longing and not infrequent devastation, you could start there.

Pop songs know this about adolescence. And so too, in some formulation or other, do the people who listen to them. Here again is Darnielle, writing for his great long-ago zine *Last Plane to Jakarta*, in a fictional portrait of a young person arriving at himself in the metal scenes of '80s north Florida that has stayed with me since the moment I read it:

The shows I saw in the mid-to-late eighties were pivotal events for me. Away from the youth-group meetings I'd been compelled to attend from a very early age, I discovered a person living within me who I didn't know, and of course it was my real self, wild and free and unfettered. . . . Our feelings were like raw, live wires, and the places where these wires formed circuits to let their energy flow freely were the non-descript buildings in which we subjected ourselves to aggressive music played at very high volumes. The Possessed shows. The Annihilator/Kreator/Nuclear Assault package tour. The incredible early Megadeth club dates, where there'd be no more than fifty of us in the room, convinced that there could not have been a moment in history more densely packed with meaning than the one in which Dave Mustaine delivered the rejoinder to "Killing Is My Business . . ." into a smashed up SM-57: ". . . and business is good!" Hoisted above the heads of our peers, riding the sweating sea of their bodies, we surfed the mosh pit and felt things that our parents could not conceivably have understood.[6]

Kipnis talks about the jolt of discovering that wanting what you want is, just possibly, not always pointless, an exercise in self-canceling futility. That is not news to this narrator, who would tell you that, when it happens, you feel certain that *there could not have been a moment in history more densely packed with meaning.*

And maybe you're like, *Megadeth? Really?* There's a temptation to say that one great thing about adulthood is the sense of proportion that arrives with it, which allows you to recognize all at once how meaningful a thing can be and, also, how preposterous. But then it's not clear to me that adolescents don't know that already. It might be that it is precisely this willingness to hold fast to desire, even in the teeth of the near-certainty that it will turn out to have been *entirely ridiculous,* that lends to teenage ardor so much of its daffy heroism—that quality Darnielle invites you to think of as a kind of absurdist nobility. Consider another *Last Plane* piece about metal, this one called "Letter to the Prime Minister of Greece," whose author demands the issuance of an official commemorative postage stamp in honor of a band called Rotting Christ, greatest ever metal act to come from "the cradle of western thought." It is delirious and unimprovable:

> I understand that a man in your position has but little time to expend on stories of how young men waste such time as will never, never come again; yet bear with me a moment longer, for I am not the madman you suppose. I am only that into which my rude elements have been shaped by the music I have heard all my life. Somewhere in the middle of high school, it dawned on me that AC/DC wasn't just campy-good, as my theater-department friends and I liked to suppose, but genuinely great; I came around to the painfully obvious conclusion that "Back in Black" was great by anybody's yardstick, and that anybody who didn't think so was a pompous ass. It was a liberating moment. I went to see AC/DC at the same venue where I'd seen Heart years before . . . and they blasted Inglewood into the middle of next week. Once a young man has understood that great rock and roll must in some sense be *savage* to be any good at all, it isn't long until the desire to be in the permanent grip of that savagery pursues him night and day, and so it was with me.[7]

Go ahead and laugh. The high-flown idiom, the nod to Poe's maniacal obsessives, the starchy formality and the presiding metal: all of it underscores the comedy. But laughter, at least here, is not disavowal and it is not rebuke. What shines through instead is a giddy testament to the life-traversing enormity of responsiveness even the dopiest-seeming objects can stir up in us. "I will say it even if your weak-kneed politicians won't," he says of one song, "anybody who doesn't find these screams simultaneously terrifying, hilarious, and completely thrilling is not fit to live on this earth or breathe its sweet air." I will confess to having stolen these phrases, folded them up and pocketed them like a pair of clean twenties, for use in bar-table debate, back-of-the-party colloquy, and many other of the favored occasions for aesthetic appraisal.

It's silly, yes, but you know what? *So is desire.* And that, for Darnielle, is so much of the alchemical magic of songs. We love them so much, so preposterously, and unlike more or less anything else in the world they can hold every bit of it, all the ardor and sorrow and yearning we bring to them. They recognize us when not much of anybody else will, certainly no lovers, and mother of god is there no overstating the galvanic power of that exchange when you're young. *They stake out a preserve for wanting.* They pry open this precious little space inside you, wherein you can hold fast to the possibility that there might yet be other objects—possibly even objects that are *people*—who will take the full measure of your love, offer you some like quantity in return. If you're over twenty-five and still listening to pop records, my bet is you know something of what this is like.

But maybe you prefer your polemics in the form of airy and brief songs, in which case I have something for you. The comedy, the affectionate generosity, the admiration for the tenacity of young people, who know so much about the desperate immensities of wanting: all of it is compressed into a song that all Mountain Goats fans know, that induces rousing in-concert sing-alongs such as I imagine would warm the heart of the kid who learned history at a Megadeth show. It is called "The Best Ever Death Metal Band

Out of Denton," from the 2002 record *All Hail West Texas*, and it is where my John story has been headed all along.

This song tells the story of two school friends, Cyrus and Jeff, whose never-named band—which they feel certain will one day bring them "stage-lights and Lear jets and fortune and fame"—is broken up when Cyrus, for having stenciled on their instruments "in script that made prominent use of a pentagram," is sent to a correctional school "where they told him he'd never be famous." It concludes:

> When you punish a person for dreaming his dream
> Don't expect him to thank or forgive you
> The best-ever death metal band out of Denton
> Will in time both outpace and outlive you
> Hail, Satan! Hail, Satan . . . tonight!

I can assure you that in all the annals of human speech and song, never has that closing call to the Dark Lord been voiced with so pure a dose of *sweetness*. It may be that these kids are about to do something awful, to follow through on what the penultimate verse calls a "plan to get even" that will transform the joke of their discarded band names ("Satan's Fingers, the Killers, the Hospital Bombers") into something terrible and real. But the song invites us still into a great tenderness for these kids—an aching sort of love—if only for the unsurrendered breadth of their desire, a world-hunger so vast that the only available emblem of its grandeur is the Archfiend himself. (Press your ear close to the song and you'll hear filaments of Marlowe, Milton, the Stones.) You listen to it, to the reedy hitch in Darnielle's voice, and that tenderness is not hard to feel. Who hasn't had that friend? Who doesn't know that song?

*   *   *

And now, the out-chorus to my John story.

Maybe a dozen years after my amiable bar chat with John Darnielle, I was living in New York. I'd had, let's say, a rough patch. Nothing calamitous in the metrics of the world, but at the scale of my own small life horrible enough. For some time, I'd been keeping close to me a memory from another Mountain Goats show, to which the same friend John had taken me, as a surprise, on the otherwise chancy occasion of my thirty-eighth birthday. (*You want to know how much John loves me?* I'd say. *That is how much John loves me.*) By then the Mountain Goats had become a different kind of famous, so it was a cavernous venue, a younger crowd. Midway through the show, spotlit and swaying as he strummed the opening chords of a lilting new heartbreaker called "Up the Wolves," Darnielle leaned into the mic. "This is a song about survival," he said. *Survival.* It wrecked me. I was glad John was there—my John—with a steadying hand on my shoulder, a reassuring nod.

Smash-cut, then, to a coffeeshop called Second Stop, long-since defunct, somewhere out on Lorimer. Like everyone else, I'm keyboarding away, earphones in, when this man strides in. We catch each other's glances, and something flickers between us. *How funny,* I think. *That's John.* Our long-ago chat had been such a warming memory—we'd even exchanged a few companionable emails thereafter—and made such a nice accompaniment to the lonely hours I would later spend devouring *Tallahassee*, his album-length meditation on wreckage, dissolution, divorce. You like to think, when you're young, that the big feelings that will eventually find you are going to be varieties of exaltation, all starshine and consummation. That's not how it goes, though.

I make my way to the counter where he's ordering and say something like, "I'm sorry, I don't think you'll remember me—are you John?" He looks me over and, with all the grace in the world, says, "Oh! You're the professor—in Maine, maybe?" Again we shake hands. I tell him I'm in Brooklyn for the summer. He says he's around the corner, recording. I tell him that's wonderful to hear, and that I'll let him get back to it.

But another impulse tugs at me. Sheepishly, with as little indirection as I can, I tell him I've had some bad times and his records, his songs, have really been there for me, even in the worst of it. I say I suspect he knows something of what that's like. I tell him how startled I am, and how glad, to get the chance to say thank you. "So, uh, thank you!" I say, in awkward conclusion.

A pause. A beat. Then, without saying anything, he deposits the two tall coffees he's holding back down on the counter. He leans in. He puts both arms around me and, just like that, gathers me in an embrace. He tells me that's a kind thing to have said. I thank him again. The door swings shut behind him. The surrounding chitchat and clatter carry on.

"He *hugged* you?" John, my John, will say down the phone later.

"Yeah, a hug. It was lovely."

"That's fantastic." A pause, a beat. "No, for real—that's fucking perfect."

The Impostor

"I'm not saying it was 'loud,'" I'm insisting to the kid. "I'm saying it was nuclear-grade. I'm saying it was like some squealing tween Armageddon. I'm saying it was *insane*."

Beside me in the passenger seat, she's playing it cool. Even now, though, an hour or so after the last encore and a number of highway miles between us and the arena, you can tell she's amped, still tingling with the adrenal postconcert elation that—old though I may be—I recognize very, very well.

"I dunno," she says, deadpan.

"Dude, it was scary! Didn't you think?"

"What I think," she allows, "is that if *I* would've been the girl he pulled up from the crowd and brought onstage? And gave those flowers to?"

"Yeah?"

"I think," she says, and there's mischievous little blaze in her eyes. "I would've played it way cooler."

"Sweetie," I say, "I have no doubt."

*   *   *

Grow up playing in bands and going to shows, spend a life in echoing arenas and cacophonous bars, and you will, I promise, know from noise.

So I hope you'll believe me when I say I have never heard any sound—no thunderclap, no shriek of feedbacking guitar—remotely as apocalyptic, as mindstunning and huge, as the EEEEEEE that went up the instant the lights went down in the concert hall and we all became aware that, in bare seconds, Justin Bieber would grace the stage.

You felt it, that sound, in your organs, your viscera. You felt it in your teeth.

Later I'd say that it was, in the original sense, sublime.

"Dude!" I had shouted over to the kid, who of course couldn't hear me, though she grinned and grinned, this frantic wonder stealing across her face.

Put it like this: I was glad to the brink of fear.

*   *   *

Much of this was just the gladness of the kid herself. A few days shy of fourteen—this, her first-ever concert, was her present from me—she was in her daily life so steady in herself and, I kept telling people, cool. Equable, even-tempered, she was the kind of kid who was forever putting to rout all the horror stories people try to sell you about teenaged girls, their volatility, their unique awfulness. She was a lot of things, this kid, but awful was none of them.

So I was surprised when, as we navigated our way through the surging crush of tweens and suburban parents at the merch table, she kept herself as anxiously close as she did. Again and again she huddled in, grasping my elbow with more nervous urgency than she'd done in, oh, years and years.

I should probably say: I had not actually lived with this kid for quite some time. She was my youngest stepdaughter. Or she *had* been—until, a few years before, with a shattering abruptness, her mother had left me. The sorrow of that dissolution was pretty well dissipated by this time, though of course other wrenching little puzzles remained.

For instance: As far as the girls were concerned, I was—what, exactly? The man who used to be married to their mom? Their ex-stepdad? It was not especially easy to say.

I won't tell you this wasn't a kind of heartbreak, my newly nameless status in the girls' lives, because of course it was. But we'd done our best, charted our way through the weird waters of this suddenly untitled togetherness. In our dinners out or on in-town walks or in any of the multitude of animated ice-cream-parlor disputes over bands and boys and records, I was by now mostly just Pete.

Pete, are you gonna finish that? Oh my god, Pete, you are so *wrong about Katy Perry!*

And so it was tonight. "Pete," the kid said, once we'd acquired our requisite Bieber-swag. "Can we find our spot? I wanna be, like, ready."

* * *

You wouldn't think a Bieber concert would be the most contemplative space. As I followed behind her through the gargantuan arena, though, I kept finding myself drifting away on little inward reveries. You know that party conversation you have with friends of roughly the same age, where everybody confesses to their first-ever concert? (Mine was Van Halen, FUCK YEAH.) I thought and thought and thought about that—that funny little world-making ritual—as we meandered through the congested corridors and angled in the vague direction of our nosebleed seats.

This, the Bieber show, was her first-ever concert. It would *always* be her first concert.

And here she was. With me.

* * *

Even in those early years, it was easy to look at Justin Bieber and see that most familiar species of fraud: the mass-marketed pop-impostor. ("He's a Canadian white kid who wants nothing more than to be Michael Jackson," is how I used to put it.) But then that's pop superstardom writ large, isn't it? There's always some-one ready to point you to its confected phoniness, its algorithmi-cized reverse-engineering. This is no less true, god knows, of teen stars—in part because, out there in the wide world, there is not much that's more belittled and mistrusted than the ardors and en-thusiasms of girls.

But you know what? I straight-up loved that first Bieber record. Have you listened to "Baby" lately? You should. It is, I would later say, chirpy tween heroin: catchy like a virus, gleaming with stu-dio polish, giddy and silly and sweet, and buoyed along by—of all preposterous things—a rap interlude by fucking *Ludacris*, tuned up for the seventh-grade set and dropped smack in the middle of it. It's a triumph.

And yet and yet: it nagged at me, that specter of fraudulence. But then, it *always* nagged at me. When you are an ex-stepparent, you live in unresting relation to the category of "impostor." How could you not? From your undesignated and semivoided position, you think a lot about what it means to be marooned from the more ordinary, more ballasting languages of legitimate family. You never cease knowing that, whatever you are or will be for those kids you delight in and worry over and cherish, for a lot of people it will just seem quasi-real, a well-meant simulacra.

You think what I guess all parents think, though from an angle very much your own: *What are we going to be for one another? What will become of all that love?*

*   *   *

But there we were, the kid and me. And there—after the terrifying cyclone of noise had decrescendoed—was Bieber himself. And *dear god*, that show. In these pubescent days, his physique was roughly that of a folded-up ironing board. He wore, over the course of the night, three tracksuits: white, black, red. His sneakers matched. At one point, guitar in hand, he clambered into a heart-shaped carriage-swing contraption and floated out over the heads of the astonished crowd.

I thought I might never stop laughing.

"Dude," I shouted, "that is 104 pounds of solid-gold SHOW-MAN right there."

Imagine a Vegas-style spectacular, all dazzle and strobe-lit enormity, staged entirely for tweens. Imagine it all italicized somehow by an uncynical joyousness. That's what it was like.

All throughout I kept stealing glances at the kid, at her in-seat dance moves and sing-along rhapsodies, those passages of pure teenaged transport. Now and then she'd look back, strike a superstar pose, mock-glam.

And then, with Bieber as witness, a new thought dawned.

Maybe he was an impostor: a bit of pop merchandise, a knockoff whiteface imitation and nothing but. Maybe that was fair.

Look at the kid, though. Look at that lit-up elation. Look at that—you'd have to call it—love.

Imposture, fabulation, fraud: maybe these were not *always* the right words. Or maybe, in the vicinity of your loves, you could do a lot worse.

*　*　*

"So what would you have done?" I'm saying, as we wend our way back to home. "If he'd pulled you up on stage?"

"Oh," she says, "I'd have just been like"—setting her expression to maximum chill—"*Oh. Oh hey, Justin Bieber.*"

Now it's my turn to fill the car with sputtering laughter.

"Dude," I say, "you're a star."

She gives me another sidelong grin, half teenaged irony and half little-kid brightness. "I know, right?"

PART III

Kids

Easy

Like all people not wholly destitute of heart, when I hear the opening of "ABC" by the Jackson 5 I experience the familiar jolt of pop elation—that swift giddiness of spirit that comes of being in company with a human thing that is also so pure a distillation of joyousness. This was true before I had kids—before, say, I'd propped their rubbery and squirming little selves on my hip and swung them in woozy circles around a living room in Maine singing, *that's how easy love can be!*—but it was a lot more true, and a lot differently true, after.

I should say, though—I don't "have" kids, not by the measure of any number of authorities. What I mean is: I was married to a woman who had two very little girls. For some years I was their stepdad. And then, one day, to my steep and unhappy astonishment, I was no longer married to their mom. What I became to them then, and am now, goes by no state-sanctioned title or much-recognized name.

For a while, though, the four of us shared a little house near the coast, and together made our way through the mazy and ordinary complications of improvised family. It was hard—for me, still a youngish man who had little experience with kids and even less with little girls, it was *very* hard—but it was also, this sudden new life, a daily adventure in ingenuity and invention. Among the rituals we devised for ourselves in the early years, in our hunger for habitable familial forms, was that of the Pre-Bedtime Dance. (When the girls were very small, this was also often the post-bathtime ritual, and so was appropriately named "Naked Dancing," which set for a me a new benchmark for delirious little-kid exhilaration.) We would dance to two or, maximally, three songs, and then their mother would take them upstairs for pajamas and books and goodnight kisses, and I would clear the table, do the dishes, maybe catch a few innings of a Red Sox game on mute. Sometimes it was the Cure, sometimes it was the Magnetic Fields, sometimes it was, in deference to their mother's tastes, the B-52s. "ABC" was never not among the selections.

A splendid literary scholar named Jennifer Fleissner recently observed that pop songs are "the new madeleine," and I can think of few truer critical insights.[1] So we would, the four of us, caper and twist and jump. The girls would take turns being twirled around, and we'd gather them up and sing, *C'mon-c'mon-c'mon let me show you what it's all about!* I can remember on one particular winter night finding myself looking at our oldest girl, the one whose rigorous devotion to family-wide *fairness* even then broke my heart a little ("We like being at *all* our houses *exactly* the same," she would remind her sister, with some sternness), and then, as she gave herself over to three or so minutes of unclouded and full-bodied joy, feeling this shock of helpless, undefended love for her.

*   *   *

Let me confess: I was not, then, as open to these dawning tendernesses as I ought to have been. Here's what I can tell you about stepparenthood: it's like a tango on a balance beam. You want to be parental, to share the often incapacitating labors of care with your spouse. But you want to be mindful, too, that these children have fathers and mothers, whom you never want them to feel you are trying, even in the most implicit way, to supplant. These are on the easiest days delicate geographies, and all the other things of grown-up life—envy, money, anger, sex, loss—conspire to intensify their fraught, fractal complexity. The quick-shifting uncertainty about whose role was whose, and what its parameters were, could play a quiet kind of havoc with your couplehood, and because of the stunned, the altogether devouring passion with which I'd fallen in dumbstruck love with the girls' mother, all uneasinesses around the scene of my marriage put me on edge. I was susceptible, too, to feeling a bit second-string. When a kid falls off her pogo stick in the driveway, her first startled cry is not likely to be for her stepdad, no matter the breadth of his care.

It tells you a lot about the embryonic state of my achieved adulthood that I had room, back then, to feel a bit hurt by this.

*　　*　　*

But even I wasn't so stupid not to recognize a blessing when I saw one, and whatever the turbulence and tedium of raising them—I had been totally unprepared for how much of the labor of child-rearing is ecstatically, mind-scaldingly *boring*—I knew these little girls, with their weird enthusiasms and slangy playground speech and sudden cloudbursts of tearfulness and hilarity, were a kind of astonishment. Playing defense against my own fears and failings, I would tell myself again and again that perhaps the only genuinely good parental thing I brought to their lives was just the example I gave them, by being so radiantly in love with their mother, of how they deserved to be loved. Still, I cannot pretend not to have had, even then, the dim sense that something else was being transacted between us. For all the impacted circumstances, for all my imbecile guardedness—for all that I had permitted to stand between me and openheartedness—it was also, I knew, simpler, more elementary. I loved them.

But it wasn't just this. Because when we'd crouch down together and make a four-person huddle of jubilant noise there on the living room rug, when we'd start to soul-clap in the breakdown where Michael shouts out *Sit down girl!* and Sophie would jump up into my arms, all bright eyes and toothy grin and unrestrained silliness, even I couldn't stop myself from knowing what, with both wonder and not a little dread, I knew. It was right there, easy, *like counting up to three.*

She loved me too.

*   *   *

You don't need to be Freud to believe that our lives are, in uncountable ways, far too much for us: too dense with conflict, want, shame, dread, bliss—with all the intricacies of accreted personhood—for us ever really to have a full grasp of them. I sometimes think this may be less a matter of repression than of, I don't know, the raw mechanics of cognition. Our days are so overfilled with this hectic clamoring of impressions—scenes, textures, a vastness of data at once physical and emotional—that memory, even at its most receptive, could never hope to take it all in. In some respects, this is welcome. There is much we do best not to retain. But in others it's pure heartbreak, a reminder of the torrent of unstanchable loss at the heart of things.

For a lot of us, I think, this is much of what makes pop songs— those fairy-dust confections, flimsy and cheap—so inestimable a

gift, a thing for which no performance of grateful devotion, however outblown or overwrought or objectively absurd, ever quite
suffices.

Once, in an airport, in the midst of a harrowing postdivorce
trip whose failed purpose was supposed to have been an Eat-Pray-
Love–like self-restoration, "ABC" came up on shuffle. And I swear
to you, as I stood in the passport line, despairing still again at Italian pretenses to bureaucratic efficiency, I nearly wept with sod-
den gratitude. I knew then, wordlessly and with a kind of elated
certainty, that pop songs had once more taken the brokenness in
me and, through their weird saving alchemy, bound it up. Because
what would we have done, the girls and I, without the Jackson 5?
How could our queer unmodeled love have found a language for
itself in the first place without that song and all it allowed? And
what would we have done, in the terrible vertiginous weeks and
months and then years after I found myself removed from the orbit of their daily lives, had we not had these outrageous gifts from
the made world, these *songs*, where so many of the nameless aspects of our devotion to one another had come to reside? How
better to hold ourselves together, even in our distance, than by
trading these songs back and forth, and inventing around them a
little private vocabulary? How better to nurture these improvised
attachments, these loves so suddenly deprived of official titles, a
proper name?

So what I heard in "ABC" in the airport that day, and in the
years after the stories of our lives together became entangled in
so many unhappy endings, was not the joyousness for which I first
loved it. It wasn't even the sound of a damaged family, such as the
Jacksons surely were, producing in seamless harmony a thing so
purely jubilant, though that's there too. For me, it was something
else. Michael would sing *1 2 3, you and me!* and the groove would

shiver up the length of my body, and every least crosscurrent of those living room nights—the smudgy faces, the fraught love, the whole atmosphere of this life I once so cherished—would come glowing back to me. Like so many of us do with the songs we love, I turned "ABC" into a kind of archive, and what I kept there, preserved against forgetfulness or the inevitabilities of loss, were just these bright intensities.

They are there still.

This, I like to think, is our happy ending.

Our Noise

We are, my youngest stepdaughter and I, at the bar.

This is years ago.

It's true there are not many other thirteen-year-olds poised on stools and leaning, as if expertly, toward the beer spigots and ranks of bottles, but nobody seems to mind. The kid herself certainly does not. She swivels this way and that, bends to her straw, checks the scene. The clamor carries on around us in an ordinary weeknight way. There are dudes twirling their big-bellied glasses of wine in scholarly scrutiny. There are clutches of ladies laughing over neon cocktails. There are couples tilting toward one another. And there is, additionally, a lank-haired and, for this little city on the coast of Maine, impressively beautiful young man working the bar, who attends to each and all with an able smooth-flowing flirtatiousness.

"Yeah," the kid is saying to me, "but he's just so . . . so *arrogant*."

"Sweetie, of course he is!" I say. "Wouldn't you be? If you were him?"

In fairness to myself I should note that I have not taken my newly teenaged stepdaughter out to a bar, or at least not intentionally. We're not at some speakeasy or portside dive. We've gone in fact to a restaurant—a fancyish French restaurant, that *she* chose—which proved to be overcrowded with diners looking for a winter night's escape. And so we have been seated here, at this elegant curving bar. And anyway, I tell myself as I fidget just a bit nervously in my seat, what's the harm? The kid herself, to appearances, is as deep in the enjoyment of this slight alteration of context as I am in the fact of her company. I'm noticing just now that she has grown over her last months into a kind of poise that I, at least, do not much identify with the early teenage years. She holds herself so unanxiously. She still can be a touch overawed by her big sister, I know, but you can see her working not to be, not to be baited out of her self-composure. She knows somehow how to look around her, to measure and assess, without seeming to gawp. She is watchful, observant, cool.

I notice, too, that she has not stopped tracking this bartender, whose striped black-and-white shirt (in campy "French" style) does not quite descend to the belted top of his skinny jeans. Tousled, bearded, lithe—you look at him and want to guess the name of his inevitable band—he is the very type of new-millennial hipster handsomeness. He's also, in a funny way, *terrible*. Preening, a bit leering, so wildly overdelighted in his small-market beauty you can't help but relish him, if a little meanly. He cajoles and chats, tells stale little jokes, receives from his patrons indulgent grins. He hands off drinks and, with the cocktail-drinking ladies, grazes their forearms with a discreet touch as he passes.

"I guess," the kid says to me. "But nobody should get to be that conceited. It's *annoying*."

"Dude, it is so *not* annoying. It's awesome! It's, like, the awesomest part of him."

We are speaking, as sometimes we do, of Kanye.

*　　*　　*

It's always easy to mock the young. Their untutored enthusiasms, their volatility, their assurance in the face of complexities inadequately grasped. Pick your liability. No one, I suspect, not even the most kindly disposed among us, would say there is nothing to cause impatience in any of this, or irritation, or an elderly roll of the eyes.

And yet and yet.

At just this moment, that default condescension has an ugly edge to it. We are greeted almost daily with news of fervent protest, and equally fervent demand, often initiated and sustained by young people. (Think of Ferguson, or Baltimore, or Parkland.) This is so much the case that the public ritual of worrying over the misguidedness of the youth has become a veritable cottage industry, the takes coming fast and hot. Some are quite thoughtful; some are, in regard to the hue and cry, thoughtfully skeptical. And then, some are just dog whistles. Witness, now, the chorus of voices bravely standing up to chastise *snowflakes*, their thin-skinnned preciousness, or—in something of an underremarked paradox—to bemoan the furious assault on time-honored and sacrosanct values being perpetrated by the ruthless young ("what about *my* free speech!"). Others have described more exactingly than I can the hollownesses of these attacks, penned often by what the redoubtable Joshua Clover calls "concern trolls and speech-bros."[1] The collective moral, for me, has been: *Try to be on the side of the young people.* Now as in the past, you can do a lot worse by way of first premises.

But if you're old, or even just older, the temptation to correct and cajole, to *instruct*, can be irresistibly great. I confess I have a lot of respect for that pedagogical impulse, perhaps more than I should. There is after all a disequilibrium built into relations between the older and the younger. Sometimes, being young means actually needing the care, the solicitude, and even the words of older people. Not always, but sometimes. Knowing when this is so and when it is not can be, on both sides, chancier than you'd imagine. For older people, the turn toward solicitude can feel at moments less like condescension than like a responsible discharge of the obligations of adulthood—like, in fact, love. You don't spend the time many of us do talking with young people about ideas, and reading their writing and writing back to them, without being pulled at least a bit in the riptides of these contrary impulses.

Here's a thing about stepparenthood, and its wrought unpatterned strangenesses: it speaks up—it instructs—at the oddest, most unpredicted junctures. And one of the things you can learn from it, I am here to tell you, is that the pedagogical impulse, no matter how generously intended or italicized by love, is probably best resisted.

The young people have languages of their own.

*   *   *

Her big sister and I have had a many-tiered debate about Kanye West circulating between us for a while, as she knows. Like more or less everyone, the girls cycle between aversion and deep attraction. I'm considerably less ambivalent (*Graduation* has just come out, and is awesome), so I tend to offer defenses of Kanye's genius spun around genre—"Can you imagine an MC *without* arrogance?" I say; "Can you imagine how dull that would be?"—and the world's ever-renewing uneasiness around Black men who refuse to cringe. Of course the girls know this without me telling them and, in respect to their resistances, I get it. The oldest is nearing the end of her first year of high school. Her days are spent in the company of fifteen-year old boys. She needs no tutorials in male arrogance and self-hyperbolization.

But the youngest, here with me in the bar and without her sister, is taking up the question and running with it. She talking about what she likes better in Jay-Z, which Kanye tracks are the most dexterous and fluent and excellent, and what she finds off-putting, exhausting, *annoying*. Great god, is there anything more killing than the inflection given by a thirteen-year-old to the word "annoying"? It straightens your spine. And so we drift, in conversation, among the limitless varieties of teenaged irritation, as I drink my beer and she attends, with winning vigor, to her steak frites, and then to mine. All the while, she keeps a watchful eye on the bartender, who minuets among patrons, striking brief poses, basking a bit in the light of all the erotic attention diffusing around him. Our conversation meanders. It shifts and grades. And this is how we begin speaking, not of annoyance in its general appearance, but of the pressing and particular annoyance of *boys*, boys both generic and in her direct acquaintance. On this topic, she has much to say.

She tells me of this one kid's fair-weather kindnesses, this other kid's jerkishness, of the modes of "dating" swimming up into sudden possibility for the world of seventh-graders. She warms to the topic. She talks and talks, and I follow. We decide together that "adolescent boy" is indeed an unpromising genre of person, though I remind her that boys too have many things to be frightened by, even if their way of being afraid is, often, dickish. Her tone is derisive and light but there is too, tracing through it, some faint urgency. I notice this and find that I feel toward it, and her, a great rush of tenderness. Like the smart kid she is, she's trying to work it all out—girls, boys, their odiousness and attraction—and she's doing it here, now, in real time. With me.

I have some sense that my role here is mostly that of sounding board and I am wary, with the practiced wariness of stepparenthood, of overstepping. But it's a delicate endeavor, especially now. By this point in our lives together, a lot that is terrible has happened around us: divorce, dissolution, separation, and, on my part, a very outsize sorrow. Before their mom and I were married, the girls invented a term for me: I was, in those in-between days, their semi-stepdad. *Semi-stepdad!* The improvisatory genius of it! How then to calibrate these distances and proximities, here in the more uncertain terrain of a relation no longer bound by a home, and marked by adult grief?

We eat, we talk. We tell familiar jokes. We speak of Kanye, in little arias of disparagement and praise. We take each other's cues.

And so, here at the bar, balancing my wariness against this glancing invitation to ampler talk, I risk a little. I say, in a stage-whisper, "OK, sweetie—check this guy *out*." And together, with commentary running largely to the satiric, we observe our so striking bartender, noting his coy smiles, his calculated touches, the whole wonderful preening theater of him. We try to locate him within a matrix of Annoying Boy Attributes, and decide he is conceited, though in degrees not yet approaching Kanye-levels. But he is also, without question, a little charming. *Adorbs* is the term we use. And also pretty. Very, very pretty.

"That's the thing," I'm saying. "Boys are annoying in so many ways. But that doesn't mean you don't get to want to, like, smooch his face."

She gives a quick braying laugh. I have no idea where the phrase comes from—*smooch his face!*—but, just as soon as it's been uttered, it sticks. It will pass between us as a term of art, a shared bit of idiom, for years to come.

"Sometimes there's a boy and he's whatever he is, he's this or that. And you just want to smooch his face. And that," I say, "is totally fine. I mean, don't let anybody be nasty to you, but you know that. But sometimes, you know. . . . Sometimes you want to smooch somebody's face."

She's bright-eyed, maybe a shade abashed, but also grinning. "Yeah," she says. "It's true. Sometimes you just wanna smooch his face."

This is how she and I learn how to talk about sex.

"Anyway," she says, "if you think *Graduation* is better than *College Dropout* you're, like, super-high."

*   *   *

Everything about that night at the bar came back to me recently, when the kid stopped over on a spring-break visit out here to Chicago. She's nineteen now, not thirteen, which is to say she has places to be, deadlines to manage, friends from a spinning galaxy of locales blinking into presence on her phone. Her time in the city was necessarily brief—quick tours through hipster districts, chatty lakeside strolls, an ice-cream parlor lunch—and, for me, a bright blur of delights.

It's hard to name the particular radiance that comes from being in company with this kid, the strange cocktail of elation and relief. It's been years—*years*—since the routines of our lives overlapped in a daily way. So many of those early seasons of separation were, as I say, rough. What this means now is that, whenever we're set to pass long hours together after a period of separation, some small ghost of that roughness revisits me. I can feel it stealing over me; I brace up. I know, by now, what it is, this little premonitory wincing of spirit. It tastes of grief, of course—I had so not wanted to lose those girls—but also, more nearly, of shame. So much had happened that was unhappy, to both of us, and here was the thing: *I had prevented none of it.*

How would they ever forgive me? Would I deserve it?

But then, within the space of a few minutes of easy-flowing chatter, whatever coiled fret I've trundled along with me to our re-encounters—it unclenches, and dissipates, and is gone. A comet-trail tracing out the darkness behind us. Rushing into its place is just the kid herself, the charmed atmosphere she makes for us to move in, and all that we have always had to hold ourselves together: talk and countertalk, gossip, old jokes, unceasing fashion commentary, dude-appraisal, disputes about movie stars, TV shows, songs. *This* is our togetherness, reknit in each new scene. And I will tell you: that the kid enters with such grace into this strange reparative labor—into the work of devising anew a way of being together—prompts in me these great surges of amazed, grateful love. No matter how often we repeat these voluble rituals of our closeness, I ride a little bubble of elation. This visit is no different.

And I mean, not for nothing, she's fucking hilarious. Right now, for instance, like many another stylish teenager with a finger firmly upon the pulse of cool, she is cultivating a connoisseur's taste for—and I swear to you this is true—*the Nineties*. The bands, the shows, the insane sartorial choices, everything. It is like an arrow speeding directly for my middle-aged heart. There she is, a vision in patterned fleece, ultra-highwaisted jeans, and the kickass Blundstone boots I identify wholly with indie rock and she with collegiate fashionability. It takes about eighteen seconds in my house before I realize, with a jolt of wonder, that we are, the kid and I, *wearing the same boots.*

The vain delight this causes me is unseemly, perhaps. It is also very, very real.

"Dude," I say. "You're up in my *wheelhouse*."

"Dude," she says, deadpan. "I know."

And this, friends, is how we come to be listening, and listening again, and then again, to a song so beautifully awful, so inextricably terrible and delighting, I'm almost ashamed to tell you about it.

We have been driving neighborhood to neighborhood across the city, and she is controlling the music, so naturally we are listening to some algorithmicized '90s ROCK programming, which soon has us sputtering with laughter and derision. *Smashing Pumpkins! Fiona Apple! Counting* fucking *Crows!* But then, slicing through the radio fare, with no sufficient warning, there it is:

Doot-doot-doot! Doot-do-doot-doooo!

"Oh, man," she says.

Doot-doot-doot! Doot-do-doot-doooo!

"Oh, *man*," she says again.

And then, "This is kind of amazing."

This is how we come to be listening to "Semi-Charmed Life," by an afflictingly bad band called Third Eye Blind.

Do you remember "Semi-Charmed Life"? My bet is, if you heard it twice—if you were sentient in 1996, and had a radio—you do. It is malevolently catchy, and so deeply of its moment it could be part of the fucking geologic record. It's like the anthemic Urtext of the alterna-bro. Put it like this. There's this picture of me, taken in about 1998, in which I appear, slouched and rumpled, in an overlarge flannel shirt, hair falling in lank scraggly curls in front of my face. On that face too is a goatee you could only describe, if you wished to be charitable, as ill-conceived. As I would say of this picture when it found its way to the spaces of social media: *Everything you might have hated about the '90s, there in one place.*

"Semi-Charmed Life" is that picture, realized as song.

Except it is also, unlike the picture, full of a weird, awful, fantastically persuasive charm. I don't mean that it's so hooky and hydraulic that you *forget* it's a song about being coked off your face and missing your girlfriend who is, like, superhot, or you *forget* that it's sung by the pure anticipatory embodiment of the future generations of techbros who would one day rule San Francisco, like fratboy pharaohs. Categorically, you do not. There is a vileness here that *seethes*, unrepentant. And yet, somehow, the song overwrites this awfulness with its own winning, unhindered, unbelievably stupid exuberance.

"Seriously," I say to the kid, who cannot get enough of it, "this is more like a staph infection than a song."

But she knows, oh she knows, and has no need to be told. In fact, the idiot infectious hilariousness of it is making her all but levitate with pop glee.

"Oh my god," she says. "I may never stop singing this song." And sing she does. *I'm not listenin' when you say*—huge indrawn breath—*goodbyyyyyyyyye* . . .

I laugh at this, and join her in the next chorus, and the car fills with our voices, and with the sounds of '90s guitar rock at its maximally confected. And for a flashing moment I'm filled with the wonderful sense of this song, this terrible song from back in my own joyous and embarrassing youth, coming into a brighter destiny than anyone could have imagined for it. By the strange swift magic the kid just carries around with her, she has remade it into something sweeter, and funnier, and altogether lovelier than it had ever been.

Hereafter, I think, it will never not have in it this visit, the kid at just this preadult instant, the two of us in this epoch of our own rekindling improvised love. Everything, from her companiable silences to her laughing volubility, from her '90s overalls down to her asskicking boots, will sound out inside of it. And this will be true even after she's gone—she'll be gone in a day—when the sudden sorrow of her absence makes me feel hollow and bereft, and the hours of missing her will start up little fires of the old, still-combustible grief.

Those hours are coming, I know it. And maybe because I do know it, I find I want to say so much about this song, to tell her about San Francisco in the middle-'90s, the MTV takeover of punk rock, the delicious wretchedness of this lyric or that. ("Sweetie, this is a dude who *believes* in the sand beneath his toes . . .")

But I try not to, not too much. Look at her. She does not much need these words. I try instead to pay attention to the laughter in her ringing voice, and to what's within it.

I want something else . . . to GET ME THROUGH THIS! she's singing, and so am I. But we're saying something else. We're saying that nothing, not even something this terrible, is beyond transformation. She's reminding me that it's not unusual for awful things to reemerge, through paths you could never have imagined, as occasion for hilarity, and closeness, and nourishing delight.

Sing along, I tell myself. Shut up, for once. Listen.

She sings and sings. She learns the words. She hits repeat.

Where I Want to Be

When I was younger—though still a bit too old for it—I had a radio show at a tiny college station near the coast of Maine. This was in the early and middle-aughts. I was a professor at this college, and our ninety-minute program was called, straightforwardly, *The Postpunk Show*—a good rubric, my cohost and I thought, inasmuch as it gave us license to play more or less whatever the fuck we wanted, so long as it appeared after 1976.

In five or six years of weekly Wednesday afternoon broadcasts I was heard, I'm guessing, by about three dozen people. If there is a more exact measure of the levels of competence, sobriety, and professionalism I brought to the whole enterprise, I don't know it.

It was great.

It was great because college radio is great—the malfunctioning machinery! the outré tracks! the earnestness and awkwardness and long delicious passages of accidently dead air!—and about this there can be no disputing. It was great because the fact of the show, and the anticipation of it, punctuated the drearier academic routines of my life, building in a block of time devoted to nothing but pleasurable amateurish indulgence. It was great because college radio *stations* are great, and you can never get to the end of the satisfaction that comes from strolling among huge haphazardly archived collections of records and CDs, annotated each and all by the ghosts of DJs past, in brief Post-it commentaries running from the rhapsodic to the caustic to the violently aggrieved. ("FUCKING FUCK YOU JEFF TWEEDY I SEE YOU MAN YOU'RE NOT FUCKING FOOLING ME," is one I remember especially clearly, penned by an evidently disgruntled Uncle Tupelo fan.)

And it was great because I was, back then, a newish and not especially gifted stepfather, and each and every familial day found me failing—badly, humiliatingly—at patience and tolerance and what I presumed to be the most rudimentary qualities of grown-up equability and ordinary goddamn chill. (Stepparenting is a complex and difficult endeavor; in this, it is exactly like any and every variety of "parenting," though at the time I had *precisely zero* purchase on this fact.) The harder days could feel like an exhausting sort of footrace between exasperation (mine) and shame (also mine), and though we never spoke of it in these terms, or never quite, it's clear that these outside-the-home hours worked as a little zone of refuge for me, a reliably recurring indrawn breath.

It was great because, in my fade-out track, I'd always play something—"Tiger Lily," "The Rollercoaster Ride"—for the girls, who I knew would be listening on their way to bed. These were my stepdaughters, whom I also loved, with whatever straining and frayed incompetence, very much.

"Goodnight, girls." I'd say. "Thanks to everyone for listening. This is Belle and Sebastian . . ."

Now, if you've ever had a radio show, there is a sweet little passage of microsociability you'll likely remember. It's when the next DJ, having arrived but trying not to get in the way as you close out your time, begins assembling lists, pulling out records, walking with noiseless stealth through the various motions of making-ready, as meanwhile you conduct yourself into the fade-out track.

Your two shows blur into one another a bit in these moments, and you find that a low-watt, comradely sort of sensation travels between you just then. You exchange pleasantries, trade notes about some new release, give warning about a glitchy mic.

"Have a good show," you say.

"See you next week," they say.

It's all very lovely, in its brief and companionable way. You do not, however, in the midst of these semiscripted cordialities, have much reason to suspect that something quietly monumental is going to happen to you. Nothing, nothing at all, suggests that a scene you will never forget is about to unfold—a scene that will then come hurtling back for years and years to come, delivered most often in the cadences of a song that is itself so gorgeous, so spirit-seizing, you'll never know for sure what it is that's kicking up all the sudden agitation that visits you then, the lurch in the stomach, the sting in the eyes.

One day, though, this is exactly what happens.

*   *   *

On some indistinct winter Wednesday we were wrapping up, my cohost and I, tidying and gathering together the detritus of our hour and a half. I'd wished the girls goodnight, cued up our concluding track. After our sign-off, the young woman with the show subsequent to ours had come in discreetly, begun settling herself in. We did the obligatory pantomime, nodded silent greetings, gave little waves.

She wandered into the boxy little studio, as we muted the mics, took off our headphones. And then, as this one lovely and lilting song began suffusing itself through the room, I saw her pause for a moment in frozen apprehension. She turned toward us, something quizzical in her expression.

Her face showed a complex recognition.

"You know," she said, "this is probably my first memory."

It was a small college, ultrasmall really, and though I'd come to recognize this young woman in the glancing way of adjacent DJs, I didn't know her, hadn't had her in class. I think she told me she was a geology major? She had an aspect not significantly distinct from that of her peers. She was bescarved, wore a great gray oversized sweater, had deposited beside her a lunky knapsack stretched to tautness by overlarge textbooks. Like a lot of kids at the college she had what seemed to me a striking quantity of self-possession—the equable bearing of someone considerably more mature than I had been at twenty—though this was wedded in her, I knew, to an easy good humor, a readiness to laugh at the bleak winter weather, the battered soundboard, whatever.

And so we joked a little then, about how "This Must Be the Place," that offbrand Talking Heads triumph from the early '80s, which had so ably accompanied my friend and I in our swoony adolescences, had been music for her *cradle*. We edged up the volume, began nodding together.

Pleasantries, cordialities, some genial laughs. A sparkling brightness played out in four-chord riffs, some keyboard vamps.

"Yeah," she said, "it's funny," and you could see her riding back into some other precinct of memory.

"I must have been maybe two? I guess I was on the kitchen floor, and I was playing with all these pots and pans. And my mom and dad were making dinner. They were moving here and there all around me. And I remember this song came on and they, like— they started dancing."

And just like that, all our sociable little jokes have evaporated. Nobody says anything. The song moves between us. We're all held in place for a moment, a tableau called *Listening*.

And you're standing here beside me, the speakers say. *Never for money, always for love*, they say. *Cover up and say goodnight!*

The recognition in her face shifts gradients, passes through different microphases of recollection—wistfulness, tenderness— resolves at last into a frank smile.

"Yeah," she says. "I remember looking, like, *way* up at them. And they're singing the words to each other, and down to me. And just . . . dancing."

And maybe you've got stored away somewhere a more shimmering and faultless image of, oh, happiness—of a charmed little human space for which *home* is only one of the words you might use. Maybe you have held inside you some scene that, in its total love-lit radiance, matches even the radiance of this song, its New Wave heartlifttingness, the overspilling jubilation of the voice that cries out, *And you'll love me till my heart stops, love me till I'm dead!* I'm not sure I do.

Even today, when I try to tell this story, something stops my throat. Some dumb part of me starts murmuring these inane wishes, pleas to no god in particular. *Be good to one another*, it says. *Please*, it says, *let no harm come to them*. Let them live forever in a world as love-bright as this one song, for its precise duration, fabulates into existence. Let nothing fade or corrode.

"That's unbelievably sweet," I say. Because this was me, there, and then—so addled with shame and failure, loves I so little understood—and what the fuck else could I say?

"Yeah," she says, "it was nice."

Then her smile gets wider, and she shrugs, abashed a bit at this detour into bygone time. "It's such a great song."

Ghost Stories

College, for me, was like coming over the ridgeline of adolescence and discovering, in one long exultant gulp of perception, that I'd lived unknowingly for years in the outer suburbs of a glittering Oz-like metropolis, except instead of emeralds and witches there was French cinema and birth control. Some people get to school and discover politics or drugs or group sex or any of the other intoxicants of spirit you encounter once removed from parental stricture. Not me. (My adolescence, though it had some of these, would've been improved by more.) I did the predictable things. I read, with dumb astonishment, a great many books, and I listened to an even greater number of records, and these I talked about with the florid intensity of undergraduate devotion. It is only barely not true that most of what I learned in school I learned by listening to *Astral Weeks*, again and again, more or less uninterruptedly, for four years. You misjudge me a lot if you think that's a complaint.

This came back to me in the last weeks as I prepared for, and then watched, my youngest stepdaughter's graduation from high school. Somehow, despite an almost daily sense of myself as having only just crossed into the country of adulthood, I have two college-age daughters. You'd think that, having been looking over the horizon at this eventuality for years, I'd have been better prepared. But no. I had especially hoped to have some eloquent counsel about the collegiate adventure ahead for this year's graduate, an independent-minded and rule-averse and indefatigably bright-souled kid, who combines as winningly as you can imagine this stylish hipster-kid poise with what I can only describe as a *sweetness* of character, a friendliness so without guile it about breaks your heart. She is, Eliza, so cool and also so kind, a mixture of which the world is not overfull, in my experience. Hadn't I something ballasting and wise for her—something, I mean, that might in the breadth of its solacing insight exceed the parameters of, say, a mix CD?

I thought and thought. I pondered and procrastinated, scratched some notes.

I made her a mix.

As a person not often at a loss for phrases, I found this wordlessness strange and a little unhappy. I reminded myself by way of consolation that, in exchanges with young people, generous silence is often the best you can do. Stepparenthood taught me this and I hadn't forgotten. But it wasn't this, exactly, that left me stymied. The more I thought about it, and of what school was for me and wasn't, and of what I could say and could not, the clearer it became that I hadn't much right to waylay Eliza with edifying sentiment.

It's only barely not true that I learned most of what I learned in college by way of *Astral Weeks*. But laboring over my little graduation mix—the next entry in a years-deep archive of songs exchanged between us—I remembered that much of what I know about *Astral Weeks* I learned from listening to *another* record, a different record, years later and in the midst of a very different life.

And I didn't quite know what to make of that record until Eliza taught me.

*　*　*

One of my dearest friends in college was a young man who had a talent, enviable and unfaltering, for making Theories. Pick any handful of objects frozen just then in the amber of your cultural consciousness: metal bands, *Bonanza*, the early poems of Hart Crane, Patsy Cline. It didn't matter. Without overmuch effort, and following whatever the cascading stream of talk, he could extemporize a narrative linking them into this cracked, kaleidoscopic cohesion. It would be fluent and fast and unserious and for me, eighteen and new to college and all but vibrating with happiness about being there, pretty fucking joyous to behold. He had an oversized concert T-shirt embossed with the cadaverous image of Robert Smith, in which he would sometimes sleep. It was he who first played me tapes of Lyle Lovett, Dinosaur Jr., Nancy Sinatra, Ornette Coleman, and—I am almost sure—the Replacements. He'd read books by people with names like Roethke and Coover and Rukeyser, though he could talk as readily about Guns N' Roses' *Appetite for Destruction* with the offhand familiarity of accidental expertise. ("So you see, Alec," deadpan, "Slash is a player *of many moods*.") He was also about the least self-aggrandizing person you were likely to meet within the egotropic climates of collegiate sociability, and he made you feel, when you were talking to him, that whatever he said was somehow half your invention.

Long before I had the words for it I decided I loved him, and it is one of not many decisions I made in the late-'80s that I stand by utterly.

From the ages of eighteen to twenty-two, that passage of max-imal male insufferability, we weren't much apart, and this was a blessing and a mercy. (It's hard to imagine how much worse I would otherwise have been, though it's clear I would have been worse.) What this meant is that we lived for a while among a set of Theories on deep rotation. These included: The Theory That Clifford Brown Was Better Than Miles Davis. The Theory of the Inevitable Return of Madonna's Repressed Italianness. The The-ory of Grace Kelly's Entrance. None of them was, finally, a great deal other than stupid, by which I suppose I just mean clever, insu-lar, designed to do not much more than entertain each other and whoever was around. And the greatest of these, the brightest star among lesser lights, was the Theory of *Astral Weeks*.

Like many of the other Theories in vogue with us then, this one followed a basic grammar: What you think of as one thing is, actually—haHA!—something else. You might think of *Astral Weeks* as a collection of gorgeous songs, neither hippie-folk nor psyche-delia nor rock-n-roll—a record so extravagant and weird, and of such enchanting unlikeliness, you hardly knew what to call it. But you would be wrong. It was my friend's insistence that the secret of *Astral Weeks* was that it told, in fact, a sprawling broken story. Once you recognized this, each song, and then the album itself, became a new thing, strange and dense but also, in a delectable way, *explicable*. The thing to do, if you were listening with this kind of Talmudic devotion, was to make sense of the story.

If you've heard *Astral Weeks* you'll know this is not a simple task, though it is exactly the kind of work to beguile young people look-ing for reasons to procrastinate, or get high, or just keep talking to each other. The record starts out in a tangle of words and sounds that, the first time I heard them, seemed to address me from some location considerably removed from the conditions of my small teenage life: *If I ventured in the slipstream,* the young Van croons, *Between the viaducts of your dreams,* and so forth. The blank-wall impenetrability of these opening sentences was, for me, matched only by a reverence for them I wished I could better explain. I remember another friend writing them out in black marker on the pull-out tablet of his dorm-room desk, the whole first verse, and if after doing so he had any greater sense of what the fuck Van was talking about he did not share it with me. It seemed a great rush of high-flown hippie mysticism, tricked out with some beautiful particulars and buoyed by Richard Davis's outrageously virtuosic bass line, carving impossible figures around the melodies and countermelodies. Listening to it was like listening in on some stranger's private language, some fully elaborated cosmology tethered just enough to the shared human earth to make it legible in fugitive glimpses, the occasional bright flash.

But then, all of a sudden, it was something else. I can remember my friend sitting across from me at some ridiculous piece of institutional furniture and, with gentle persistence, explaining over and over again one point. He's saying, "They're at a wake." I am all vacant unresponsiveness. "*Showing pictures on the wall*— they're at a wake and they're showing slides of whoever's dead. They're pointing at him, at the singer, because he's in the picture." Nothing. "The singer's the person who's dead. Do you get it?" Indeed I do not. "It's the singer of the song and he's imagining whoever it is he's in love with, and, and . . . he's asking what she'd do if he was dead. Dude. *Listen.*"

And Van is singing, *Would you find me? Kiss my eyes? Lay me down in silence easy?*

Branching mythologies would follow, until we had it, a theory, a story. Here was a record that starts out at this imagined wake, and then for most of the rest of its duration tours exultantly through

the stations of a youthful love affair, only to end back where it begins, which is in the contemplation of death, with the singer conjuring up an eerie shrouded figure. (*Slim slow slider*, he says on the
final track, *horse you ride is white as snow*.) But then came the larg-
est fact, the claim that made everything vibrate on another frequency altogether: *Astral Weeks* ends like this because the death
with which the record contends is not, as in the opening, imaginary. *It is not the singer who is dead*. The record is sung to, and for,
and about a lover who has died. *Astral Weeks*, for all its enveloping
gorgeousness, was a memorial, an eight-song edifice of grief. It
is the sound of a young man contending with the blank fact, obvious and all but inconceivable, that those we love will die, quite
independently of the force and implacability of our love for them.
It finds the singer unleashing these cascades of joyous sound because it's all he has by way of bulwark and protest. It offers noise
as life, cacophony against dying.

It was college. It was talk like that.

I assume that at some point you'll have made a similarly baroque liturgy out of your love for some like object. Young people
in particular excel in making rituals of their devotion. And I certainly was devoted to *Astral Weeks*. But I will say that in the midst
of all that juvenile veneration what struck me most forcefully was
not the record's interfusion of joy and annihilating grief. No. All
my wonder was saved instead for the quantity of *work* just a few
swift sentences, properly placed, could do. For quite a long time I
could have told you staggeringly little about what you might call
the substance of *Astral Weeks*. Love it though I would surely have
said I did, the record itself was for me really not much more than
a radiant atmosphere, a wash of sound whose sum was this giddiness of spirit it produced in me. And that was fine. I won't say this
felt inadequate, or like a deficit of pleasure, because it did not. But

once touched with the wand of just a handful of words—a crackpot narrative, a theory—the record found itself transformed into different kind of thing, something alive with sex and love and the strange, mostly abstract sorrows of adulthood.

For years, that transformation was most of what I'd hear. Play a track and I'd be dropped back into that long-ago moment when a friend I loved wrote this piece of quasi-scriptural revelation back into the world for me, and made it a thing we might talk back and forth about, in words anybody could use. And I'll tell you: this was, for me, an estimable and ramifying joy. It occurred to me that you could set even this record's flights toward the mystic, its weird exhilarations, down amid the ordinariness of your daylit life and they would, in the exchange, shed not a bit of the glowing otherworldliness for which you fell in love with them in the first place. You could turn your experience of dumbstruck delight in a thing into something else—theories, words to trade—and it would *lose nothing*. It might in fact be said to gather into itself a new kind of density, something lit from within by the presence of other people, and your love for them, and theirs for you. This is what I meant when I would say, as I did say many years later as he stood beside me on my wedding day, that my friend had given me my first glimpse of what criticism could be, and why you might want to make a life out of it.

*　*　*

"*Marriage is a noble daring*," John Dryden wrote, and I thought about that phrase a lot during my married years. I liked it, not least for its edge of cynical satire. Had I been paying closer attention, I might have caught the implication, not only about bravery and tenacity, but about the omnipresence of *fear*. Only slowly did I come into the sense that as your happiness scaled up and grew intricate and involved, so too, in exact proportion, did the quantity of your life given over to dread. I spent a lot of time afraid of something happening to the girls. I spent a lot of time afraid of something happening to our lives together.

Something happened.

*   *   *

Allow me, now, to introduce a theory: Van Morrison's *Astral Weeks* and *In the Aeroplane Over the Sea* by a band called Neutral Milk Hotel are the same record. You can best approach them, I mean, as belated versions of each other, wedded so elementally that you misappraise them more by speaking of them separately than as one. It isn't that time does not flow between them, these records from 1968 and 1998. It surely does, and shows itself as time often does: in style. You can talk a lot about these deep histories of shape and form, punk and folk, and I can probably be induced to talk back to you. But these are, I would submit, matters more cosmetic than otherwise. In their essence, in whatever secret algorithmic core the aural data-miners have yet to uncode, they are the same.

I don't mean only that they both trade extensively in a kind of heady mysticism, the bending of language toward obscurity as it approaches some threshold of the unspeakable, though that's not nothing. I take it, in fact, to be one good way into *Aeroplane*, a record that has since its release gathered about itself an extravagant, nearly impenetrable cloud of devotion, a kind of obscuring dudestorm of love. (Sometime in the early 2000s one of the premiere venues for this sort of thing—*Pitchfork? Magnet?*—declared *Aeroplane* the "greatest record of the '90s," which given the demographic tilt of its readership was not a lot different from declaring it a holy relic, sacred and inviolable.) And sure enough, *Aeroplane* can at first seem like forty-odd minutes of Dadaist devotional poetry tracked over a thrumming guitar and sung in a piercing nasal tenor that stops short, though not much, of being assaultive. The record starts, in "The King of Carrot Flowers, Part I," like this

> When you were young you were the king of carrot flowers
> And how you built a tower tumbling through the trees
> In holy rattlesnakes that fell all around your feet

though you can dip in more or less anywhere to find like obscurities. Here as on *Astral Weeks* we are in the presence of something only marginally not idiolalia, some language obeying perhaps the insular logic of a dream but no apparent other.

Sit with it long enough, though, and it changes. Sit with it, maybe, through the accreting years of your life, as you drift from juvenile ardors into some marginally wider reckoning with the possibilities of sorrow, and you might begin to feel your way into its recurrences, the patterns the songs can't release, the presences that insist on themselves. The one you are least likely to miss is that of Anne Frank, the figure who haunts the record as an object of devotion no less than grief, appearing in visions by turn violent and erotic, haloed in the distorted beauty of the singer's dreams. (*She was born in a bottle rocket / 1929 / with wings and rings around the socket / right between her spine / all drenched in milk and holy water / pouring from the sky.*) Whatever else she may be for the record—and she is woven into dream-logics we do best not to hazard—I take Anne Frank to be the bearer, to the singer of *In the Aeroplane*, of all manner of incomprehensibilities. The most undoing of these, as on *Astral Weeks*, is also the simplest: it is just that in the contest between your love and death—in the battle that pits your ardor and your fear, your courage and your longing and your bliss, against the all-devouring force of dying—you lose. *Always.* And forever.

You can hear this all over the record, on tracks that teeter between horror and a frenzied, carnal exhilaration. You can hear it on what is perhaps the most compressed jolt of violent joy in all the annals of postpunk, a song called "Ghost." "Ghost" is "Sweet Thing"—a love song in which a passion for the beloved spills out into an awestruck love for everything that is—tuned almost wholly to the note of terror. The song shudders and blares, all brass and martial drum and huge distorted guitar. And the singer says of Anne Frank, *I know that she will live forever . . . she won't ever die—* very much like a young man trying to cry or shout or otherwise conjure into being a world in which that might be true.

So this is my theory, brewed up for the most part over quiet nights in a serene and unhaunted little house in Maine, where I sat listening to music through headphones given to me by my wife and stepdaughters, with connotations both ironic and affectionate ("These will help you tune us out!"). Anne Frank is at the center of "Ghost," and of *Aeroplane* generally, because it is a record made from an encounter between a singer and some herald, some shattering prevision, of the absolute indomitability of mortal loss. Exactly like *Astral Weeks, In the Aeroplane Over the Sea* is a record trying to work out how you can live in a world whose deepest fact, as Philip Roth somewhere says, is *the stupendous decimation that is death sweeping us all away,* which the singer seems to be discovering, in fright and in wonder, as he sings.[1] What you're left with, on both records, is a piece of pure, maniacal exultation—a prayer, you could say, of grieving, violent love for the world.

* * *

Though I learned a lot in college, enough that I feel an indefensible tenderness toward what are objectively embarrassing episodes of boyish self-seriousness, I did not learn to love the world in this way. That came later, somewhere in the long stretch of small hours in a house near the coast of Maine. It's part, though only part, of what Eliza and her sister gave to me, a hard sort of gift for which I will never reach the end of my gratitude and which I would not give in return, even if I knew how, which I don't.

And so, short on words, I made a mix, and let me say right now it is a fucking *triumph*. I stitched it together and thought of how long it had taken for me to come into my sense of both of those records from my youth, and though I'm delighted that Eliza has a lot to say about them—the day she texted me just to talk about Neutral Milk Hotel is, I assure you, marked on the calendar of my heart—there is no saying what these songs will become to her, or when, or how. And that's as it should be. Still, listening to them now, I find it hard not to harbor these predictive wishes for her, as for her sister, wishes that tend to come in impossible combination. It's hard, I mean, not to want them to encounter enough of the world to fall in reckless blazing love with it and, also, to know *nothing* of loneliness or sorrow or unedifying pain. Or no more than they do already.

Put a hope like that into words and it reads like the nonsense, the category error, it is. But songs make for a different kind of wishing. They do different work. This is why mixes are not keepsakes or archives of parental wisdom and, jesus, even less are they roadmaps to the byways of Cool. Young people have little need of any of these things. They're more like prayers, the pleas you send up into a future irretrievably other to ourselves. That they be vibrant and thriving. That they be fearless, unharmable, the equal of any grief. That they be joyous and tough and, in the teeth of all that is broken, loved. And loved and loved and loved.

If there was something else worth saying, I didn't find it. If there was someone better to do that saying—better, I mean, than Van, Jeff, Ella, Neko, Stevie—I didn't find them either.

Rhapsody for the Crash Years

Time hovers o'er, impatient to destroy,
And shuts up all the Passages of Joy.

The most beautiful pop song from the ugly year of our sorrows 2016—sorry Beyoncé, sorry Adele; sorry RiRi, sorry Anderson Paak, sorry (not-sorry) Drake; a thousand times sorry to you, Solange, whose "Cranes in the Sky" distilled into shimmery radiance so much of the stunned heartstrickenness of these ghastly months—the most beautiful song of this dread year, as I was saying, came from a twenty-three-year-old Chicagoan named Chancellor Bennett. Sometimes he goes by Chano or, more colloquially, Lil' Chano from 79th. You'll know him as Chance the Rapper. He won a Grammy a few months back which, if it means not a thing else, means you *will* know him. He's legit-famous now, bona fide.

Amid the blight, the compassless malignity of the past year, we must take our solace where we may. I suggest you take it here, in the ascent of a performer as deliriously good as Chance, as brilliant and as winning, into superstardom. It's like a bubble of pure happiness, riding the surface of so much frothing horror.

It can be hard, though, to stay dialed in to the straight-up joy of it all, at least for me. And I'm not talking about any indie snobbishness, some I-knew-him-back-when recrimination. It's something else. I'm thinking of the strange way that things that once had such power to please us have come lately to seem, you could say, *arti-factual*, tokens of a time now lost. They flash up like visitations, these once-near pleasures. It's as if they speak to us from inside the locked chamber of some vanished moment, wherein we had contrived to imagine that other futures than this, than the *after-lives* of 2016, were possible.

I think of it, I suppose, as one among the lesser symptoms of the immense ugliness of now: a queasy out-of-jointishness of time.

This, as it happens, is something of what the most beautiful song of 2016 is about.

*   *   *

I've been semi-infatuated with Chance the Rapper since—and this is a fact I can carbon-date—April of 2014, though, alas, I can't take any early-adopter cred for it. Chance is the first artist of whom I had heard nothing, not the faintest intimating breath, be-fore having a track of his propelled unbidden into my aural orbit. What's more, I was introduced to him by neither indie rag, online product aggregator, nor the happy misfiring of some clairvoyant algorithm. That introduction came, far more ignominiously, from *my kids*.

If there is an opposite of hipster cred, a coolness antimatter, surely it is this.

By "kids" I mean my youngest stepdaughter, although if I'm being technical about it I ought to describe her and her sister as my *ex*-stepdaughters, since it's been years since I've been married to their mom. That's not what we'd say, but then technicalities have never been our thing. For some time ours has been one of those loves that goes by no ready-to-hand name, though we've held our-selves together, we three, just fine all the same. It's not always the easiest or least heart-pricking thing, loving children to whom you are attached by no ballasting title, no state-certified designation. But the truth is it's also been an improvisatory and joyful sort of adventure, a thing we have conspired to invent, moment to moment, with scraps of memory, familiar idioms, whatever's around.

Songs—exchanged over many years, in millions of mixes, over many kinds of distance—have of course been much of what's around.

Back in April of 2014, a new kind of distance was about to dawn. I had just then accepted a job that would take me away from them. This was exciting, but it filled me, too, with fretful disquiet. The oldest had just gone away to college but the youngest was a junior in high school, still living there where I was, in Maine. She was the first person to whom I confided the prospect, the suddenly real possibility, of this life-upending departure. Her response, over dinner out one late-winter night, was a thing I would keep with me over many turbulent months. It was memorable, emphatic: "I think you should go," she said, a bowl of noodles steaming in front of her. "You *love* Chicago."

And so, that April, for my birthday, in one of those sudden flourishes of care with which teenagers can rattle you out of all your older-person knowingness, she surprised me with a mix. The sweet and wondrous joke of it—a *mix*! *She* made a mix for *me*! Here, in her own hand, was an addition to that treasury of songs we'd amassed over the years. This one was called CHICAGO.

And what should close it out but a beautiful lilting rap track, a singsongy number strung over an elegant little piano vamp. And that voice! The overspilling exuberance and cartwheeling dexterity! A jazz track bending toward hiphop rhythms and given over to one young man's kaleidoscopic riffs on an array of bygone delights. (*Remember jacket shopping after listening to* Thriller?) The inventiveness, the seamless grading of the rapping into floating melodies and back, and above all the fucking *sweetness* of it: I fell for it, hard, by the second listen.

Come to find it was by a gaspingly young man named Chance— only three or so years older than the kid herself, she told me— and when I realized he was from Chicago, my heart, my bruised middle-aged heart, shook with pride and startled happiness.

And this is precisely how wrought up I was about the prospect of leaving, of maybe abandoning these girls I so loved, who were not in any official sense my children: it took me hundreds of listens, spread out over nearly a whole fucking *year*, even to notice that this song wasn't on that mix just because it was a Chicago song. It was also, this song, about something.

The track, which is called "Everything's Good," opens with a little conversational interlude, a recorded conversation between Chance and his father—his father who in this recording is telling his son how proud he is of him, how he'll do anything to help him out should he need it, how he loves him.

"Thank you—love you," Chance says.

"Alright, son, love you too."

And then the song proper commences.

Whatever else it describes, "Everything's Good" is a song about a young person loving his dad.

Oh, I thought. *Oh*.

It came over me one bright day training home on the Brown Line, the north side coming into leaf around me. I closed my eyed, tuned myself in to Chance's exuberant fluencies. A wave of something—call it an unclenching of heart—went right through me. I opened my eyes and it was a new day, a new Chicago.

*　*　*

One of the truly great critics of the last decades, a scholar named Hortense Spillers, observes that "the dancing voice embodied" is "the chief teaching model for black women of what *their* femininity might consist in." She suggests that in "the motor behavior, the changes in countenance, the vocal dynamics, the calibration of gesture and nuance" of Black female vocalists, we can find edifying transcription of ways of being in relation to, but also nimbly *apart from*, the given scripts of Black American womanhood, their distortions and confinements, their punitive enclosures.[1]

We don't much struggle to hear, in the dancing voice Chance commands, something similar being transacted in relation to Black *masculinity*, with its multiple and contradictory entailments, its simultaneous presumptions of danger and indolence, violence and incapacity. Chance routs such presumption with a voice long on irrepressibility and exuberance, to be sure, animated by joyous swagger. But there's so much else as well, a density of affects circulating in fine-tuned calibration: tendernesses and sudden vulnerabilities; delicate professions of humility, of gratitude; a kind *reverence* unchastened by its proximity to secular pleasures. And with this, also, in its timbre and especially in its quick flights from speech into melody and back, a vivid strain of melancholy. An always-present nearness of grief.

And listen, I get that you might say too, of the relatively low frequency at which anger is kept, that this is a voice leaning more Black-bourgeois than otherwise. (The deep impress of early Kanye, for instance, is hard to miss.) That's fine as far as it goes, I guess, though I confess I have a pretty limited patience for white listeners eager to dismiss some rapper or other as, in this want of performed *hardness*, insufficiently authentic. ("Yeah I prefer something a little more *street*" is the calling card of young gentrifiers nationwide.) Listen to a capering hyped-up track like "Angels," about his (and my) beloved, besieged Chicago. (*Too many angels on the South Side . . .*) Here is a song that understands unplaced joyousness to be less the opposite of protest, of heartbreak or indignation, than an underused resource for their expression.

*   *   *

The most beautiful song of 2016, which is called "Same Drugs," tilts more melancholic than otherwise. Imagine the sound of a church where gospel reverence and the joyousness of being a kid doing drugs come together in unstraining harmony, and you get some sense of the sonic atmosphere of this song. Another piano number of extraordinary melodic sweetness, borrowing something of the stateliness of gospel balladeering—complete with a crooning chorus, *strings*—it finds Chance in a mood of youthful retrospection, contending with the movement from precincts of childish wonder to, oh, whatever it is that might follow.

For this song, though, youthfulness comes not in the guise of bucolic innocence lost, some confected unworldliness. It is offered instead as a different sort of haven: the scene of adventurousness, and daring, of a secret shared pleasure in transgressiveness. The chords ring out, and there's Chance:

> We don't
> Do the same drugs no more
> We don't do the, we don't do the same drugs
> Do the same drugs no more

It could just be a sort of joke—*we do* different *drugs!*—but the keyed-up yearning in Chance's voice makes the lines say something else as well.

And it's a love song, sort of. The girl to whom Chance sings these lines is called "Wendy," and in this swift little gesture the song folds itself into the mash-up of mythologies that traverses the whole album, in which Chance figures himself by turn as Simba, Peter Pan, Jesus Christ. (It is, in its range, a fantastically winning roster.) Then there's the bridge: the piano drops away, a gospel choir rises up in the silences between each line, and there's Chance's voice:

> Wide-eyed kids being kids, why did you stop?
> What did you do to your hair?
> Where did you go to end up right back here?
> When did you start to forget how to fly?

As an old person, you can listen to this and be jolted by the directness of its encounter with real loss, its hard intimation that the next phases of post-youthful life will mean diminishment and constraint, a translation of whatever was magical about their secret hoarded days into something more ordinary and unglowing. Adulthood isn't all deadness; there are *still* drugs to be had. But there is division and distance. And there's the intimation, too—*what did you do to your hair?*—of an expanded, enforced demand for compliance not just to adulthood but to the supervision of *white people.*

The world, in all, has come for them, and it's the world we know: narrowed, flinty, mean. Overbrimming with occasions for Black grief.

For all that anticipated sorrow, though, there is not much you'd call fearfulness here, no turning away from the call of the life yet to come. What you find instead is a soaring insistence on the still-uncanceled possibilities of wonder in the world. *That* is what sounds out in that dancing voice embodied: it is the voice of a young man so eager for the world, and for the chances of grace yet to be found there, but pausing on the brink of it, taking measure, counting out his losses.

* * *

In mid-2016, in my little Lincoln Square apartment, that one line flared up before me, filling all the rooms of thought for a few days: *When did you start to forget how to fly?* What a song! I thought—to be able to risk, and to get away with, a line that could so easily fall a treacly sort of flat.

And with it came the piercing thought that somewhere in America—upstate New York, rural Maine—were two beautiful young women, neither of them little girls anymore, readying themselves however they might for the turbulent passage from youth into, oh, whatever comes after it.

I'd hear it, and they'd wheel into clarified vision, the both of them, seen in all the brightness of the poised, dauntless, venturesome people they were on the way to becoming. There they were, with all their undimmed eagerness for the world. And I thought, too—I admit it—of the losses that were coming for them, different from Chance's, to be sure, but in some glancing conjured relation to them. The kinds of diminishment, hurt, demanded compliance. The pains that nothing—not Chance, not me, not even the most gorgeous assembly of pop confections—could keep from them.

I remembered, in a quick short flash, the summer day I left Maine. The movers had come, the apartment was empty, and when I found the youngest out in the city, hugged her goodbye, I was startled to see tears standing in her eyes. She was seventeen;

I hadn't seen her crying in—what?—years and years. My breath caught in my throat.

"It's gonna be great," she said, and gave me a steady gaze. "You're gonna be great."

* * *

All of this came hurtling back to me one night last summer. By then Chance had *hit*, was in fact set to play a massive show, essentially a Chance-themed festival, at a baseball field on the south side. Those tickets vanished in a hot minute, gobbled up by scalpers, to be resold at 1000 percent markup. In distressed response to this, Chance staged a surprise pop-up show, announced at noon on Twitter, at one of the little venues where he'd gotten his start.

This venue is a handful of blocks down the road from my apartment.

I happened to be idly Twitter-scrolling at the right time. One frantic bike-ride later, and with a sense of the semimiraculous beginning to dawn around me, I found myself standing on a corner on North Clark Street, two tickets in my hand. We went.

The "we" here, I should say, is me and the woman with whom I'd spent much of the previous year falling into an escalating, self-surprising kind of love. Somewhere along the course of that otherwise nauseous and darkening year it had happened—if "happened" is the word for something as diffused into the atmosphere of days. You go along, and go along, and then one day realize that every morning is Stevie Wonder singing "Hey Love."

To see a show with someone you're this kind of newly-in-love with is, as you probably know, its own subspecies of joy: every least thing, from the train ride to the beer-stuck floor to the swirl of sound that eventually engulfs you, partakes of the radiance you two are making together. It was that kind of night, elating, a sweet interfusing of old loves and new.

And there was Chance himself. The girls had seen him before (*of course* they had) and he was just what they'd said: a hyperkinetic wunderkind, pinwheeling across the stage in a gleeful master-of-ceremonies romp, an atom bomb of tweaked-up and fantastically persuasive charm. Watching him, that whole bright theater of kindling brilliance that was his onstage self, you knew you were in the presence of someone about to be a star, a *superstar*, to ascend any minute into, say, Rihannaish-levels of fame. There was an exhilaration in this, certainly, and we were held by it, all of us singing back to him each and every rapid-fire riff and phrase.

But there was also—and there was no way you could ignore it—this other sort of gravity at work, some wordless counterbalancing force. These intimate venues, these local shows, these human-scaled gatherings of friends and fans: they were speeding away from the young man standing before us, without question. And as he thanked us, and sang, and laughed, and yelped out verses in call-and-response little set-pieces, you could watch him reckoning with them, with this, as things very soon to be of his past, bits of a life superseded, gliding away into irretrievability.

Later I'd say that I could not recall a show so overspilling with joy that was also so elegiac, so crosscut by anticipatory loss.

*　*　*

It's something we all know so much better now, isn't it? The sense of bright possibility blinking out? That bittersweet undertow?

*　*　*

We took the train home, leaned against one another, felt humming between us that sweet sensation that comes of being out in the vastness of the city night, riding its circuits, nodes on its flashing grid. An August warmth hung in the air. We talked about the show, the winning delirium of it, about Chance, about the top-knotted frat-dudes lined up in front of us on the floor. (*Our bro-overlords*, she likes to call them.) I texted some blurry pictures to the girls, who texted back in excitement and mock envy. Outside the windows, our city—this beautiful, fucked-up, unruined city—pulsed and flowed.

The fall seemed a long way off, a rumor that hadn't arrived.

PART IV

Sentences

So-Called Normal People

A dozen or so years ago, when she and I still shared a home, I gave to my oldest stepdaughter what I think both of us would now agree was the greatest of Christmas gifts. She had just turned thirteen. I had wrapped, and put under the tree for her to find, the DVD box set of the complete run of *My So-Called Life*. Those who were for whatever reason wrought-up in the earlyish '90s, tender and susceptible and weepy, will recognize this for the stroke of haphazard genius that it absolutely was.

In the drowsy quiet of the week between Christmas and New Year's, she sat glassy and transfixed, beset by a TV-induced hypnagogia. For a handful of days, episode by episode by episode, she attended to the show in the posture of a person considering how best to plunge, as completely as was possible, through the flickering surface of the screen.

Now and again, and however unobtrusively I could manage it, I'd take my place on the couch beside her and co-watch. Unobtrusiveness, I should say, does not come naturally to me. Did I hold forth about the great glory of Brian Krakow's wide-eyed stare and halo of pale ringlets? Or about the pure heartbreakingness of Angela Chase's recessed and depressive wordlessness, matched so perfectly to her plaid-on-plaid ensembles? Did I waylay her about the unrivaled delight of the Buffalo Tom episode, in which the band name "Buffalo Tom" is uttered something like forty-five times in the span of an hour ("Are you going to see BUFFALO TOM?," "Is BUFFALO TOM playing?," "I love BUFFALO TOM!" etc.)? Or about how genuinely saving it all had been for me—a little carved-out interlude for cleansing tearfulness—back in the trying early years of grad school? I promise you that I did not. Or, at least, I tried very hard not to.

There were other moments, though. Around the middle of the season, again as you may photorealistically recall, a series of vexations about sex—who has it, why, with whom, what it means, what *not* wanting to have it means—come vividly to the center of the plot. Virginity, shame and desire, the terrible intractability of boys: it's honestly all quite beautifully done. This seemed as good a moment as any to hazard a remark or two.

"Dude," I said, as we slouched shoulder-to-shoulder, taking in good-girl Sharon's disquisition on the whys and wherefores of high school coupling. "This is really so good."

A long pulse of silence.

"And, I mean. Is there anything you feel like maybe talking about?"

I remember, with saturating clarity, what happened next. Without turning toward me, without the least flutter of her person, she exhaled a single unemphatic word.

"Nope."

I think about it a lot. And whenever I do, there it is: that same small-scale detonation of admiration, amazement, hilarity, clumsy heartstruck love.

*   *   *

It was hard *not* to think about it when, about a decade later, I gave her another gift. By this time she was a recently graduated young woman working and living on her own in Mexico. For my part, I had learned to navigate at least a little less fumblingly this sort of transaction, with the kid and her sister. Giving aesthetic objects to young people is a procedure of some delicacy. If you're being prescriptive or insistent ("now *this* is cool") you are, allow me to suggest, doing it quite dramatically wrong. And anyway, the era in which I had any sort of cultural insight to bequeath unto them had long, long passed over into myth. I had been stealing music from them for a while now.

But I still passed along novels.

And so, because I'd read it and been captivated, because its swift lucidity and unnerving emotional clinicism were not quite like anything I'd read in recent memory—and because it was a novel about the jolting turbulence of being a woman in her early twenties in the now-ish world—I sent on to her my copy of *Conversations with Friends*.

There is, let me say, an especially sweet pleasure in talking to your grown-up kids about books, and why they love the ones they love. And, sweet jesus, did this kid love *Conversations with Friends*—or, at least, did she find it surpassingly resonant, as well as suggestive, provoking, disquieting, limitlessly good to think with. She had so much to say! I loved all this talking-over—of which more in a minute—but I loved even more what she told me she had *done* with her own set of agitated readerly responses to the novel. In a gesture primed to induce in me frenzies of overidentification, she just . . . passed it on. She got herself another copy, mailed the first one to a friend, and set into motion a buzzing circuitry of what would soon prove to be eight or so young women readers, gathered around their library copies or hand-me-down editions, each of whom found something in it to notice, to laugh over, to object to and be puzzled by and otherwise engage in intricate prolonged dispute about.

What I mean is: she enjoyed a book, and then convened around it a kind of scene, a small brimming *world*. And then, through the crosscurrents of talk it generated and the disputes it animated, she and her friends looked to nurture and extend and substantialize that world, there in the midst of that first hard season of postcollegiate dispersion.

She told me all this, and there it was again: admiration, amazement, hilarity, etc.

*   *   *

And so, on a gray and blustery winter day in Philadelphia, we strolled around together talking, at voluble length, about Sally Rooney. What, I wanted to know, got her and her friends so into it? Some of it was what you'd expect: the verisimilitude of the portrait of postcrash life out in a narrowing world of mostly desultory work; the offhand poise in respect to forms of intimacy—queerish, non-monogamish—not easily parsed in the familiar grids and taxonomies, but unexceptional in their milieus; the volatile crossings, so acutely rendered, of rivalry and desire, love and need, in the intensities of female friendship. Above all these things, she said, her friends thought Rooney just got something ineluctably *right*. And this something lived for them in her singular ways of relating to these various matters—her style, I might at this point have blurted—which made the novel less a series of thesis-like propositions (about gender, about sex, about work) than a fantastically charged atmosphere, a scene of things known and half-known in the act of living through them.

I remember being struck by her vehemence on one point in particular. Frances, she said, was irresistible: so smart and so nervy and so cool. But she was also, this heroine, kind of terrible! "She gets so *mean*," she told me, as we wandered about in the settling afternoon. "And it's not always like it's by accident." That, she said, was fascinating to her and her friends, and something that they thought and thought about: how spiky with unkindness Frances could be; how that didn't make her fumbling married lover Nick any less exasperating, though it maybe made him a bit more sympathetic; how it deepened a kind of dispassionate mysteriousness in Frances that made her hard to stop considering and reconsidering, talking about and then talking about again.

"That seems, uh—yeah, that seems very right," I said, in edifying colloquy.

Read around a little and you will soon find critics making strong claims for Rooney as one of our most agile inheritors of the vexed canon of nineteenth-century novelistic practice.[1] That strikes me as a perfectly good way into Rooney's scenes of vibrant, prickly coupling, which are always both so near to the intimate forms on offer in a long, long history of domestic fiction, and so much a detuning of them. Now, I have not *quite* been trying to suggest here that Rooney is drafting artfully as well, if with an icier millennial comportment, upon the affective mechanics of the prestige-teen-TV favored by bookish Gen Xers. Or not exactly. Famously, back in the '90s, Eve Sedgwick used to tell her graduate students that the Victorian novel, when stripped down to its essentials, told one story, and one story only: "Heterosexuality is a disaster." Angela Chase, god bless her flannel heart, knew this, or at least had powerful intimations, whether or not she'd read George Eliot.

Fair to say that Rooney's novels are no less fascinated by the disaster areas Sedgwick has in mind—though they bring to that scene of queasy fascination an erotic torque quite their own. So much of what we find there, along with their portraits of creativeish precariats decathecting promises of a smooth capitalist future, are depictions of the routine and painful incapacities of men, when faced with the forceful desires of women. Again and again, Rooney shows us cerebral young women interested in something near to—or that simply is—masochism, a surrendering to an erotic power that might hurt in galvanizing, pleasing, self-solidifying ways. But those women persistently encounter men who cannot begin to endure the steep demands—of responsibility, care, trust—made upon them by such acts of eroticized submission. The recurrence of men overawed by women in their desire: this is so much a theme in Rooney's books you might expect to find Jordan Catalano, shrugging and mute, loitering over in the corner of one of them.

Not hard to imagine, in all, why these novels might grip the attention of a group of young women charting their paths through postcrash worlds of sex, talk, work, love. That, at any rate, is just some of what I heard that gray afternoon in conversation with the worldly, openhearted, so-much-beloved twenty-three-year-old who is my oldest. Sally Rooney wrote novels about young women who saw with unclouded penetration into the confounding disasters of heterosexuality—but who were not, for all that disquieting clarity, much interested in foreswearing desire, or in pretending themselves unbeguiled by the duplicitous allurements of sex, no matter its fractiousness and fearsome capacity for brewing up sorrow. Rooney wrote books about—and also clearly for—young women figuring out how to address themselves to these vivid irreconcilabilities.

There is much more I could say about our meandering afternoon talk. And yet, with the memory of Christmases Past before me, I don't think I want to—except to add that whatever I now have to think about Sally Rooney is shadowed, in an unrevocable way, by my sense that she is a writer at the vibrant vital center of a conversation in which I am very much not an essential participant. It is a conversation into which I can enter only partially, and whose parameters and terms and intensities of investment are oblique, necessarily, to most any of those my middle-aged companions and I might mobilize. And this seems to me the case quite apart from the curiosity or the admiration or, as the case may be, the aching urgent love with which we, the no-longer-so-young, might turn to those scenes.

I don't mean to suggest that these young people are accordingly more right about Rooney, or more incisive, or that we must regard their readings as transpiring in some black box of insider knowledge, incommunicable to us in its esoteric codes and idiolects. Young people, as Rooney reminds us, are as full of extravagant self-misapprehension as anybody. But those worlds, surely, have their separate clarities as well. Sometimes it's best to sit there, shoulder-to-shoulder, and keep your mouth shut.

Say Chi City

If you want to fall wrackingly, despairingly in love with a place, here's what you do: leave it.

When I was young and wintering out my graduate years, marooned in the penitential bleakness of upstate New York, I grew fond of declaring that, once I turned thirty, I was going to go ahead and start straight-up lying when asked where I was from. "I'm just gonna be like, FUCK IT," I'd insist, typically in barlight diffuse or glaring. "Me? I'm from Chicago."

You will perhaps harbor similarly counterfactual allegiances, wherein the dull facts of biography come unstuck from the more salient truths of your heart.

Chicago has been my heart's home since I was old enough to want any such thing. I arrived in 1989, left four years later, pined for it over nearly a decade of insufficiently lengthy visits: for its density and its neighborhoodiness, its unhealed fractures and its fugitive moments of precarious repair, for its cheapness, its flatness, its day games and industrial canals, its colliding southernness and midwesternity, its lakeside vistas, hot dog stands, pierogis, taproom voices—its *bars*, sweet Jesus, its bars!—the people I loved, the people I almost loved, as the song goes. I spent the next ten years punctuating my life with micromoves to Chicago (a summer here, a semester there) until, at last, by the grace of some propitiated lakefront god, I got a gig there and returned, for real, for good, in 2014.

But nothing is simple. And so it has been my pleasure, in these last weeks, to read and to savor and to dwell inside Liesl Olson's greatly rewarding *Chicago Renaissance: Literature and Art in the Midwest Metropolis*. I have done so from the midst of a fellowship year here in the woods of central New Jersey, in yearning exile once again.

Olson's thesis is, like the city itself, multifaceted and straightforward. It is that Chicago has a central, underappreciated place in the high canon of Anglo-American modernism, which is legible in everything from Pound's imagism and Stein's famously elliptical prose to the fictions of Sherwood Anderson and Ernest Hemingway, the new-fashioned realism of Richard Wright, the post-Sandburgian verse of Gwendolyn Brooks. Around all of these major figures and several of their major works, Olson builds a series of case studies, in each of which she traces out the impress made by Chicago, its industries, its institutions, and the persons living and working in them. So we are reminded that Pound's indelible "In a Station at the Metro" appeared in *Poetry* magazine—"the most important 'little magazine' of literary modernism"—launched and nurtured by Chicagoan Harriet Monroe, who corresponded and wrangled and fought with Pound over many years. We come to be reacquainted, too, with the story of Gertrude Stein's visits to Chicago in the early '30s, where she was both celebrated by the internationally minded Arts Club and quizzed, down on the South Side, by Mortimer Adler, the professor who would establish at the University of Chicago the now-famous "Great Books" curriculum. In each and all cases, with persuasive agility, Olson vivifies the many presences—patrons, editors, visitors, authors, as well as venues, places, entire demimondes—that speak through the artifacts of Chicago modernism.

That Chicago became a fomenting element in modernism, that the Great Migration and the Chicago Black Renaissance were crucial to that foment, and that its major texts give rich testament to the intricacy and multiplicity and genuine cultural vibrancy even of this heartland city, located so far from New York and Paris: these are some of the central theses of Olson's book.

But the truth is you don't come to *Chicago Renaissance* for the theses as much as for the rendering, in roving and aptly selected detail, of the history of Chicago arts across a remarkable slice of time. This is the period of its astonishing transformation, wherein a largeish windswept American prairie town metamorphosed, with a shocking rapidity, into a global metropolis and, for some, "the exemplary modern metropolis." ("Between 1870 and 1900," Olson reminds us, "Chicago's population quintupled from about 300,000 to more than 1.5 million.") *That* story is what Olson is after here, and it is a story she tells with verve and fluency and an historian's archival acuity.

What thus holds the book together, carrying us between passages of close reading, are a series of meticulous cultural micro-histories: accounts of self-created venues for aesthetic dispute and disquisition, like the Dill Pickle Club, the Arts Club, the George Cleveland Hall branch library at 47th Street, the Radical Bookstore; of especially pivotal parties and dinners (such as the one in Hyde Park on November 27, 1934, that found Stein and Adler falling into vehement disagreement); of transatlantic trips (because this is a book about modernism, people are *forever* meeting up with one another in Paris) and generative meetings and oblique but consequential connections. Olson gives us, in all, a generous portrait of a world of interlinked *scenes*, and this local, especially fine-grained sort of literary historicism affords her a strong purchase on her objects, and on the subject of modernism more generally.

Olson's approach pays out in a range of ways. We learn a good deal, for instance, about what we might call the imperial-nostalgic brand of racism that runs like a live current through the heart of these largely monied, variegatedly bohemian scenes, visible as much in the Orientalism of *Poetry* and the fixation on "vanishing" Native cultures among the "Cliff Dwellers Club" as in Stein's primitivist fantasias of white renewal via Black vitality in a text like "Melanctha." This latter was a text that greatly moved Richard Wright, who would go on, as Olson details, to offer prescient counsel on the matter of Black speech and "jive": "Jive is a way of talking invented in the main by urban Negroes who see to have nothing much else to do but play with words. . . . Jive now can be heard on the lips of white boys at Yale and Harvard."

Most crucially—and for this reader, most compellingly—Olson shows too that these scenes were made by, supported in, and sustained through nothing so much as *the labor of women*. We do well, Olson argues,

> to recognize the people who built the cultural infrastructure for modernism in Chicago. This was a particular kind of labor, mostly unpaid, and largely underacknowledged. Much of it was done by women. They ran bookstores, organized galleries, launched periodicals, and hosted salons. These are people who saw possibility in Chicago and knew how to build an audience for modernism.[1]

Olson's book restores these women, and their immense labors of imagination, to the center of the story of modernism in Chicago, and what emerges is a kind of composite portrait of aesthetic achievement, wherein Chicago modernism, whatever the series of names we associate with it (still mostly male, still mostly white), appears as a complexly *collective* endeavor. For Olson, this is how we can best retell the story of the cultural life of a wind-blown middle-American city in its growth into an artistic center and global hub.

This is a fine and winning sort of story of Chicago, one long in the unearthing—it is a blessing to have the stories of Harriet Monroe and Fanny Butcher and Eva Bell Thompson and their allies so vividly told to us—and ought to be received as such. But I wish to conclude by remarking that there's another story in Olson's chronicle as well, winding through the interstices of its generous and multiplicitous narrative. That story is a good deal more cautionary. As Olson figures it, Chicago modernism is an intensely coterieish affair, and virtually all the members of that coterie come from, or are soon intimately linked up with, money. It is in this sense a story of the bracing work, aesthetic and civic both, done by the blessed of capital, an oligarchy of lawyers and industrialists and real estate barons and their circles, dented perhaps but not doomed by the Depression, and enjoying the comforts proper to the classes gifted with the plenty of expropriated labor. None of this is lost on Olson. ("If the Armory Show tested the Art Institute's principles of democracy," she writes of the scandalous exhibition of Duchamps and Cézannes and Gauguins and van Goghs in 1913, "it did so only through the most powerful men in Chicago.") She registers acutely the high-gentility of so many of her subjects, while keeping an eye as well on what they helped produce. "Cultural uplift has its good," Olson notes, and more than makes that case.

But to any Chicagoan living under the Reign of Rahm, all this has an unhappy familiarity. Mayor Emanuel, former ballet dancer that he is, after all *loves* the arts, and loves burnishing the golden gleam of the city's many famed cultural institutions. He also loves cops, as well as privatization, school closures in nonwhite districts, and sweetheart land deals for billionaires. He is an especially vivid version of the liberalish ethos that celebrates diversity while sanctioning the state murder of Black people, champions the arts while erecting an unrivaled regime of securitization, and sings the high virtues of culture such as they are available to the smaller and smaller ranks of the über-wealthy able actually to *live* in Chicago, and so take part in its many edifications. The monied patronage that helped to birth Chicago modernism is, in its current iterations, inescapably interwoven with the very forces that have done so much to hollow out what for many of us were the greatest, most cherishable things about the city. Ride the Red Line, up from Englewood and through the Disneyfied grown-up frat party that is Wrigleyville, and the idea of *neoliberalism* will become for you, I promise, something other than abstract.

Not that I would wish you to believe Chicago has ceased to be Chicago. If you care to bask in the afterlives of the aesthetic achievements Olson details so capably, go read Stuart Dybek. Or watch *Go Fish* again, perhaps while scrolling idly through images of UIC kids shutting down a Trump rally in 2016. Or listen to "Drive Slow," or to Noname, or to Open Mike Eagle, or for that matter just gaze wonderstruck—with the rest of the world—at the righteous joyousness of Chance the Rapper, White Sox fan, child of Chatham, Chicago ambassador extraordinaire. Or maybe just go to 31st Street Beach on a warm summer Sunday. All of it will convince you of the ongoing vitality of this, our "beautiful, fucked-up, unruined city," as I recently had occasion to call it.

And then, when you hear some execrable politician rolling the word *Chicago* on his forked tongue, and making it a byword among racist concern trolls, I hope you will think instead—as I have been so much, in this un-urban New Jersey fall—of a beautiful poem by Anthony Walton. It is called, simply, "Gwendolyn Brooks," and I think Olson would concur that we can do worse than to give it, and them, the last word:

> Sometimes I see in my mind's eye a four- or five-
> year-old boy, coatless and wandering
> a windblown and vacant lot or street in Chicago
> on the windblown South Side. He disappears
> but stays with me, staring and pronouncing
> me guilty of an indifference more callous
> than neglect, condescension as self-pity.
>
> Then I see him again, at ten or fifteen, on the corner,
> say, 47th and Martin Luther King, or in a group
> of men surrounding a burning barrel off Lawndale,
> everything surrounding vacant or for sale.
> Sometimes I trace him on the train to Joliet
> or Menard, such towns quickly becoming native
> ground to these boys who seem to be nobody's
> sons, these boys who are so hard to love, so hard
> to see, except as case studies.
>
> Poverty, pain, shame, one and a half million
> dreams deemed fit only for the most internal
> of exiles. That four-year-old wandering
> the wind tunnels of Robert Taylor, of Cabrini
> Green, wind chill of an as yet unplumbed degree—
> a young boy she did not have to know to love.[2]

Our Man in the Fifteenth

It's been a big media week for many-decades-departed French intellectual historians. Michel Foucault—whom some of you may remember from a graduate course you took in 1994—found himself name-checked, on the op-ed pages no less, in a pair of major English-language dailies. As protests in the wake of the police murders of Breonna Taylor and George Floyd convulsed not just the United States but the planet, as a pandemic continued its awful decimating work, as the possibility of an unprecedented economic contraction loomed evermore asteroidlike in the night skies of even the most Panglossian market forecasters, and as temperatures tipped up past 100 degrees in the Arctic Circle, a couple of Professional Opinion-Havers paused amid their reflections to invoke the author of such chart-toppers as *The Archeology of Knowledge* and "Theatricum Philosophicum." As one friend observed, "2020 does not quit."

The redoubtable David Brooks, in a mea-culpaish column from June 18 entitled "How Moderates Failed Black America," noted in passing that conservatives like to blame spasms of dissent on the intellectual foment brewed up by "campus culture," which he then described with enviable concision: "People read Foucault," he wrote, "and develop an alienated view of the world."[1] And then, on June 19, in Rupert Murdoch's venerable daily *The Australian*, Adam Creighton came out of the gate harder still: "Want to spent [*sic*] three years reading Foucault and dreaming about vandalising Captain Cook statues?" he wrote, with the squeaking pugnacity proper to austerity economists everywhere. "Fine, but don't expect a cent from taxpayers."[2] (This line afforded the piece its deathless title: "Want to study Foucault? Don't expect a cent.") High theory as such may be back on its heels, and something of the '90s luster may indeed have faded from the project of genealogical critique. And yet there is apparently no gainsaying the mystically aversive power that our man Foucault continues to wield—more than a third of a century after his death—upon the planet's burbling reactionaries.

It's a mug's game to venture too earnestly into the cobwebbed psychic recesses of the world's rightist punditry. As here, however, the temptation to do so is often great, and I think you can see why. One need not be fluent in the byways of Lacanian psychoanalysis to see a certain, let's say, symptomaticity at work. Were you a person paid to speak for those who cherish, with vague but vituperous nostalgia, the allegedly commonsensical status quo, Foucault might well be a target difficult to resist. There he stands—gay, bald, *French*—discarding the holy verities with the provoking *panache* and *savoir-vivre* proper to the Fifteenth *arrondissement*. Possessing something of the risible-yet-menacing obscurity of Derrida, though spiced with a nearer proximity to the heat of insurrectionary politics—memories of '68 and all that—"Foucault" offers a ready metonym for what writers only marginally lazier than Brooks and Creighton derisively call "postmodernism," though among the more blithely antisemitic the term of art continues to be "cultural Marxism." *Foucault*: as malign incantations go, meant to summon up the dread permissive power of antifoundational speculation and Gallic attitudinizing, it will serve.

What, along these lines, could be more pithily perfect than Brooks's lament? *People read Foucault*—yes, go on—*and develop an alienated view of the world.* It is a compacted little scene of seduction, rendered with exactly the dopey sweater-vest unsexiness you'd hope for from a David Brooks column. No need, here, for teachers, or for the laggardly efforts of reflection, or for that matter any near experience with the liberal world's uncountable varieties of incentivizing rationality, managerial coercion, disavowed violence, oh no. On this model, the circuit travels, with an impressively instrumental immediacy, from text to consciousness to statue-toppling political resolve. I wish for all my fellow professors seminars that run so smoothly.

It all inclines toward the ludicrous, certainly—the roster of genuinely incendiary authors you might name before landing upon Foucault is, in the first place, very, very long—but I'll give credit where it's due. Neither Brooks nor Creighton seems to have in mind Foucault's work on policing, or the wedding of hypereconomized political life to regimes of security; they are not thinking, so far as I can tell, about his writings on control societies, the carceral state, the management of populations as aggregated into racialized subgroupings, differently exposed to quantums of opportunity, protection, violence, death. But they are, in their way, getting something right about Foucault's project. For it is indeed among his ambitions to suggest that there is an outside to the empire of liberalism and its many self-sanctioning rationalities. In his interest in the volatile interplay between that unconverted outside and the forces that seize and make it knowable, and in his altogether cold regard for the narrowed horizons of that empire's emancipatory promises, he takes his place within a long and vital dissident philosophical tradition that runs from Marx and Nietzsche out to W. E. B. DuBois, Frantz Fanon, Sylvia Wynter, Gayatri Spivak, Hortense Spillers, and many, many another. And this, among the pundit class, does not sit well.

Nor has it done, for some time. In his sharp book from 2016, *Foucault in Iran*, Behrooz Ghamari-Tabrizi reminds us that, for a certain style of critic reenergized by what he aptly calls "the civilizational ardor of the post-9/11 moment," Foucault stood out as a villain among villains. In his essays on the Iranian Revolution in particular, he had committed a capital crime, which for these critics was a failure, prevalent among "poststructuralists" generally but led by Foucault, "to reckon with the catastrophic consequences of deviating from the project of the Enlightenment."[3] To have shown a sympathetic interest in the Iranian Revolution—to have been "kindled by witnessing a moment of *making history* outside the purview of a Western teleological schema" and to have written in resistance to "bifurcated conceptions of Islamist versus secular politics based on a temporal map of Enlightenment rationalities"—is, for critics of this sort, as good as to have cheered on the hijackers.[4]

Echoes of this civilizational horror are there to be heard in today's aghast invocations, though for our part we might hear too a different set of ironies. How, after all, does one assess that "civilizational ardor" in the context of 2020, what with "growth" fetishism giving inexorable way to impending economic and environmental collapse, fascoid populisms rising vertiginously, and the creaking edifice of postwar liberal-imperial consensus looking more and more ready to topple? The murderer's call, we might say, has always been coming from inside the house.

Now, I do not mean to suggest that, since reactionaries say his work is malignant and galvanizing, it therefore follows that Foucault must be regarded as *indispensable* to any left-oriented or liberationist intellectual project unfolding in the present tense. I find him greatly enabling, it's true—of which more in a moment—but god knows that's not because I imagine his is the key that fits all locks. His use to you will depend, as with most theorists, on the questions you wish to ask, as well as your orientation toward them. It's not hard to imagine an interest in, say, police power that might be better served by reading George Jackson, or Angela Davis, or Ruth Wilson Gilmore—which is not, at least to me, a dismissal of the work of *Discipline and Punish*.

And anyway, such disclaimers as these are perhaps unnecessary, inasmuch as a more left-oriented critique of Foucault is by now fairly well-established. In the meme-ified way of contemporary things, these critiques have acquired, some of them, a certain ready-to-hand familiarity. For those opposed to what is called "identity politics," often as linked to the '90s-style queer theorists most identified with works like *The History of Sexuality*, Foucault stands in for a reduction of the sphere of the political to the realm of the subject, as she or they or he has been "constructed" or "discursively constituted," and a drawing-away from the cross-identitarian solidarities that make for mass movements. Then, too, are the related and frequently recurring online inquiries— *Foucault:* WAS HE A NEOLIBERAL?—that bloom and wither like annuals, and tend to be about as tedious, as italicized by undergraduate tendentiousness, as you'd guess. (If you insisted that *Jacobin* had published some eight or nine of these in the last half-dozen years, each with the identical thesis, I could not find it in my heart to fact-check you.)

A more recent and more interesting version of the critique identifies "biopolitics" with its use in the context of a critical substrain called New Materialism, and pays attention to a certain vaporization of the realities of capitalist political economy in the constitution of life—in favor of a vague "ethics" oriented toward all iterations of "life" down to the least microbe and molecule—such as might be found in, for instance, the work of Bruno Latour.[5] This latter critical turn, for me, amounts to a wholly salutary refusal of the ethics-not-politics drift in Latour, but one that is also, much like the line on identitarianism and the subject, of equivocal value for thinking about *Foucault's* work, rather than its holographic appearance in the recountings of his less agile admirers. Latour, after all, represents Foucault's project with about the acuity that Marx's is exemplified by, say, Zizek.

These assessments may be more and less acute—as I say, they vary—but again that's not because there is nothing to be said about the *relation* between biopolitics and political economy, governmentality and empire, security and the circuits of capital. There very much is. Foucault's work persistently lays a certain kind of stress on the questions he takes up, often in the effort to shake them free of their embeddedness in what he takes to be the more rote traditions of Marxist analysis proper to pre-'68 France. That, along with the habitual tuning of his own style of critique toward layered irony and away from direct judgment or rebuke, makes for a contentious legacy.

For me, that contentiousness—the labor of translating back and forth across paradigms and their preferred conceptual idioms—is where much of the ongoing value continues to reside, in part because it tends to reveal surprising harmonies as often as it does dissensus. So, for instance, while the Marx of the 18th Brumaire encourages us to see conflict and contradiction working crosswise *at every social strata*, unfolding in real time with byzantine complexity, Foucault asks us to envision a world stratified by forces both vastly conglomerated and infinitesimal, that calcify in structures but also operate beneath their codes, according to rationalities that coexist sometimes smoothly and sometimes uneasily, in fractious multiplicity. That's only one very generalized example, but it does at least begin to get at why Marx and Foucault have not seemed to me theorists meaningfully understood as, say, opposites. And, more to the point, they have never seemed less so than *right now*.

Think, in this vein, of Jasbir Puar's resonant work in her 2017 volume *The Right to Maim*. There, in the key of anti-imperial critique, she reads Palestine not as some sort of outlying state of exception in the global order of things, but as something nearer and more unnerving. It is for her rather *a theater of security-experiment*, in which control societies test out, through varying styles of life-halting or -inhibiting violence, the modes of regulation proper to (as the phrase goes) surplus populations. Explicitly, *The Right to Maim* looks to join a Foucault-inflected project of biopolitical critique to an acute vision of the political economy of global capital, in an era marked both by precipitously decelerating growth and by an environing climate crisis. We could put it, in compressed terms, like this: If *longue durée* historians of capital like Giovanni Arrighi are correct, and so too are the climate scientists, then we are speeding toward a moment in which vaster and vaster swaths of the planetary life will be, from the purview of capital and its states, at once negligible as consumers and unassimilable to the swollen ranks of waged labor—will be in this sense *surplus*—and thus in need of securitized management and optimization. *The Right to Maim* tells the story of the life of a racialized religious minority, then, as a mapping-out out of *future* trajectories for imperial liberalism in the season of the Long Downturn: a glimpse, that is, of the shape of power in the world to come.[6]

Perhaps it goes without saying, but I will say it anyway: exactly nothing about this pandemic, with its swaths of laborers and of the institutionally underserved exposed to the probability of death in the name of an economy that must be "open," seems to me ill-suited to an analytics attending, as Puar's does, to the interwoven strategies of racist policing, labor discipline, the conjoining of spaces of circulation with those of enforced immobility, and the hyperfetishization of security. One might struggle to imagine a moment in which biopolitics and political economy, as conceptual frameworks, have seemed *less* agonistically opposed.

Not that this reading of a kind of provisional theoretical comity will be an especially conciliatory note to the guardians of what Brooks calls "campus culture," for whom one antiliberal—or "postmodernist," or expert in "grievance"—is basically as good as the next. Certainly it will not be heartening news to our tough-talking man Creighton, with his withering eye upon the under-productive graduates of "queer or diversity studies." (Creighton who—incidentally!—was in 2019 a journalist in residence at the Booth School of Business at the University of Chicago, where Brooks is of course a proud alum and board member—proving once again that, for such august institutions, the holy work of neoliberal apologism is long, and never done.) For pundits like these, we professional humanists have only alienation in our flinty hearts, and a dour determination to pass it on to the youth.

And yet, if you're at all like me, you can't help sensing something else, something stranger flickering up in these brief and talismanic invocations. These hailings of a figure not really known but conjured, half-seen, evoked in furtive seductions, producing in his wake a kind of malign enchantment . . . they bring a quick smile, don't they? It is for all the world as if, against the promptings of reason and sober judgement, these writers had caught a flashing glimpse of the joy in struggle, and in the kinds of being-together it precipitates, and maybe—who can say?—in the possibility of an entire *way of life* coming into new vitality there. And what they see, or think they see, is a prospect too alluring, too queer, too luminous altogether, not to revile.

Hollow

In the midst of Henry James's magnificent heartbreak of a novel, *The Portrait of a Lady*, there is a curious turn of phrase—a phrase, you could say, for conjuring. Famously, *Portrait* is about a young woman granted an almost unlimited freedom of action who is determined to live a life of bright and searching intensity and who, in part as a result of that gift of freedom, brings herself to ruin. In the midst of the unspooling of this drama, one character pauses to wonder, of our tragic heroine Isabel Archer, "what queer temporal province she was annexing."[1]

It may be that you can read that striking bit of idiom and not think of Joni Mitchell—or for that matter of the novelist Paula Fox, or of the fraught prospects of '68, not only for women but for women especially. (Among them: freedom, sex, ruin.) That's how I hear it, though. It prompts in me a weird cluster of questions, and they go roughly like this: Is it possible that a song written by a woman in her early twenties can map out the arc of the nearly fifty-year career trajectory that would follow it? When this happens—*if* this happens—what's the name for this kind of anticipatory resonance, its queer temporal provinces? How does one begin to make sense of it—the song itself, the career, the worlds from which they emerge?

These questions come to turbulent life, I think, inside a single song, which closes out Joni Mitchell's 1968 debut record *Song to a Seagull*. That song is called "Cactus Tree." Now, as Mitchell enthusiasts will be quick to tell you, "Cactus Tree" was neither her first nor her most indelible hit from the '60s. (She had already written both "Circle Game" and, even before that, "Both Sides Now.") But "Cactus Tree" holds something of a place of pride in Mitchell's body of work nevertheless. Nearly a decade later, in a track from the masterwork that was *Hejira*, from 1976, the speaker in Mitchell's "Amelia" pauses in her flight from romantic catastrophe. She spends the night, she tells us, at "the Cactus Tree Motel."

From the seeds of that winking little aside—what I take to be its backward-looking acknowledgment of *something*: achieved clarity, continuity, a strong early attempt at an abiding set of preoccupations—much can be grown. Here's my claim, which is both straightforward and counterfactual: many if not all of what would come to be the signature conflicts of Mitchell's work, the most enlivening and also the most dismaying, are prefigured, in compressed clarity, in this one ultra-early song. That queer folding together of a future-to-come into the past's present-tense: this, I think, is a lot of what there is to hear now in the four-minute bolt of radiance that is "Cactus Tree."

Here's a subclaim, which is perhaps marginally less counterfactual: the poise with which the song holds its conflicts in calibrated balance, coming as it does in a songwriter so young, about breaks your heart. In that way, it's the note-perfect soundtrack for Paula Fox's novel of '60s upheaval and devastation, *Desperate Characters*.

* * *

It's worth saying from the start that there are ways of not much liking this song. Were you to insist to me that "Cactus Tree" had no place whatsoever in your private pantheon of Mitchell tracks, and could not rightfully be compared to "River" or "Case of You" or "Refuge of the Roads" or "Free Man in Paris" or any of the other likelier possibilities, I would not have a lot of heart to dissuade you. The reasons are clear enough. If, for instance, you have any sort of allergy to what we might generously call Mitchell's youthful *poeticism*, if you take to the song any quick impatience with phrases a little too artful, a hippieishness a little too contrived—in that case, "Cactus Tree" will not make you happy. When, at the outset, the singer speaks of a man "bearing beads from California / with their amber stones *and green*," the preciousness might set your teeth on edge.

Let me say it directly: I understand the distaste for this sort of pat prettiness, I do. You do not need to convince me that these are figures not quite able to mask their self-enchantment, or to overcome the atmosphere of coffeehouse confectedness they conjure around themselves. I get it. Nor do you lose points with me for identifying precisely that confection, so vivid in what is sometimes called Mitchell's "folk waif" period, with a style of specifically sixtiesish, specifically countercultural affectedness. Pick among the expressions of high-flown hippie piety that drift back to you even now—*maybe if we think real hard we can stop all this rain!*, to take the famous example from Woodstock, works as well as most. Any one of them will give testament to the distinctive style of pseudopolitical toothlessness that, in its laxest moments, it is difficult not to find aggravating.

An ungenerous accounting of the counterculture, you may say—and perhaps that's right. But then anybody who grew up listening to punk rock, or just beguiled by the array of detonating refusals to be found there, will likely have a clear enough sense of what I mean, if only because so much of the eviscerating force of punk was aimed directly at the played-out pieties of hippiedom, its neutering of the conflictual uglinesses of politics, its garish self-satisfaction. Love it though I do, I am for all these reasons not the sort of person who will blame you too severely for consigning "Cactus Tree" to some playlist of worn-out period pieces, entitled DO NOT REVIVE.

Hear me out, though. Because "Cactus Tree," it turns out, is not as fully in thrall to these limping figures as you might fear. So much of the sparking liveliness of the song derives, in fact, from the cagey way it crosscuts just those flights toward flower-child effusiveness with a language much more exacting and unadorned. Take the following lines:

> There's a man who writes her letters
> He is bleeding from the war
> There's a jouster and jester
> And a man who owns a store

I dissemble not at all when I say that, in the Introduction to Poetry classes I used to run back at the college where I worked, I taught this stanza. I taught it as an exemplification of the point made by modernist critics like Josephine Miles and John Hollander and Mary Kinzie, about the extraordinary ligaturing work done by effective rhyme. Part of the function of rhyme, these critics say, is to fold together anticipation and surprise—you know *that* it's coming, inside the structure of a rhyming poem, but you do not know *what* is coming. By yoking words and phrases from contrasting rhetorical registers, poets can dramatize that effect, use it to ring complex changes in tone, texture, meaning.²

Standing in front of rooms full of the credulous young, I liked to say that Mitchell's song is one of the finest materializations of this principle you're likely to find anywhere this side of, I don't know, Pope—or at least Elvis Costello. Watch what happens to the phrase *bleeding from the war*. Watch how it becomes infinitely more vivid, so much more a condensed emblem of horror, by virtue of its swift conjoining with a piece of idiom that could not speak more utterly of the homely, the unexceptional: *a man who owns a store*. There are fanciful precincts (the *jouster*, the *jester*) but then that clinching line lands you someplace worlds and worlds apart. It sets bloodletting, in a breath, down among the fixed rudiments of the everyday.

The point here is not to marvel at Mitchell's rhetorical poise, honest—though I confess that, poetry teacher that I am, I find it hard not to be moved even still by the grace with which Mitchell's deft punctuation of flowery indulgence with taut plainspokenness effectively anchors even the gauziest of her abstractions back to the ordinary and unglowing human world. Nor is it even to note how that poise will work to similarly stirring effect in later songs, though such moments are certainly goddamn great. Think only of the heartlifting wonderfulness of "Refuge of the Roads," where the narrator has a lover who has managed the neat trick of giving her back herself "simplified"—until it all goes abruptly, terribly wrong, the moment he begins (in Pamela Thurschwell's delectable phrase) "mansplaining enlightenment." *Heart and humor and humility*, he tells her, *will lighten up your heavy load*. ("Heart and humility might be nice in the abstract," Thurschwell notes, "but not coming from him, not to her."³) Nothing exposes the windy paternal indulgence of the lover's phrases, his high-minded sententiousness, quite as killingly as the narrator's curt reply to all this: *I left him then.* You can hear it a thousand times—most of you probably have—and still, like the poem says, the heart moves roomier.[4]

Everything about "Cactus Tree" hinges on just that counter-balancing agility—and by "everything" I mean above all the song's frontal address to that greatest of hippie shibboleths, *free-dom.* On first blush, it's easy enough to take "Cactus Tree" for something of a second-wave anthem of liberation. Appraise it at the right angle, and it seems very much to be the song of a young woman living in the enjoyment of the freedom proper to what it calls this *decade full of dreams,* and especially in the enjoyment of its erotic freedom—the freedom, say, to have just this heteroge-neous array of lovers, taxonomized in their startling variety, verse by verse. (Here they are, the great Whitmanian catalogue of them: the sailor, the climber, the man in the office, the letter-writer, the veteran, the jouster, the jester, the man who owns the store . . .) The point could not be clearer: *they will lose her if they follow,* we are told, and that is that. Whatever it is that "freedom" may turn out to be, it takes form for this singer as the putting-away of a whole host of antiquated and specifically patriarchal proprieties. "Cactus Tree" gives voice to a few of the pleasures, the bright and persuasive delights, that might follow from that sort of deliberate cutting-off and breaking-loose.

And yet. However richly the song figures the rewards of what might be called "liberation," "Cactus Tree" will not hold up as a cheerleading account of, say, '60s-left cultural radicalism—least of all as it moves through the outerlands where sex, gender, and politics come into their fraught crosswired relation. All of this comes into focus in the compressed power of the song's ending:

> She will love them when she sees them
> They will lose her if they follow
> And she only means to please them
> And her heart is full, and hollow
> Like a cactus tree

Full, and hollow. In part because of the clarity with which the song sees the joys of freedom, the genuine human delights, these final undercutting lines, about a certain hollowness of heart investing all that tumultuous pleasure, arrive like a punch in the solar plexus. Everything that comes before is recoded, less disavowed than disenchanted. Not that the song emerges as some sort of reactionary counteranthem as a result; it doesn't. Mitchell isn't interested in dismissing liberation as such, and even less in belittling the erotic possibilities of freedom for young women at the end of the '60s, and no just reading of "Cactus Tree" can make it say that. But it is a song fiercely invested in *mistrusting* that freedom: in worrying over the languages in which it gets articulated, and in returning us to the griefs those languages try and try and try to dissemble.

*   *   *

In her undisavowing mistrust—expressed as an attunement to the hollownesses of proffered promises of freedom, particularly as they are shaped around the lives of women—Mitchell is of course not alone. Consider the example of Paula Fox and, in particular, her ferocious, compressed, and bleak novel *Desperate Characters*. Here is a novel that transpires over a few days in 1968—the season of the release of *Song of a Seagull*—though in a setting a good deal removed from the multiscenic and wide-open locales of "Cactus Tree." To the heroine at the center of *Desperate Characters*, 1968 feels, contrarily, claustrophobic—even if the scenes of her confinement are especially comfortable, sumptuous even.

The novel commences with a startling if tiny burst of violence, unleashed on the threshold between the tastefully high-bourgeois Brooklyn interior belonging to "Mr. and Mrs. Otto Brentwood" and the wild outer world it keeps at bay. Mrs. Brentwood, Sophie, is bitten on the hand by a feral cat that had been scratching around their back door and which, against Otto's wishes, she had gone out to feed: "it sank its teeth into the back of her left hand and hung from her flesh so that she nearly fell forward, stunned and horrified, yet conscious enough of Otto's presence to smother the cry that arose in her throat as she jerked her hand back."[5] Over the course of the rest of the novel, the wound festers. Sophie resists having it treated—that early note about Otto's chastening and censorious presence carries through the whole of the book—and because of this the possibility that she has been poisoned, that she has contracted a strain of rabies that even in the midst of all this cosseted security might actively be *killing her*, never dissipates from the novel. It is, throughout, alive with a corrosive menace.

The story the novel tells is of a period of stilled unhappiness, edging out toward crisis, in Sophie's marriage and in her life more largely. Much of the local turmoil in the book involves the fact that Otto's longtime partner in law, Charlie, has broken up their firm, exasperated by Otto's stolidity, his conservatism, his want of sympathy for Charlie's own burgeoning countercultural political commitments. Charlie understands himself to have been, in a word, *radicalized*. "You won't survive this," Charlie complains bitterly one night to Sophie, "what's happening now. People like you . . . stubborn and stupid and drearily enslaved to introspection while the foundation of their privilege is being blasted out from under them."[6] It's worth saying that no one in the novel is convinced by this, or believes that in Charlie it expresses anything other than a dilettanteish cocktail-party self-besottedness. But Charlie's crisis, and Otto's struggle with his partner's abandonment, however glancingly they both seem to touch the malaise of the world, open out onto the crisis that, for Sophie, *had* had a radical power, a capacity to shake her out of her accumulated habits of being, and into a newer, rawer relation to the world without. This was her affair some years before—undisclosed to Otto—with a man named Francis Early.

In the middle of the novel is a chapter in which Sophie recollects her affair, its stages, its eventual nonclimactic dissolution. It is, without question, the scene of Sophie's most enlivening intensities, her least befogged passages of contact with the world—and also where the resonances of the book, alongside Mitchell's song, are most clear. Sophie will later realize that "her involvement with Francis had shoved her back violently into herself," though this violent inwardness makes also for an outward attunement, a fine keenness of regard for the suddenly unblurred details of her life. She is, across the registers of her person, vitalized:

> She had never looked better; the whites of her eyes were as clear as a child's, her dark hair was especially lustrous, and although she didn't eat much, she seemed to be bursting out of her clothes, not because of added weight, so much as of galvanized energy. Strain, she thought, became her, tightened up her face which was overly plastic, lightened her rather sallow olive skin. She didn't have a moment of repose, thinking, thinking, thinking about him.[7]

If a sort of gendered conformity adheres to these passages, there is also a "Cactus Tree"-like achieved vividness of life here: a fierce and burning clarity that for a time unclouds Sophie, in a way that even the potentially lethal bite with which she is afflicted cannot.

Here too, though, what's so striking about Sophie's retrospective account of her affair with Francis Early is the way that, while holding close to its transformative power, she understands it still to have been unavailing, its own kind of cloudedness—and not just because it came to an end, failed to issue in some new scene of intimacy that might replace the airlessness of her relation to Otto with something larger and freer. That sex-sharpened promise of liberation seems rather, for Sophie, exactly the ruse with which she must somehow contend, the humiliating lie that she recognizes but cannot prevent herself becoming entangled in. She sees this even *before* she commences her affair. After an exchanged, electric touch has sent them into a taxi, speeding to Francis's apartment, the not-yet-lovers enjoy a frozen moment together, in which Francis takes her hand, so that "a tremor passed over her and her mouth went dry." But then comes one of the most lacerating sentences of the whole novel: "She had, then," we are told, "an anguished fore-knowledge that she would be a long time missing him."[8]

An anguished foreknowledge: the unnerving possibility here is that, without being in the grip of any unconverted bourgeois conventionality or staid gender obedience, Sophie knows to *disbelieve* the promise of liberation that is shortly to arrive to her, wrapped up in the transporting power of sex. Like Mitchell's narrator, she will take the measure of that liberation, and when she does it will be accounted as something richer in possibility, and less mired in self-deception, than Charlie's enthusiasms, or her husband's stolid resistance to them. But it will be insufficient nevertheless, unavailing, hollow.

All this gives a stinging resonance to a scene that comes earlier in the novel (though *after* her affair), at a party on the night Sophie suffers her terrible bite. There she encounters "a couple in their early twenties" who are bedecked in countercultural markers—he has frizzy long hair and an army fatigue jacket covered in buttons, she a "heavy bracelet around one of her ankles"—and who bristle at the *squareness* of the party:

> They looked at her as though they'd never seen her before, then they both padded softly out of the living room, looking neither left nor right. "That's a beautiful anklet!" Sophie called out. The girl looked back from the hall. For an instant, she seemed about to smile. "It hurts me to wear it," she shouted. "Every time I move, it hurts."9

When we first come upon it, the moment seems a bit of sharp observational comedy, mordant and undercutting. In the reflected light of Sophie's affair—the affair that was vivifying, clarifying, and unredeeming—it glows with a terrible inner darkness. The options for freedom, on either side of the generational divide marked out by 1968, are not without compelling force. They might even be beautiful. For the women, however, in and out of scenes of domestic confinement—in whatever proximity to the available idioms of liberation—they are also more and other than beautiful. They constrain. They *hurt*.

The novel's stirring conclusion unfolds in close relation to such submerged revelations as these. "God, if I am rabid, I am equal to what is outside," Sophie says aloud to herself,

> and felt an extraordinary relief as though, at last, she'd discovered what it was that could create a balance between the quiet, rather vacant progression of the days she spent in this

house, and those portents that lit up the dark at the edge of her own existence.[10]

Rabidity, for *Desperate Characters*, is the condition that adheres Sophie to the world: the heart's rabid desire for love even at the cost of steep self-deception; the world's rabid malignancy, its narrownesses of care and brutal, deforming inequities. It is a novel that does not want for sympathy, a warm-blooded seriousness of regard for anybody's hunger for a freedom capable of cracking open these narrownesses, even a little. But it is wedded just as much to its own dearly bought mistrust, an unwillingness to be beguiled by the languages in which those supposedly broadening freedoms are cast. Undisavowing, unbeguiled: it's a narrow patch of ground. Mitchell and Fox stand there, determinedly, together.

*   *   *

As we know, an undercutting skepticism with respect to liberatory languages can calcify into unlovely forms. (Pamela Thurschwell, the best reader of Mitchell I know, offers another great phrase for that especially spiky sort of wariness in relation to worlds of liberation and confinement both, as they are shaped by patriarchal presumption: she calls this subgenre of critique "irritable feminism.") There's Mitchell's sometime racism (think of her late-'70s ventures into blackface), her sometime polemical antifeminism. "I was never a feminist," she says to Malka Marom in one of the interviews collected in *Joni Mitchell: In Her Own Words*. "I was in argument with them. . . . And even though my problems were somewhat female, they were of no help to mine."[11] Fair to say, I think, that these are no one's favorite versions of Joni Mitchell.

I would not want to dismiss them too hastily, though, or to contextualize them away. As a song like "Cactus Tree" is there to remind you, they are interwoven with the very aspects of artistry, the cultivated mistrust and vibrant ambivalence, that make her precisely the kind of extraordinary that she is. I think instead of that backward-looking moment in "Amelia," whose narrator beds down at the "Cactus Tree Motel." If this is a moment of recognition, a queer sort of nod across time, what it confirms is nothing so much as the power and the lastingness of Mitchell's roving inquietude of mind. Wary of complacency, impatient with romance, uneasy around boomerish high-mindedness in all its guises, but especially as they tender themselves to women: this is the Mitchell who suffers and exults through the whole of *Blue* but also *Court and Spark* but also *Hejira* but also everything. Quite as much as the soprano radiance of her voice, the thrumming insistence of her guitar, that prompting restiveness is what rings out even now in a song like "Cactus Tree," written when she was all of twenty-three. Listen close: there's a whole future in it.

Killing Joke

Some things you fall for a little too fast, and a little too hard. Not that long ago a novelist friend urged this novel on me, the way your novelist friends are wont to do. "You'll like it," he said. And then, in response to what may've been something unpersuaded in my aspect: "In the first place, it's extremely funny."

An ardor for the antic, a weakness for that weakest of rhetorical maneuvers (the *joke*), a more general wearied impatience with the familiar Franzenish self-delectation of *serious* writers, even the obviously good ones: none of this is anything to brag about. Even I would admit that a susceptibility to the comic sentence, artful and barbed, is nobody's idea of an unerring standard. But this friend, he had my measure.

"Sure," I said. "OK."

And this is how I found myself plunging into the kind of heedless idiot novel-love with which many of you are likely familiar—a besottedness as precipitate as it was without margin and, it would prove, unshakable. The occasion was Sam Lipsyte's 2004 book *Home Land*.

Lipsyte has a new novel out called *Hark* (we'll get to that), and in the notices I've read, many of them a bit disappointed if also, to me, a bit petulant (we'll get to that too), people talk about Lipsyte's previous novel, *The Ask* (2010), as his breakthrough, his arrival, his Major Statement. It's a great book, sure: skewering and desolate, especially unmerciful in its attention to those armies of the monied busily despoiling new-millennial New York. But it is not his masterpiece. For propulsive lunacy and tottering demented grandeur—as well as for nihilistic farce, Bush-era vituperation, vigorous self-despising, Jersey in-jokes—you can do no better, I promise, than *Home Land*.

The premise of the novel could not be simpler: *Home Land* takes form as a series of "updates" sent to a high school alumni association by one Lewis Miner, a.k.a. "Teabag," a graduate of the class of '89 who, as he tells us at the outset, "did not pan out." As conceits go, this one is pretty threadbare. But it allows Lipsyte the latitude to fabulate an entire narrative edifice—meandering, "plotted" in the truly loosest senses, lurching toward its end at a reunion party—out of his very greatest novelistic gift, which is, for want of any more Latinate designation, the riff. (In this, he resembles no one so much as Paul Beatty, another ultragifted contemporary comic novelist.) I mean no disparagement at all when I say that *Home Land* is a good deal more like a 250-page Lenny Bruce routine, spangled with bursts of Rothian grandiloquence and the staccato crackle of Grace Paley dialogue, than it is a well-wrought urn of deliberative domestic fiction. It gallops and careens, characters accruing and entangling, riffs begetting further riffs, in a baroque succession of digressions and micropolemics tending to the bitter, the despairing, the delirious.

Those riffs sound like this:

Which reminds me, I've yet to comment on the latest issue of *Catamount News*, wherein it was announced that my old flame Bethany Applebaum is making a mint helping the doltish progeny of the rich gain admittance to our nation's leading universities. Bravo, Bethany! Tuck those little one percenters in all safe and cozy. Keep that ruling-class razor wire sharp and shiny!

Bethany, your father was head of the lathe workers local. Would he pop and lock in his grave knowing you've dedicated your life to helping these entitled cretins? You busted your hump to get to Cornell. All that panic and self-cutting, those blood-speckled scrunchies on your arm. Is this your way of giving back to the gate-keepers? Or is your cynicism a huge holy shimmering thing no mortal could view in its entirety?

Please write in and let us know!

Or again, still less mercifully:

Philly Boy, congratulations on your continued success at Willoughby and Stern. You've always been a persistent guy, Phil, a real plugger, whether the task at hand was to find a hole in rival Nearmont's vaunted line or a fag to bash after the Friday night game . . .

I'm also fairly certain at least a few of our contemporaries share my fantasy of cornering you in Eastern Valley's dank shower room and firing a hollowpoint round into your skull. We could picture the startlement in your eyes, the suck and flop of your dead-before-it-hits-the-floor body hitting the floor, your brain meat chunked, running out in rivulets of soapy water across the scummed tiles, clogging up that rusted drain the school board never saw fit to replace. Your pecker would be puny with death.

We'd never do such a thing, of course, not like those suburban murder squads of today, those peach-fuzz assassins

in mail-order dusters who lay down suppressing fire in cafe-
terias ...

The temptation to keep quoting and do nothing else—except perhaps pause over the rich effects of words like "progeny," "scrunchies," "hollowpoint," "suppressing fire"—is for this reviewer great.

I hope you can see why. There are few writers I know so fever-
ishly allergic to the bloodless sentence, the ossified idiom. There
are fewer still more spectacularly agile in their resistance to "con-
forming to usages which have become dead," as Emerson puts it—
even when, as here, that resistance risks callousness, obscenity,
cruelty, or any of the other disavowed affects proper to the empires of American optimism. Lipsyte is nothing if not a nervy, tra-
ducing sort of writer, and I take this to be part of what it means to
think of his ludicrous virtuosity neither as ornament nor flourish,
but as a bedrock element of what has been, for him, a years'-long
effort to bring the submerged violences of the ordinary American
scene into queasy-making clarity: to contest, in the Emersonian
mode, the consolatory conventionalities of a poisoned world that
wishes not to know overmuch about its own malignancy.

Granted, this may not be your thing. Hyperverbose loserish
white-guy freakouts, tuned to the bleak and the lewd, are by now
their own sorry genre, and you may well have developed a distaste
for it. Fair enough. Nothing, at this point, is easier than claiming
"critique" as an alibi for more garden-variety sorts of (typically
male) odiousness. It's certainly the case that none of this would
cash out as much were Lipsyte's vision not appreciably wider and
more acute, and were the aspects of character he portrays not
themselves ultimately other than merely cartoonish—and were
they not also, as *Home Land* will put it, "acquired in provinces of
real human pain."

Lewis, for instance, has lost his mother, dead from cancer before the book opens, and that loss throws into cold relief all his accumulated failures—of nerve and of decency, at work, love, life. Her failures had been grander and braver. A late-arriver to '70s feminism, she wrote plays, convened readings groups of like-minded Jersey suburban women, "became a witness to what she'd come to conclude was her bondage." "Laugh at it now, Catamounts," Lewis says, "God knows my father did, but it was dangerous and new to Hazel, and what can you admire more in a person than a will to danger?" For all his undisguised perviness and anarchic discursive vigor, Lewis knows himself to possess no such will, and none of the scalpel-sharp world-despising of the novel would cut the way it does were it not superseded by what we might too blandly call its shame—a corrosive self-contempt which, let me hasten to add, is of a variety that Lipsyte has no interest either in redeeming (as in the familiar Apatowian arc) or in heroicizing (in the tired guise of the damaged but valiant male antihero). In Lipsyte's corner of the north Jersey cosmos, misery is blighting— the worst of us just pass it around, pass it along—not improving. And it is also, for all its putative universality, cruelly ill-distributed out in the mortal world, broken up as it is into its grief-gathering subdivisions of color, of sex, of money. (*The Ask* waxes magnificent about "the true machinations of money and power, the nuanced, friction-free nanotechnics of privilege.") Sharpened clarity on this point makes it satire, and not just existential bellyaching.

For most of us non-oligarchs, then, the livable options are not many, and they are not great. "We're at a crucial juncture in the history of our homeland, Valley Kitties," Lewis perorates in the frantic conclusion. "It's now or never. It's now *and* never. We must choose once and for all: police state or police state!" One response to this is the kind of grim laughter the book everywhere traffics in. But it's not the only one. "Sometimes, alums," Lewis says elsewhere,

> I'll be walking down the street, catch myself chanting softly, "Blow my friggin' head of, blow my goddamn friggin' head off."
> Doesn't everybody, Catamounts?

If you like a novel that makes a churning and batshit litany out of such soul-sickness, while not *quite* being able to muffle its own sentence-making joy, you'll maybe like Sam Lipsyte.

* * *

As I say, I love Sam Lipsyte, and nothing at this point is likely to push me off my mark. His new novel is called *Hark*, and while it's not as satisfying as a lot of his previous ones, I don't think, there is still a great deal to recommend it. The sentences, for instance, are still his.

Hark is the story of the small cadre of souls who gather around Hark Morner, the inventor of a set of techniques called "mental archery"—something between pilates, meditation, TED-talkish pseudophilosophizing—whose great and, Hark insists, sole purpose is to enable people to focus. Over the course of the novel its central characters assist, and bear witness to, Hark's ascent from self-help pamphleteer to corporate inspiration-monger to something less manageable and more, it seems, messianic. A message-board commenter, who will have a large role to play in the plot, says,

> It's a personal philosophy, maybe a little self-helpish (and damn, can't we all use a little self-help—the fucking corporations and the government and the fascists and the tech lords

aren't going to help us, trust me), but it's a really powerful message that uses archery as a metaphor.

And there is, unsurprisingly, a lot of ripe comedy to be plucked from the collision of planetary collapse and evermore uncontested oligarchic dominion with the improving bromides of "personal philosophy," Goopish affirmations, vigorous stretching. "Now we need a fresh song," one tech overlord assures Hark. "A vibrant life poem with which to propel ourselves into a succession of profitable quarters."

There are, I think, three particularly striking things about *Hark*. First, it is not in the fanatical first-person. It features a multitude of centers of narrative consciousness, and this makes for a story that feels more spacious—less claustrophobically compulsive— than many of Lipsyte's others. In direct relation to this, too, is a spaciousness in the novel's regard for what we might call its characters' practices of belief. Hark himself, for instance, remains something of a well-drawn cipher in the book, a vivid blur, and in Lipsyte's novel-wide willingness to demur from mercilessness, to withhold satirical fire and thus preserve some unvoided space of mystery about him—this unfunny man who professedly neither gets nor traffics in irony—we can feel a deliberate and, I think, telling recalibration of the novelist's own marrow-deep impulses toward mockery.

"How strange," muses the middle-aged and hapless Fraz, the most familiar of Lipsyte's narrators,

to be Fraz, a fairly sharp guy raised by atheists, and still want to believe in this stuff. But it's more than desire. Fraz does believe. Better to believe than accept his mother and father's miserable certainty, their sour invitation to the void. Better to believe than to fetishize doubt, that dubious lodestar for all those sweat-bright wrestlers of faith.

It's not that belief has become appreciably less absurd, or less easily convertible into the idioms of corporate wellness-peddling, the extractive machinery of venture capitalism. Still the novel wonders: What if a killing and all-devouring irony *isn't* the way to survive the world?

But then, in a not-at-all-metaphysical way, the world may not be ours to survive. And this, for my money, is the third curious thing about *Hark*. It takes place about a dozen years in the future. One mark of this is Tovah Gold, one of Lipsyte's most splendid creations, who first appeared in some shorter fiction, including the breathtakingly great "The Climber Room." There she had been in her late thirties, navigating the plummeting awfulness of dating New York men and wanting children; here, she has twin ten-year-olds with Fraz, is the breadwinner, still writes poetry, sustains a nondismissive wariness in respect to "Harkism" throughout. But that time-tracking device is appended to others, which make for a kind of background noise in the novel—until, a little bewilderingly, that noise is much of what there is to hear.

We learn that not only has the planet deteriorated in predicted and predictable ways, and not only has an ascendant oligarchy further severed itself from the collective life of the species. We discover, too, that Europe has for some time been convulsed by a vast bloodletting. "War is everywhere," Fraz writes in ad copy for Mental Archery,

Europe is about to be conquered by a group many call the Army of the Just, a force made up of the same mix of veterans, conscripts and soldiers of fortune that have filled the ranks of marauding militias for millennia. That this horde claims no particular religious or political ideology beyond the abolition of poverty and oppression, and includes members of diverse races, religions and creeds who have gathered from around the world and sworn to fight both globalist power structures and ethno-nationalist movements across the continents is especially striking.

You don't say? By the end of the novel, that war has begun its transatlantic migration.

Reviews I've read have complained that as the book heaves toward its conclusion it grows scattered, and a shade arbitrary. I'm not going to tell you that's wholly unfair. I will say that Lipsyte seems to me to be trying to think his way into something obscure but pressing, something at the dark edges of the frame of the world of his striving city-dwellers. I don't just mean the climatological terror that, Amitav Ghosh notwithstanding, we lately *have* found many, many ways of narrativizing. I mean rather the unnerving twinned conviction that the brutalizing arrangements of the global present—with its misery-quintiles of sex and color and money—*cannot hold*, and that the thing required to uproot that arrangement will be, when it comes, of an unimaginable scope and scale of violent horror: a full fucking *hemoclysm* (thank you, Sam Lipsyte, for teaching me this term) from which ultimately very few are likely to be spared, no matter their conscious consumption, their preference for diversity in the ranks of overlords, their devout recycling.

"The fact is," one of the novel's tech-bro titans tells Fraz,

I myself spend a lot of money on philanthropy. As does my company. But we're not interested in any large-scale, systemic shift in how things are done on the planet. For that, the downtrodden are really going to have to come and take our fucking shit and kill us. And so far they are too scared to try. Actually, it's getting kind of boring.

Near the very end, we meet a pregnant young woman who gets high with Fraz, remarks that she's been in Europe. "Eat shit," she tells him. "I'm a vet. I was in Ibiza. Saw the deathpits. I was on a nuke squad in Mallorca. I'm just trying to get through the day." Boredom, then, or world-scale horror.

I'd be a poor reviewer if I claimed for *Hark* the singular achieved power of *Home Land*. It is a thing considerably weirder and more diffuse, its riffs semi-chastened, though it is still outlandishly funny. And some readers, especially partisans of the cool Cuskian formalism many of my contemporaries seem to admire (though I do not), may find turns like the above overdrawn, rote, an apocalypticism too easily come by. I do not find them so, but then I am an avowed sucker for what Lipsyte is selling. Still, nothing in the novel suggests to me it's wrong to believe Lipsyte is always worth reading. In every bit of his work you will find a writer striving to be unbeguiled by the prevailing fantasies proper to what I will just go ahead and call imperial liberalism, as it staggers toward its terrible planetary ruin—fantasies about the benevolence of power, the sure victory of comity over antagonism, upheaval without suffering, change without blood, all boats rising, a thousand points of light. His characters look around and see (or try not to see) worlds offering less and less in the way of noncataclysmic "outcomes," as the few remaining Pinkerite techno-optimists might have it. This, in *Hark*, is where their listing toward some renovated possibilities for belief comes from. Who are you to say they're wrong? Who am I to laugh?

PART V

Ends

Whose nerves are always on a knife's edge?
Who's up late polishing the blade?

ELVIS COSTELLO, "Man Out of Time"

. . . the postulate was, that there is a group alive, clustered on his
threshold to watch the last flicker of light on a black sky, to hear the last
word uttered in the stilled workshop of the earth . . .—whether in austere
exhortation or in a phrase of sardonic comment, who can guess? For
my own part, from a short and cursory acquaintance with my kind, I
am inclined to think that the last utterance will formulate, strange as it
may appear, some hope now to us utterly inconceivable. For mankind is
delightful in its pride, its assurance, and its indomitable tenacity. It will
sleep on the battlefield among its own dead, in the manner of an army
having won a barren victory. It will not know when it is beaten.

JOSEPH CONRAD, *Notes on Life and Letters*

My Thoughts Are Murder

Who can be serene in a country where
both the rulers and the ruled are without principle?
The remembrance of my country spoils my walk.

HENRY DAVID THOREAU

As with much else, you could I suppose just blame the Eighties.

It was 1989 and there were perhaps five or six of us there in my friend's living room, unspooling the lax teenaged hours together. Were her parents home? I imagine they had to have been. Someone must've greeted us when we returned from the video store, must've overheard our tittering nervous laughter. Someone could have traced the fine thread of incredulity running through our fitful conversation, or heard within it the dawning sense that this, here, was something a pace or two beyond us, a thing stranger and smarter and more unmanageable than our clever-kid wit could quite encompass. Something about it was upsetting, certainly. But what I most remember is finding myself, in a moment to moment way, awash in this steep, stunned exhilaration.

Then someone on the TV, a handsome boy in a menacing overcoat with an expression of arch, razored irony on his face, uttered the following sentences.

"Football season is *over*," he said. And then, "Kurt and Ram had nothing to offer the school but date rape and AIDS jokes."

All at once, the air went out of the room.

I replayed it: *nothing to offer the school but date rape and AIDS jokes.*

DATE RAPE AND AIDS JOKES.

I repeated it and repeated it to myself. Could I have heard that correctly? It was so mean, so *vile*, and, also, I knew, so bottomlessly true: true beyond any possibility of contradiction.

It became on the spot a little private novena. A motto. A shield.

The actor was of course a young Christian Slater, who was speaking to an even younger Winona Ryder—speaking about the two jocks they had just, amazingly, shot dead. After that, nothing was quite the same for me.

*   *   *

Like a lot of people I know—perhaps like a lot of you—I make my living standing in front of young people and trying to persuade them of the beauty, the brilliance, the complexity or daring or compelling critical force, of this or that piece of literature. It is, if not the very greatest of human gigs, pretty fucking close to it, at least for me. There are of course less heartening ways of describing what I do. Credentialing, you could say; outfitting adolescents with marginally useful skills in preparation for jobs that have long since vanished anyway; or—as we used to say, with some justice, when I taught at a small private college—*painting a thin veneer of culture on tomorrow's ruling classes.*

All of this is perfectly fair, though I'd insist nevertheless it is as great a job, as lit up by quotidian wondrousness, as any I can imagine myself having. The days, the laborious classroom days, are by turns tedious, irritating, and then—just when your teacherly patience has begun to collapse in on itself, and the chalk feels heavy in your hands, and the words prattling and dry in your throat—out of nowhere there comes a moment of jolting radiance. Someone says something amazing. The conversation, so pinched and grinding, suddenly ascends into unforeseen precincts of thought. Or, best of all, you get to watch as some kid, who hour by hour has maybe only been diffident, half-bored, medium-engaged, comes out with a formulation that, even as she's making it, seems actually to surprise her, to take her a step or two beyond herself and into a new and unlooked-for idea. You can see the look stealing across her face: *Look what I just figured out.*

As I say, there's not much to compare to moments like this, when the ordinary workaday world cracks open a bit, and seems for an instant to gleam with bright possibility. Anybody who's taught even a little, at any level, will, I think, know what I mean.

The last weeks in the classroom have been, for me as for many others, rough. The young people in my classes are by and large bewildered and scared, and who can blame them? Where I now teach most of the kids are nonwhite, many from immigrant families, many more making their way through this urban public university with the aid of an array of government-secured grants and loans. What would happen to their families, and their friends? What would happen to their education? "My mom can't stop crying," one student said, "she's so scared." It was *frightening*, they said—these tough, tenacious, dauntless kids—to be a Muslim, to be Black or brown, to be queer. It had always been, of course, this they knew. But the near-to-hand world felt, they said, newly fragile.

Like a lot of you, I said what I could. I said that I would do whatever I could, whatever we could imagine, to have their backs. I told them I'd do my best to be in it with them, whatever that might come to mean, and that there were, I knew, ranks of other old people like me who'd be in it with them as well. And then, that said, we went on talking about Elizabeth Bishop and Derek Walcott, about James Baldwin and *Member of the Wedding*.

How awful, I thought, how fucking shameful, to have so little to offer these kids, these everyday pains in my ass who were also, in ways I could never predict, so much an amazement.

But then, in the class I'm teaching called THE QUEER CHILD— because such is my devotion to the perversion of youth and the destruction of all the holy verities—before turning back to the sentences of Carson McCullers, one student told us she'd been out at a major postelection protest the night before and it had, she said, worked a kind of magic on her leaden despair. She felt energized, clarified, an on-the-street solidarity buzzing all through her.

"It's like," she said, and then cocked her head to one side, as if scanning the middle distance for the right words. "For the next four years I'm just going to be Blacker and gayer than anybody's ever seen."

You never know, in the classroom, when the radiant moments are coming. But then you find your breath coming tight, and your eyes stinging, and you think, *Here: here's another one.*

*   *   *

Months before this, when the world seemed a different complexion of broken, and malignity a different kind of institutionalized, I'd scheduled for the last day of our class what I thought was an ingenious pairing. We would watch *Elephant*, Gus Van Sant's trancey art-film restaging of some Columbine-like scene of high school carnage, in concert with that landmark of my long-expired youth, *Heathers*. Dreamy landscapes of high school sociability, punctured by outbursts of lethal adolescent violence: GO!

Of course it's been hard to teach, to stand up in front of anyone in the guise of authoritative knowledge, in these ugly and disorienting weeks. *Waves of anger and fear / Circulate over the bright / And darkened lands of the earth* is how Auden puts it, in a poem that the twenty-first century has managed to turn into cataclysm-kitsch, a cliché of bookish political despair.[1] Anger and fear, yes. But, with these, a tremendous nauseating uncertainty. It ramifies, this stunned unknowing, in dozens of directions at once, and brings with it a sickening sense of the world slewing unstoppably toward some still more malignant and cruel version of itself.

To take only one near example, most everyone at the moment seems to need, quite reasonably, two not wholly compatible things. There is the need to return to some ballasting sense of continuity, some normalcy, in the texture of things, so that we might in this way stay attached to the world in its dailiness, where so many of our struggles are sure to transpire. But there is, alongside this, the need to resist, absolutely and implacably, any least normalization of this, our new Nonconsensual Real, presided over by the Short-Fingered Führer. Nothing about how to execute this double-move is easy or self-evident. (For a few days, Facebook, where over the years I'd taken such solace, became a cauldron of aggro microdistinction, as justly frightened and angry people set upon one another for leaning just a bit too far to one side or the other of this impossible toggle.) We're all out here, in real time, trying in our different ways to figure out how to do it.

But then something, some stupid time-dusted artifact, cycles into your syllabus, and an unforgotten feeling comes burrowing back into you, and suddenly, strangely, the monster that's been squatting on your chest day and night, pressing the air out of your lungs and making sleep fitful and haunted, seems somehow . . . different. It doesn't disintegrate, this monster, in some kind of pixelated CGI detail, alas. But you find yourself regarding it, taking it up and even talking back to it, in a new way.

*   *   *

I will fail to describe to you the seizing delight with which I re-rewatched *Heathers*. (I certainly failed to make it as clear as I wished to my students, who liked it—loved it, even—though in a hesitant, notably inarticulate way.) I promise you it was not just nostalgia, though I'll confess too to taking a substantial pleasure in the memory of how hard, with what searing indelibility, some scenes in the movie had landed on me when I first watched it. Two generic douchebag jocks approach the outcast kid at his solitary corner table and, in an idiom that in 1989 sounded in my ears like a small documentary slice of daily reality, remark sniggeringly to one another, "Doesn't the cafeteria have a NO FAGS ALLOWED rule?" To which, with a weary shrug, the faggy kid replies, "But they seem to have an open-door policy for assholes though, don't they?" And then, and then, in the midst of this dreamy and hyper-stylized high-school-cafeteria scene, *he pulls out a gun and shoots the both of them.*

Can you imagine the bliss, vengeful and nakedly compensatory, with which I watched this first unfold before me, the sputtering disbelief in me speeding toward a joyful sense of the world growing larger, funnier, more savage, and somehow also more habitable than it was only moments before? It was a bright amazement that only redoubled itself later—*nothing to offer but date rape and AIDS jokes*—as I came into the incredulous realization that the most hateful young men scattered around the scenes of my adolescence *could be named.* They could be named, they could be described in mordant and piercing terms, they could be grasped in the grain of their malignant doltishness and made into objects of an offhand and malicious ridicule. Can you imagine the new possibilities for being in relation to the world that crackled in the air around me, all of them keyed to this kind of caustic cleansing hate?

Those of you who were in whatever manner a notch or two queerer than the aesthetic ideal of the '80s adolescent: I know in my heart that you can.

I'm here to tell you that some of that incredulousness adheres to the film even now, transmuted and in fact amplified by the years. You realize, watching it again, that here is a film that, for all its hyperstylization and hypergenericization of teenage life—its overdrawn typologies of high school, its commitment to what Winona winningly calls "convenience-speak" in the 7-Eleven-ish store where she flirts with Christian Slater—is nevertheless not that interested in getting you to disavow wordy, disaffected, sex-having adolescents who set about murdering the more dull and cruel of their classmates. In 2016, this is in multiple respects *remarkable*. A glinting and unchastened malice shines through every moment of *Heathers*, not less but more visible now. Not that the warping unreality of the aesthetic of the film, its staginess and garishness and kaleidoscopic hyperreality, does not mantle all the proceedings in a somewhat militating irony, giving us a way to take the murderousness of these clever-kid killers at something other than, say, an earnest, neorealist face value. Remarkably, though, the movie does not deploy its ironizing stylization in quite this familiar, indeed by now virtually canonical, way, as a kind of hedge against itself. (SIDEBAR: To watch *Heathers* in 2016 is to be reminded of all the tonal possibilities, the great breadth of affects and inflections, that Quentin Tarantino just fucking destroyed, swallowed up quick in an aesthetic that allows for a more or less frictionless style of cheerful bloodletting.) Part of the reason *Heathers* amazes at this distance is that it does something ampler, nervier. It stages not any neutering opposition (genre v. blood, pulp v. pulp) but instead an uneasy, precarious balancing of cruelty and irony and something nearer to tenderness.

So, for instance, even when Christian Slater's J. D. (himself a condensation of every white-boy rebel in cinematic history you could care to name) turns more and more villainous, and Winona-Veronica must foil his plot to incinerate Westerburg High in a series of timed explosions, the movie declines to repudiate utterly its affection, less for him, I think, than for the impulses toward murderousness he carries into the plot. Winona is our final-girl, and so of course we don't want to see J. D. blow up the school; the camera's climactic slo-mo turn through the cheering young faces at a pep rally underscores this, a tender vision of youthful fragility and exuberance protected, in this one sweet instance, from any ironic undercutting. But we are invited nevertheless, with her and with him, to regret *at least a little* that he does not. (Veronica's talent, you might say, is to improve his violence—make it less the stuff of possessive misogyny, say—not refuse it.) *Pretend I did blow up the school—all the schools*, he says just before staging his own blaze-of-glory immolation, and we get it.

How could we not? From its first moments the film is saturated in this kind of all-devouring irreverence, a blaspheming, ill-tempered, fuck-each-and-every-one-of-you kind of antipiety that J. D., with his half-digested Nietzsche and Oedipal meshugahs, both perverts and exemplifies. Oh, oh, oh, how this movie hates! And not just the bullies, the homophobes, the cretins, and the jocks. The venomousness with which it regards liberals—the clarity with which it sees the naked self-aggrandizement in performances of white piety—is, I promise you, altogether joyous to behold. The grownups who aren't parodies of unknowing or cynicism ("Dammit—I'd give at least a half-day for a cheerleader") are smug feeling-vultures, ready to transform any mode of adolescent grief or pain into a circus of *care*, a spectacle of pious white people flexing the muscles of their compassionate blamelessness.

And then, and then, there is perhaps the cruelest line in a cruel film. "I love my son!" says a mawkish father standing by the open casket of the murdered son who, absurdly, wears in death his football uniform, helmet and all. "I love my dead gay son!" The comedy here is coldblooded, *arctic*. It would be years and years and years before the violence of the line came into real focus for me, how mercilessly it bullseyes the treacly way Americans, by 1989, had taken to professing their ardent love for handsome young gay men, *so long as they were dead*. (See, for the apotheosis of this, *Philadelphia*, from 1993.)

So *of course* we half-wish to see the school and everyone in it enveloped in some fiery apocalypse. How can we not, when the movie has tuned us to the world with such vigilant, all-encompassing spitefulness? Oh we do, we do, we do. Even if we don't, ultimately. Mostly.

*   *   *

Here in the waning hours of *annus horribilis* 2016, just this mélange of affects and uncanceled possibilities—all of it, every comic and cruel moment—has proved an astounding comfort to me. And, maybe, something better.

*   *   *

No one seems to me righter about the current moment than my wonderful Communist friend Frank. ("Have I mentioned the guillotines?" he likes to say. "And that they will run day and night?") He says there are three things that will get us through the next four years—Principle, Solidarity, and Organization—and this seems to me inarguably correct. These *are* the ideals to which we will need to aspire. Saying as much, though, does not to tell us how we might live in and through them, their formulation, their enactment, their nurturance.

Heathers does.

Heathers invites us to live in the world in a state of vigilant and never-satisfied spitefulness.

Heathers invites us to prosecute our lives with, let's say, a vengeful joyousness.

Heathers invites us never to forget that our enemies, whatever their awful power over us, are clownish and laughable and vile, as callow as any Heather, as unimaginative in their stunted hatefulness as any Kurt or Ram. (Ram, beside the casket of a dead Heather: "Dear Lord: why'd you have to kill such hot snatch?" AND THEN VERONICA AND J. D. KILL HIM.) They are scary, of course, these piteous flailing narcissists, their power gone suddenly nuclear-grade, fragilizing life for the whole of the world, with echelons of our comrades and loved ones ready now to be harmed by their fumbling cruelty, in familiarly asymmetrical ways. But *Heathers* also reminds us that the genuineness of that terror ought not to back us off one inch from an unfaltering sense of the extremity of their gasping loutish fraudulence, their profound human ridiculousness.

I mean, truly: these motherfuckers? These Twitter-flunkies? These Bircher assholes? These billionaire con-men and bloviating trolls? These bullhorn bigots playing make-believe with real bullets? *These* motherfuckers?

Say it with me, friends: DATE RAPE AND AIDS JOKES.

Which, only by happenstance, was not the slogan of one party's presidential campaign. The *winning* campaign.

*   *   *

None of this unelects the impending demagogue, I know. None of it renovates, or for that finally stakes through its fat corporate heart, the Democratic Party. None of it protects queer kids, immigrants, the Black and brown commons, the vulnerable, the ranks of the systematically and historically fucked. I know, I know, I know. And for all these reasons you'll see me in the streets, beside my students, and probably beside a lot of you, though I will not be standing there grimly, carrying the terrible weight of an irreparable despair. *Grimly?* No. Our side of the cafeteria has always had the better jokes, the more world-affirming malice. *Heathers*, with its barbed and killing laughter, knows this, and so do you, and so do I.

But I want to say that *Heathers* also proffers for us the fortifying reminder that our enemies deserve nothing—*nothing*—that is not derision, venomousness, and whatever quantity of only half-foresworn murderousness circulates between and among them. It insists that, the necessity of ballasting and humane tenderness notwithstanding, there maybe isn't any need to squander the energy of our despising, nor to surrender it even a little, even when it lists in the direction of an impulse more rending, and eschatological, and cataclysmic. "My thoughts," Thoreau famously remarked in 1854, "are murder to the State, and involuntarily go plotting against her."[2] *Heathers* is a movie that puts some evil joyousness back into the plotting, and sets a kind of detonating laughter in your throat. It is better now than it has ever been, and getting more so, I suspect, by the hour.

Mercy Hours

Like many of those whose working lives involve explaining things to young people, I traffic perhaps more than I should in superlatives. Often, these are inflected with a kind of vehement implacability. Since I teach literature, they take a familiar form. The *most* devastating breakup scene (James, *The Bostonians*). The *most* damning and vengeful American fiction (Melville, "Benito Cereno"). The most brutal drive-by aside (Eliot, ". . . the mother too often standing behind the daughter like a malign prophecy"), the most pulverizing interpellation (Baldwin, "*Look, baby, I know you*"), the most compressed sweetness (Bishop, "Why, oh why, the doily?"), the most sorrowful single word (Larkin, "undiminished"). And on and on. I imagine you have some of your own. It's a teacher's trick—a mnemonic device meant to induce recognition via hyperbole and insistence, as well as through the attack and counterattack that typically follow. There are worse pedagogies, even if, as substantive declarations go, they are each more or less ridiculous.

And yet. Live with these habits of untethered vehemence long enough and you may find that, whatever the quasi-charlatanism entailed in them, certain of those claims will not surrender themselves—but, to the contrary, will appear somehow to have ripened over time into fact, or at least the factlike. Some of them just come wheeling back upon you.

So it was I found myself insisting to a friend the other day that the *greatest*, the finest, most tender and demolishing literary scene of straight-male friendship transpires smack in the middle of the otherwise impressively bleak Patrick Melrose novels, by a writer named Edward St. Aubyn.

For real, I texted him. *I fucking mean it.*

The Melrose novels, as perhaps you know, are an extravagantly praised series of books tracing the life of a modern Englishman born into Old Money luxury, as well as into a family of spectacular, elaborate, life-envenoming cruelty. Patrick's father is David, a figure of towering malice who spends a part of Patrick's childhood raping him, while his mother (herself another of David's victims) drinks her way into an only slightly perforated unknowingness. These facts direct much of the "action" of the five novels, though the tone is another thing entirely. Committed throughout to the undislodgeable adjacency of horror and sparkling comedy, spiked with cauterizing wit, the novels read something like Evelyn Waugh for nihilists—though it is a nihilism humane enough for expansive laughter and, more saliently, for an aching, all-pervading sorrow. If this is at all your sort of thing (gutting comedy, acrobatic despair, razor-wire sentences), you know the praise is earned.

The most perfectly achieved of the five novels, for my money at least, is also the funniest, and is called, with characteristic duplicity, *Some Hope* (1992). It finds Patrick at thirty, no longer trapped in the slow-motion suicide of his heroin addiction but cleaned up, wondering what a life devoid of the terrorizing intensities of narcotics might look like ("He had been weaned from his drug addiction in several clinics, leaving promiscuity and party-going to soldier on uncertainly, like troops which have lost their commander")—and also, on the narrative's night in question, wondering whether to attend a party being thrown at an estate in the country, which promises to feature some of Europe's ghastliest, most venal, most venerable titled aristocracy, including, as it happens, Princess Margaret. It's all as vicious and ravaging as you could wish, a manor-house satire tricked out for early-'90s malefactors.

But another, less farcical plot threads through. For before he can bring himself to enter this scene, Patrick feels he must speak to "his greatest friend," Johnny Hall, with whom he had once been allied in drug use and is now collaborating in the project of making the desolate ordinary world somehow endurable. He wishes to tell Johnny about the fact, undivulged for so long, that stands at the disfiguring center of his life.

> But which words could he use? All his life he'd used words to distract attention from this deep inarticulacy, this unspeakable emotion which he would now have to use words to describe. How could they avoid being noisy and tactless, like a gaggle of children laughing under the bedroom window of a dying man?[1]

These unshared apprehensions aside, they meet. Sober now, they drink mineral water, order their dinners, and begin to speak.

Whereupon Patrick does indeed tell Johnny. Johnny, for his part, responds to his friend's confession with shock, attentiveness, and a muted willingness to witness and to converse, though without the pretense of any near-to-hand fix for his friend's anguish— all the hallmarks of a kind of tactful, patient, persevering care that, were the players not Englishmen, you could just go ahead and call "love." But in the middle of their conversation, as the hyperarticulate Patrick labors to convey to his great friend what has happened to him, there is a piercing turn. It goes like this:

"I'm exhausted by hating him. I can't go on. The hatred binds me to those events and I don't want to be a child anymore." Patrick was back in the vein again, released from silence by the habits of analysis and speculation.

"It must have split the world in half for you," said Johnny.

Patrick was taken aback by the precision of this comment.

"Yes. Yes, I think that's exactly what happened. How did you know?"[2]

How did you know? Patrick says, as if he has only just realized the ruinous, inarticulable grief that has so damaged him might in fact be communicated, in sorrow and compassion, to another person—might be made over into something slightly less, because shared. *Patrick was taken aback*: infinitely guarded and ironically unflappable Patrick! As if he only then recognizes, in its breadth of meaning, that the person with whom he is speaking loves him, and that this might, somehow, matter. No matter how many times you reread the thing, there it always is: this startling little detonation of tenderness.

But then, some days it's not so little.

And so it was partly out of surprise, and partly out of a steep and genuinely usteadying sort of confusion, that I sent those chirpy texts to my friend. I did so from my couch in Chicago, where I sat with my throat catching and my heart turning over, coming inexplicably unglued over a passage I very much knew was coming, in a book I'd read maybe half a dozen times.

It is a sensation that perhaps you know: a cocktail of *oh god how gorgeous* and *the fuck?* I am by nature an overreactive person, it's true, but this? And so, puzzled, rattled, fizzing with a sense of dislocated weirdness, I did what I often do with my excesses of blurry emotion, which is convert them into jokey, semi-needy texts to my own great friend, whom I have loved basically all my life, and who fields them with an expert fluency.

That these novels precede Brexit and the permanent Tory majority, he shot back, *is strong argument for uselessness of the "novel qua novel."* What, I ask you, is not to love?

So how's pandemic life going over there? I wrote back, stepping into our calming groove. *What are you listening to?*

*   *   *

It's hard to imagine a gentler quarantine than the one I'm having. My job is secure, praise be to the state of Illinois. I am not travel-stranded, I am not sick or especially vulnerable to sickness, I have kids who are grown, friends nearby, a lake to visit. It's true that, like a lot of middle-aged people, I am periodically *out of my mind* with worry over my parents, who are near on to eighty and for several bewildering days seemed to suffer a mysterious cognitive blockage, some generation-wide systems-error that rendered them curiously blasé in respect to the terrifying epidemiological situation. But even that gnawing fretfulness feels comparatively mild because, along with all these other unearned securities, I am locked in, here, with Julie.

I wish you could meet Julie. In her person you would find the unlikeliest convergence of graces. If, for example, there is a soul striding the shattered earth who better holds together her discerning and indeed ferocious clarity of mind with what I can only call an aptitude for *joyousness*—an attunement to the pleasures of all the days: a bright sky, pie for breakfast, a touch—I swear to you

I do not know them. (When I was first falling over myself in love, one of my stepdaughters said, "Julie's great because she knows what it is to be happy, *and she's not uptight about it*.") And then, too, nothing of that pleasure-alertness distracts her from a life-anchoring sense of justice—its urgency, its scarcity—that exceeds my own by many, many powers, though this she carries with so scrupulous an absence of piety you could easily miss it. These are impossible harmonies, really. But there they are, in fleecy running pants and a purple spotted bathrobe, each of these pandemic mornings.

Just this past summer we got married, which is to say: we are, currently, newlyweds. Since our planned spring trip to visit my family in Naples has been canceled, you could call this our weird honeymoon. A *luna di miele*, I've taken to saying, keyed to the Age of Disasters.

Of course, when I say *I wish you could meet Julie*, you should know that I am lying, at least a bit. It's nothing to do with her affability. (Unless you're an asshole, I'm pretty sure you'd like her). The matter is more, let's say, defensive. For there is a battered and persisting little part of me that delights in thinking, *maybe it's best that Julie's singular magic is clearest, mostly, to you*. It's the same part that is eager to remind me how supremely easy it is to imagine better versions of a companion—more pliant, more beautiful, more selfless, more competent and calm and stylish and wise—than the one I inevitably am.

I like to think everyone is in occasional contact with ghost-selves such as these, voices that crackle away inside us like fugitive broadcasts from a distant outpost, bristling with malign counterfactuals. Years and years ago now, in another life, I had been married, and had loved that person with a clutching urgency that at the time I would have just called a happy, if anxious, besottedness. That person, who it is fair to say came to experience our to-getherness rather differently, left me, with an unforeseen suddenness that did not do much to ease the labor of recovery, no. Everybody, I like to think, knows a version of this, most of them more harrowing.

Staticky voices, dialing in and out of range.

I don't mean to overstate. On most of the days, for me, there is just the faintest distant hum; if they are pronouncing something, these voices, I cannot make it out. Nor do I feel a pressing need to try. Why would I? Even now, even in the midst of these stricken weeks, Julie is here, and I am here. We have our work, our ever-involving phones, family to call, friends to text, songs to send on in solidarity and consolation. And then there are all these books, clamoring to be read and reread, which on occasion deliver us—or *some* of us—to sputtering wrought-up tearfulness. We're fine.

"Doomstruck incredulity and the enveloping dread aside," I found myself saying the other night, "we are absolutely fuck-ing fine."

*   *   *

That was how I put it on a digital date with a pair of far-flung friends. There was, between us, much need of solidarity and con-solation. The partner of one friend is severely immunocompro-mised, effectively rendering the outdoors off-limits to her and a scene of escalating fear for him. The other friend, who suffers from a chronic illness, is likewise susceptible, in different but equally scary ways. I can tell you that talking together, even in this unnerv-ing tech-mediated way—saying out loud what we feared, but also reminding each other how much our ration of small shared plea-sures still delighted us, how our jokes still lived, how pleasant it was to be so laughingly fucking *annoyed* by the same social media presences—talking together like this was exactly as replenishing as everybody says it is. For real: if it's doable, do this. Let a million pixelated Zoom squares bloom, is my feeling. Even if what transpires there proves, in its way, unraveling.

"I'm not as sick as I've been," my one friend said, "and I'm being super-careful. But my body is totally reactive. I can feel all my symptoms creeping back into me." We condoled over this, which seemed so worrying and stressful. And it was then that my friend said something astonishing.

"All this helplessness and fear, all the *uncertainty*," she said. "Everyone's sinking into their trauma responses. Everyone's body knows this is a crisis."

There was a pause, and I swear it was like the light in the room shifted gradients. I felt myself breathe in, and breathe out. And then the previous days, with their weirdnesses and agitations, danced before me for a moment, reassembling at last into a sort of dry clarified relief.

I thought about the texts I'd sent, the insistent jokes, the reassuring old routine. I thought about why, of every goddam book to read in this book-clogged apartment, I'd land upon *that* one, with its impassioned commitment to the artful transformation of horror into comedy, old grief into consoling form. I thought about the strange low-watt elation that had visited me, when it became clear that the next weeks would for the most part consist in being here, at home, hour after happy hour, with Julie. And I thought too about how awkwardly that elation had sat alongside something else, something nervy and chest-tightening and obscure.

Which, then, was less obscure. Because as my friends spoke to me, as the low murmur of voices I said I couldn't hear started to come unjumbled, I caught quick clear sight of myself, as I'd been living out these first pandemic days at home. It was just the usual me: joking, fretful, basically very happy. But also, there on the lower frequencies: huddling into myself, seized in a semifetal crouch, as all the while my mind spun out a series of interrogatives. *Is Julie unhappy? Is being here with me going to be unbearable for her? What I am doing, right now, without wishing to, that is going to make her stop loving me? How will I ruin everything?*

"Yeah," I said, weakly. "I think that's really, really right."

*   *   *

It remains the case that, by every metric that matters, we are fine, we are more than fine. (The next night, as I found some words to say much of this to Julie, she said, "Sweetheart, it's truly ok. If I'm annoyed I won't leave, I'd just *tell* you. Because I don't like being annoyed.") As I say, we have one another, and our home, and more by way of security than anyone in this despoiled garrison state could be said to deserve.

And we have our books, crouching on the shelves all around us. Each one set to unloose its minor chaos, ready to act as venom and antidote, the bandage and the wound.

Meanwhile, from where we are the back windows look south toward the towers of downtown, out over the low buildings and jumbled rooftops of the neighborhood. When you're home a lot the view acquires an uncanny familiarity, like a face you see in the mirror. Just after sunset there's a lovely metallic glow, pinkish and gold, that comes off the housefronts, as one by one the lights pop on and you see for a minute the illuminated interiors.

There's something sweet and also queasy-making about it.

Inside every lit-up room, I've started to think, there's a person-sized haunting going on. There is somebody low-key reliving the absolutely, the superlatively *worst* shit that has ever fucking happened to them. It's setting itself up in their shoulders, at their temples, in the cells of their pumping blood. You watch the lights blink on, the next and the next and the next, and then night settles in and the glow turns cathode-blue.

Whenever I watch this now, I find there's this text I really want to send, though I'm wary by now of trying anybody's patience. *There is no greater* second *paragraph, I want to say, in any novel, ever.* And then this:

> The obscure fragments of his dream, which seemed to have taken place beside a lake, were confused with the production of *Measure for Measure* he had seen the night before with Johnny Hall. Despite the director's choice of a bus depot as the setting for the play, nothing could diminish the shock of hearing the word 'mercy' so many times in one evening.[3]

The shock, I want to say, *of mercy.*
Have you ever seen anything sharper or sadder? For real: tell me.

In the Maze

The story told in Stanley Kubrick's adaptation of *The Shining*, from 1980, is a familiar one. In that olde-timey Sophoclean key, it offers up the drama of a family gone awry. That family is the Torrances. *The Shining* tells us that what's thrown this family awry is the violence being done inside it, a violence directed most harrowingly at Danny, the child, by Jack, the father, and unprevented by Wendy, the mother. That—give or take tricycle rides, axe-murder, writer's block, cascading waves of blood, all the iconic rest of it—is the story *The Shining* tells.

And yet, whatever its diffused atmospheres of ominousness and accumulating dread, *The Shining* is not actually so vague as this, at least where "familial violence" is concerned. For the film tells us that Jack is not just a man who has dislocated his son's arm while drunk (however important that story has been to the preservation of the family). It tells us not only that Jack is, in more intimate ways, abusing his son. *The Shining* tells us too—with a terrible clarity, that is only barely not frontal declaration—the *kind* of abuse to which Jack is subjecting his son. It's all very, very awful, a horror in the most primal senses. But it is not especially unclear.

So for instance: Late in the film, when Jack has gone properly and murderously mad, we follow Wendy in her flight through the cavernous Overlook Hotel as she encounters spectacles of weird terror. A cobwebbed room of skeletons, scenes of blood and fright. Perhaps the most unnerving of these: she sees before her a man in a bear suit—a kind of pajama suit for grownups, with the union-suit flap open at his backside—kneeling and with his head pressed in the lap of a man in a tuxedo. Interrupted, they both sit up and stare startled back at Wendy, and us.

Jarring but, more properly, uncanny. We have seen the figure of the bear, exactly that bear, before. Very early in the film, Danny has had an "episode" and we join him and his mother and the doctor in his bedroom. He is lying in bed, without pants, his bare white legs and supine passivity making him a figure of arresting vulnerability. A shot of Danny from in front of and above him reveals him to be lying on a pillow. That pillow is a cartoonish bear's head—in color and in shape and in form precisely the bear's head worn by the man kneeling before the man in the tuxedo. Wendy is seeing something she, too, has seen before.

The rest is, as I say, not especially subtle, though it is grueling. We can enumerate the telltale marks of the specific violence being done to Danny one after another. He has a little friend named Tony, who tells him things—who is the voice of his seeming clairvoyance, to use a term we'll come back to—and Tony lives in Danny's mouth. Or again, after something violent has happened to Danny offscreen and he wanders, semicatatonic, with a zombie-like lentor, toward Jack and Wendy, we discover bruises wrapped around the side of his neck, and Danny himself, with scary intentness, sucking his thumb. In repeated scenes of frozen shock we see Danny, iconically, in direct close-up, horrorstruck, his mouth unspeaking, open. In perhaps the least merciful moment in the film, we see Danny upright in bed, trembling, his face slick, his mouth slack and open.

In *The Shining*, we don't not know what's happening to Danny. Kubrick, you could say, has transposed a novel about an abusive alcoholic father (Stephen King's *The Shining*, from 1977) into the story of a sexually abusive father, whose particular modes of sexual use of his son it also knows, and invites us to know.[1] Again: *very* awful; not unclear. And so know we do—even if, also, we don't, or can't. Even if it's in no sense certain that you can call what happens in the course of that hours-long dwelling-with *knowing*.

*   *   *

One thing to admire in new-millennial living is the happy parade of fully apocalyptic facts, arranged with listicle-like clarity, ever-available for your stupefied contemplation. The Trump era did not invent this, though its psychotic commitment to antireality— half sweaty grift, half unhinged projection—could surely be said to have goosed up the doominess. Did you know that the scribes at the United Nations estimate one *billion* displaced persons by around 2050, if middle-of-the-road projections of warming, melt, desalination, and sea-level rise hold true? Did you know that global spending on what is called "security," public and private, has jumped better than 10 percent per annum across most of this, our chronically insecure century? Perhaps you recall that great moment in *Society Must Be Defended* where Michel Foucault observes that the security state is, functionally, "a suicidal State"?[2] Or the cheering reminder, in the 2009 conclusion to Giovanni Arrighi's *The Long Twentieth Century*, that "to a far greater extent than in previous hegemonic transitions, the terminal crisis of U.S. hegemony ... has been a case of great power 'suicide'"?[3]

Suicide, then, on every palsied hand—although, if this is suicide, it is one of a distinctively modern sort. What I mean is: Do you know what the American numbers on incarceration look like? Or life expectancies as rolled out internationally, across geographies of impoverishment? It's like the old line on the serial killer. He keeps trying and trying to kill himself, the state-appointed shrink says. But it's always someone else who ends up dead.

That's one little aria of expanding cataclysm, though you hardly need me to make such a list for you. You've got a phone, maybe a subscription to *Nature*, the *New Yorker*. None of these things—global contraction, infrastructural collapse, security-mad court-ratified neofascisms clamoring to keep pace with accelerating and irreversible planetary ruin—is a matter of information, *data*. Revelations these are not. No canny team of gumshoes needs to unbury the facts, crack the case. These are not problems of knowledge.

Or not exactly. Such grim litanies tell us so little, after all, about what it's like actually to live under to such conditions, so near to what the redoubtable Mike Davis, pulling no punches, recently called "an already anticipated genocide."[4] I sit on the train, phone semaphoring in my hand—or maybe I'm at home, or maybe, better still, there in the office, with pictures of my twentysomething daughters angled toward me in mute inquiry. There's the familiar sequence: a noisy revving of mind, all clamor and queasy churn, and then, after this, a lapse—a sort of slow-dawning, sickhearted nullity where *thinking* had been.

How do we even begin to describe the frozen state of apprehension that prevails here—the style of unceasing awareness that also keeps sidestepping recognition, slipping the noose of knowing? To put it again in olde-timey terms, these borrowed from Freud: how do we live with what we cannot manage to know, yet do know, yet also don't? "Repression" is the term of art, yes. But I'm not sure that's right, or that it gets at the overwhelming simultaneity of things known and unknown—the kind of cognitively super-saturated unknowing—that pulses at the terrible heart of what we might call, only a little fancifully, the psychic economy of Anthropocene living.

The Shining appears in 1980, which if you ask a twenty-four-year old may as well have been 1919. And yet if there is a stronger, stranger, more entirely pulverizing meditation on exactly these questions, I'm not sure I could say what it is. How do we live with the unsurvivability of our lives? With the horrors already arrived to so many lives proximate to our own? Give yourself over to thoughts like that and I swear it's as if *The Shining* came out, in sky-sweeping arc-lit debut, sometime last week.

*   *   *

The Shining, as I say, is a movie depicting sexual violence—incest—in a register so minimally beneath the threshold of explicitness that to call that plot "occluded" seems a falsifying way of speaking. Perhaps the first thing to remark is: none of this (the negligible obliquity, the garish horror) is what makes the film interesting, or acute, or artful, gorgeous, indelible, transporting, or much of anything else. ("It's a movie about—*AHA!*—incest" is not an interpretive line that's going to get you very far, I promise.) The threat of sexual violence suffuses the film. But *The Shining* is so much less about the brute fact of Jack's abuse, I think, than it is about *a familial labor not to know*: the conjoined, competing efforts of three people to keep the terrible knowledge of what is happening to them somehow at bay. *That* is the drama all its virtuosic formal contrivances are there to crystallize. That is what makes *The Shining*, rather than just scary or obscene, as devastating as it is.

Every member of the Torrance family puts his or her shoulder to this desperate wheel. Danny, for instance, is so note-perfect a rendering of the abused child as figured in the high canon of twentieth-century psychoanalytic literature that you half-suspect Kubrick of having a copy of "Confusion of Tongues" open on his desk. There, in that famous paper from 1932 (the actual title is "Confusion of Tongues between Adults and the Child"), Freud's compatriot Sándor Ferenczi argued that the child, having suffered abuse, splits his self in two. ("When the child recovers after such an attack," Ferenczi writes, "he feels extremely confused, in fact already split, innocent and guilty at the same time."[5]) And there, piteously, is Danny, speaking now and again in the voice of Tony, his sometime-other, his broken-off counterself.

But Ferenczi's strange essay pursues a differently suggestive set of claims as well. Abused children, he contends, find themselves in the grip of a multitude of crosswired fears: the fear of further harm *but also* of loss of love *but also* of the confusion and shame radiating toward them from the adult. Such children, overwhelmed as they are by this torrent of interwoven terrors, and frantic to protect themselves against them, become in Ferenczi's arresting conception *clairvoyant*—possessed of "strange, almost clairvoyant knowledge."[6] The child's world all at once bristles with fright and violence, Ferenczi says. And this, in turn, prompts in the child what he describes as a defensive, diligent, ultra-fine-tuned consciousness—a scrutinizing hypersensitivity to the slightest shifts in mood or feeling, alterations in the environing social atmosphere, the subtlest drift in intentions expressed or, as may be, *unexpressed*. Ferenczi's abused child seems eerily to *know*—like a tiny, terror-stricken analyst—and to be possessed of an unnerving talent for discerning wishes as yet unvoiced by the nearest grown-ups, disturbances that may remain unconscious on their side.

"Clairvoyance," then, is Ferenczi's name for the abused child's predictive hyperattunement to the microfluctuations of the dangerous adult world. And there, in *The Shining*, center stage, is of course nothing but this style of fear-battered seeming clairvoyance. It is called *shining*, and its chief figure is Danny—or rather Tony, who with a kind of hyperreal discernment acts as Danny's warning system, forever gifting him with visions of violence and disaster. *The Shining* might in fact be said to do Ferenczi one better, or at least to expand the range of his insight. For if the film offers up *shining* as an aptitude belonging distinctively to the abused— exactly as Ferenczi suggests—it asks us to note as well that *not all violence is sexual*, and not all trauma is, as it were, familial. Danny's compatriot in shining is Dick Hallorann (played indelibly by Scatman Crothers), who is the movie's figure of an explicitly racial difference, and the repository of an explicitly racist harm. (Jack's rampaging reclamation of his fallen potency—"White man's burden!" he declaims to one of his prodding visions—commences, you will recall, with the murder of Hallorann.) Danny is not alone in having worlds of brutality to survive.

Nor is he alone in devising intricate ways to live with—to have and equally *not* have, as knowledge—what is happening to him. If it's true that everywhere you touch *The Shining* it vibrates to the note of unacknowledged sexual violence—the movie, you could say, is narrated from the perspective of that knowledge; it hovers at everyone's shoulders, unblinking—it's also true that everywhere you look you find a struggling will not to know. It is there in Jack's fleeting fantasies of spectacular omnipotence. He is a man haunted by shame and racialized emasculation. Forever conjuring himself as the indomitable White Man, lording his domineering power over women, children, racial others, he must contend with the undermining intimation that he is exactly none of these things—that he has always been the caretaker, lowly and

foul. (What triumphant sexual conquests he imagines for himself transform, in an instant, to horror.) Then too there is Wendy,
whose halting narrative about Danny's long-ago broken arm in-
troduces her character—a monologue she offers to the summoned
doctor, whose hard, unmoving stare is our first indication that this
is the agreed-upon cover story, the event standing in for other less
speakable violences. Students to whom I teach the film tend to
hate Wendy, her ragdoll haplessness, those brittle pantomimes of
cheery normalcy. I try to dial them into how heartrending it all
is—this cowed, terrorized attempt to perform a passivity so absolute it might actually salve the wound of Jack's unmanning, bolster
the façade of functional family order. Like Danny, like Jack, she
struggles to stage, as something that is not knowledge, the ruinous
things she knows.

Here it is perhaps worth saying: If you've ventured at all into
the turbid waters of critical commentary on *The Shining* you will
have discovered how oddly contagious the film's prevailing will
not-to-know has proven to be. All the hyperformalism and unending technique-fetishism, the conspiracy-mindedness, the *numer-
ology*: it's as though commentators have contracted the Torrance
family's impassioned drive toward unknowing like some sort of
virus. Hence, the delectating fanaticism with which any form of
meaning the film produces *apart* from the content of its specifically sexual violence is seized upon and catechized. (If you care
to see what this is like, I commend to you the remarkable documentary, about interpreting *The Shining*, called *Room 237*.) Better, it seems, to dwell in lore, numbers, form, design—anything—
than on whatever it is that gathers at the edges of every meticulous
vignette, every just-so frame.

*   *   *

One now-familiar line on Kubrick appraises him as the maestro of a certain kind of coldness, not untouched by sadism. He specializes, it is said, in existential frigidity, of a sort that holds human folly and desire at a formalized, god's-eye distance. (It is this disposition that would impress itself so definingly upon inheritors like, say, the Coen brothers). All that may be exactly right. Yet *The Shining*, for all its grimness and gore, has always seemed to me the least cold-blooded of films. If it remains surpassingly difficult to sit through—and I think it does—it's not because of its callousness. It may be the reverse.

Consider the squareness with which Kubrick sets our gaze not just on Danny's fear, or Danny's pain, or Danny's horror—all of these are vivid enough—but upon something altogether harder: Danny's *ambivalence*. Danny is frightened of his father, this we know; there is the famously chilling scene in which he sits on Jack's lap, paralyzed, like a lifeless doll (an "automaton," in Ferenczi's again apt phrase), asking if his father would ever hurt him or his mother. But with a care that astonishes me every time I rewatch it, *The Shining* shows him to be afflicted by something else again: a confusion—a kind of anguished incertitude—in respect to the family that is, also, hurting him so grievously. Danny dreads his father, yes. But watch how Danny is also forever *courting* his father, vying for his attentions: going to his room, soliciting his responses, hiding with the staged ineptness of a child who wants to be found. He is forever recalling to us, you could say, the intimacy in this family—or, as the Freudians among us would have it, in *family*—of devotion and terror, love and violation.

For instance: One of the implications of what I've been saying is that there are in fact no supernatural elements in the film—no ghost-bartenders, no butchered pinafored twins—only projections and fantasies, the grisly psychic life of the denizens of the

Overlook Hotel. On this score, there is one, precisely *one*, narrative question that seems most hard to square. How does Jack, wounded and locked by Wendy into the hotel storage room, get out? There is no rampage without his unnarrated release, and nothing but the supernatural seems to explain it. A mystery, then, but also—as with the rest of the film—not really a mystery. Because of course it's Danny. It's Danny who lets him out. It's Danny, who is frightened of his father, who is being tormented by his father, and who loves his father. It's Danny, who is casting about for ways to contend with the presence of all these things, all at once.

What better culminating figure for such confused anguish than the maze in which the film ends? As we know, Danny ultimately chooses the love of his mother, as against Jack, and in their reunion and escape the Oedipal drama concludes. But what are we to make of what's come before, the flight into the dark? Watch it again: it is for all the world a scene in which we cannot quite be sure if Danny is fleeing from his father, in headlong mortal fright, or *playing* with him, embarking in a game of hide and seek, a fort-da flee-and-follow in which being loved and being annihilated merge.

Talk to me all you want about Kubrick's coldness and cruelty. I won't even say you're wrong. I'll just keep saying that *The Shining* treats Danny with an almost unbearable tenderness. The film dispenses with the consoling fantasy that the only conceivable relation to abuse is refusal, untinctured by longing, uncertainty, childish solicitude—and this is part, though only part, of what makes it *so fucking hard* to watch, to sit through without pinning your attention elsewhere, to the fluency of the tracking shot, the eerie score, Nicholson's feral virtuosity. *The Shining* does not ask us to imagine Danny is unwilling to entertain the possibility that annihilation is a bearable condition for preserving his father's love. It does not ask us to believe Danny is unbeguiled by his father, or unneedful in relation to him, as a condition for recognizing him as wounded, victimized, catastrophically abused. When I say *The Shining* seems to me a film of tremendous, human-hearted sorrow, this is most of what I mean.

* * *

How do we live with the unsurvivability of our lives, the profligate disposability of lives proximate to ours? It's the sort of question for which there are only bad answers, which is to say that it marks, properly speaking, an *impasse*. Here we find a set of dilemmas whose only conceivable amelioration lies in massed collective action. But they are dilemmas that, in turn, throw into stark relief the absence of any habitable venue for collectivity at such scale, any currently available way to convene it, make it go. What follows from this isn't even despair, necessarily, nor for that matter iron resolve, though these may well send up their flares. It's that other, that more familiar thing: a vast benumbed thwartedness.

In a lot of precincts, as you will have seen, the prevailing line on unsurvivability is that people do not *really* know, that what news of it there is comes out garbled, more noise than signal. As fantasies go, this one's pretty inexpensive. If only some charismatic demi-Messiah would arrive, media-ready, bearing the holy and unignorable light of dire outcomes! Then would our attentions turn and the right prevail, or at least a less incinerating wrong.

For a lot of reasons, this has seemed to me a bathetically misbegotten bit of wishfulness. It's misbegotten materially because the owners of the resources of the world are not looking to profit-share, and this is not because they do not comprehend the concept of carbon, or have not been sufficiently persuaded, prevailed-upon, or shamed. It's wrong more nearly because what sets the world to flame is neither shamelessness nor unfeeling so much as it is the entire agglomerated infrastructure through which it is fucking *lived*. "It is life," as my friend Brian curtly says, appraising the "causes" of climatological endstrickenness, "as currently constituted and as constituted for five centuries," and that is that.[7] The science, the tech, the markets and the humanisms, the feature-not-bug inequity, the daily miraculousness, the inbuilt cruelty, hanging firmament, majestic roof, etc. The murderer's call, as I've grown fond of saying, has always been coming from inside the house.

But I think it may be wrong in a queasier, more intimate way as well. When knowing buys you nothing, nothing at all, what could seem more natural than the quiet reassembly of what is known as something else? A surmise, say. A prediction, an unfatedness. When there is no remotely commensurate thing to *do* with your knowledge, what could dissuade a person from setting all those soul-gnawing facts in some place apart, a chamber just a few doors down from the crowded rooms of what you know? It is, god knows, the easiest thing. Even if the everyday labor of it makes for its own kind of desolation, is maybe its own subgenre of horror.

Anthony and Carmela
Get Vaccinated

One obvious thing to do when you move to central Jersey for a year, nearer to your East Coast family but further from your workaday Chicago life, is to commence a grand and ceremonious rewatch of *The Sopranos*. If you have a name like mine—if your mother's maiden name is Scognamiglio, with its two silent *g*'s—then it is perhaps something more than obvious.

This was a few years back and, as it proved, the timing wasn't right. I stalled out after only a few episodes, though not out of boredom or disinterest. A few moments into the one where mobster Tony Soprano takes his daughter Meadow on her college trip, and they tour through the expensive private campuses of Maine, the strangest of storms descended upon me. I'd start to laugh (because *The Sopranos*, as you will likely recall, is nothing if not continuously and unmercifully funny). But for some reason instead of laughter what began to come out was this series of sputtering half-choked sobs. And then, in a moment, these became unchoked, whereupon I found myself dissolving into shuddery mists there on the couch, as Julie looked over at me with dawning alarm and said, "Oh sweetheart—what's the matter? What happened? Are you ok?"

All I could manage by way of reply was to say, "Look at James Gandolfini—he looks *so young*."

In fairness to me, he did, and he does. Also, a lot had happened that year. We'd moved, Julie and I, but we'd also moved in together, and the dumb grinning happiness of that was like a bubble rising in my throat all the time. If you've come through a very bad time, and then found yourself inside something considerably brighter than you thought was in the cards for you anymore, you will know what that kind of lachrymose susceptibility is like.

But it wasn't only this. On the way east we had stopped over for a few weeks with my parents, whose summer had not been altogether easy. My father, who like my mother was at the time a blessedly heathy person in his later seventies, had begun to have the debilitating back problems that would result, eventually, in surgery. He was in pain, which scared him, and this in turn seemed to scare my mom, who had worked for decades in a nursing home and who, I thought, might have been grappling just then with the first frightful premonitions of a possible decline in the man to whom she had been married for fifty-plus years. Things were loud, which was usual, and tense, which was not.

I spent our weeks in what now seems to me to have been an almost mesmerically adolescent trance: clinging to Julie, wishing my dad could be a little more temperate, my mom a little more patient with his disquiet. *Be different*, I thought, with the teenaged peevishness proper to middled-aged people returned to their childhood homes.

Which is only to say that those onslaughts of weepiness in the face of a young James Gandolfini, returned to such titanically charismatic life—this was not, even as it was happening, especially hard to diagnose. Like the books and shows and records that populate our lives can sometimes do, *The Sopranos* had sent me tumbling into the arms of a recognition that I'd have preferred to avoid, at least for a while. Might it be possible to devise some less preposterous way than this to enter into the awful knowledge that your parents, whom you love with such needy and baffled intensity, will in fact one day die? I suppose it might. But I can tell you that, watching Gandolfini then, it was for all the world as if the nonnegotiable fact of my father's mortality had come wheeling into sudden view there before me, like a constellation rising in a pale and terrible sky.

I cried some more and thought, *I'm ruining this for Julie*. This was not true, but one great thing about your self-evasions is that they do not need to be.

*　*　*

About such dire mortal facts there is now, it would seem, little point in evasion. It's been a year of polychromatic dread, as any child of even moderately elderly parents can tell you—though so too, really, could anybody at all. Still, if by the ill-fate of lockdown you found yourself thousands of miles from those aging loved ones, you will know the rituals: the anxious calls, your inveigling questions, the swift descent into dismay, bargaining, *pleading*. ("Please do not go back out to the market for better basil, *please*.") I met a friend in the park for walks and we talked about our parents. How are yours this week? I asked.

"They keep going over the wall."

It was, we decided, entirely like being seventeen again, though from the other side. Let's try to be less impatient, we told one another. Only later would we fully grasp how poorly patience kept company with these varieties of plunging helpless fear.

But let me be truthful. The honest fact of the matter is that the story of my lapses in even the most rudimentary sorts of patience in respect to my parents, and to the whole familial generation of which they are a part, is not a new one. I had had ages of practice, decades. I was *fluent*.

Here, from the archive of these failures in achieved maturity, is one of the very choicest items, which has lived near to me over the stretch of many years: For the entire period of its run, the older faction of my family hated—and I mean *hated*—*The Sopranos*. And this, in its turn, catapulted me into such lunatic extremities of exasperation and invective you simply would not believe.

Talk about pleading. You should've heard me. So here's this show, I would say, and people talk about it as among the greatest pieces of narrative art of its age, an end-of-century masterpiece. And it offers not just Italian American experience, and not just southern-Italian American experience, but *East Coast southern-Italian American* experience as the veritable Rosetta Stone for the understanding of national life. And you're all over here like, *Meh, not for me.* You have got to be fucking kidding me with this.

"Peter," my mother would say. "Don't talk like that."

The problem with *The Sopranos*, as my mother had it, was that it was all so ugly. By which she meant the torrential swearing perhaps most of all—but also the violence, the offhand bigotry, the crazy proliferation of *guns*, the routine infidelity, the casual and all-pervading degradation. Verisimilitude did not enter into it. "Have you ever seen anyone in this family raise their hand in anger, your whole life?" my aunt once asked, in a way that rhymed with what my uncles deplored, in one voice, as its grossly stereotyped depiction of Italians: the mobbed-up guys with their tracksuits and Brylcreem and goomahs, duffel bags of ill-got cash stashed in every crawlspace. "People didn't laugh at Archie Bunker," my dad said, not unreasonably. "They thought he was real. They loved him."

Violence, vulgarity, degradation: objections like this, you might say, betray nothing so much as class anxiety of the most garden-variety first-generation sort, and you know what? That's not really wrong. My grandfather on my mother's side was a left-leaning young man in Naples, and was permitted to marry my grandmother on the condition that he not take her to America. It was the '30s; they went to America. There they had four daughters, the first of whom began speaking English when she arrived at grade school. (This was my mother.) But his was a union factory, and though a two-bedroom house in Stamford, Connecticut, was not especially spacious for a family of six—two of whom, I would later learn, spent years mired in the unhappiness of too little money, too much misapprehension between themselves and their American children, and too terrible a longing for the lost Naples of their youth—it *was* a house, un-redlined, and their kids went to good postwar public schools, and some of them even went to college, and thereafter moved to nearby and whiter suburbs, so that by the time my cousins and I came along they had achieved, by this combination of luck and work and circumstance, a set of respectably middle-class lives. (In the metrics of the show, if we were never going to be Cusamanos we might yet be aspiring Melfis.) This was our ultraconventional white ethnic story.

But then here was this show, this enormous national *sensation*, and what did it do? It identified Italianness, true Italianness, with so many aspects of the worlds they had left behind them. They resented that, my uncles and aunts, and honestly: why would they not? We, their children, had never seen anybody raise their hand in anger, it's true. It's not clear to me they could say the same.

You might think this alone would've persuaded me that theirs was something maybe a bit more freighted than the blinkered ethnic chauvinism for which I was eager to mistake it. But no. The name they chose for their layered sense of misrecognition, woundedness, and resentment was "offensive," and to this, in my wisdom, I took offense. I resented their resentment, their class-aspirational refusal of the call of Livia and Corrado and Janice and Artie and Sil, and again it's not hard to see why. However they phrased it, they had planted themselves interferingly between myself and a love for the show, a devout and grasping and evermore encompassing adoration, that managed somehow to be even *more* reflexive than their frowning distaste.

Talk about prestige. *Rosetta Stone for the understanding of national life*, I'd say. *Narrative architecture of the nineteenth-century novel*, I'd say, and more to the same effect. Laugh if you must but I promise you this only begins to capture the hypnotic delight, the breadth of longed-for and apparently irresistible affirmation, that came from finding so much of the detritus of my dull and suburban and resolutely unliterary upbringing transformed, like that, into the stuff of *art*. "It's not television," the ads should've said, "it's high goddamned modernism." The college episode that ends with a quote from Hawthorne? Studious Dr. Melfi, who looks for all the world exactly like my Aunt Nettie, walking Tony through the fundamentals of psychoanalysis, symptomaticity, the terrors of Oedipal conflict? *Come the fuck on.* Here was my own bit of feverish and disavowed aspiration, and it is no great wonder—though it is, for me, a matter of unexpired shame—that it came directly at the expense of a family that had been nothing but kind, nothing but supportive and unmocking and really just low-key proud, as I ventured further and further out into the weird seas of academic life. You wouldn't think it would be so hard not to be unkind to the people who love you. But what are you going to do?

I wish now that I had had better purchase on something *The Sopranos* was laboring to tell me from its first moments, which is just that they had become Americans, my family, and that there was something unnerving in that ordinary, that longed-for attainment. It could not, for them, have had about it the dull inevitability with which it presented itself to my cousins and me. I think a lot about a resonant pair of lines from the poet Robert Pinsky, an exact generational peer of theirs, who says of his childhood: "I once thought most people were Italian, / Jewish, or Coloured."[1] He is speaking of Long Branch, New Jersey, in the early '50s, though it could as easily have been Stamford. Think of growing up inside those worlds, those wraparound enclaves. And imagine awakening one day to discover that scattered around the scene of your life were grandchildren with names like Kelly and Josh and Ashley— and also, of course, Giovanni. How would it be possible to have lived those lives and *not* experience the cheerful and bland Americanness of your progeny with some volatile mix of pride, defensiveness, and an all but impermissible regret? Call it, if you'd like, an unconfessed ambivalence. You would not in any case feel especially warmly toward a goddamn cable TV program that had come along and managed to agitate every last disquieting thing about it, no matter how beautifully or complexly or even lovingly it did so.

We are talkative and we are loud, my family, but this is not to say we have a lot of words for the knottier impasses of feeling such as these. We proceed by other means. Back in the days of that private-life cataclysm I mentioned earlier, my family was at a loss with what to do with the awful wreckage of self I kept trundling home to them. In the midst of one such collapse my beloved Uncle Joe came over to see me. He did not say, "Peter, I'm sorry to see you so devastated but I promise, though you cannot believe in it, you have a future." He did not say, "You will never be a failure to me, or to any of us, because we love you more than you can possibly know." Instead he said, "I saw this, and I thought it'd be about right for you." And he handed me a box that contained a pristine pinstriped Mickey Mantle jersey, number 7, which I have been wearing to baseball games between Chicago and New York for more than a decade now.

So no one ever put the matter of *The Sopranos* to me in any but the shopworn terms of resentment and offense. I like to think I would've heard them if they had, but there is reason to doubt it. Pained and puzzled generational ambivalence? "But the show is *so smart* about that," I can hear myself saying. "The two kids are named Anthony Jr. and *Meadow*, for Christ's sake."

*   *   *

For only the second time in fifty years of chances, I missed Christmas this year. By "Christmas" I do not mean the 25th of December. I mean the weeks of preparation, from the extensive laying-in of supplies to the making, and freezing, of pounds of cavatelli (pronounced *gavadeel*). I mean the week-before collective trip to Arthur Avenue to gather the needed goods, and the subsequent day-long labor of rolling the prosciutto and salami and cappy ham and assembling the trays of antipasto into elaborate color wheels of meat and cheese. I mean the Seven Fishes on Christmas Eve (with my Aunt Diane's unsurpassed meatball sauce on the side for those who, like my uncle and me, don't love mussels). And I mean the day itself, for as long as I can remember a party staged for thirty or forty at the house of my Aunt Louise and Uncle Joe, folding tables fitted geometrically into every corner, which commences yearly with my uncle offering a toast marking out the milestones (the marriages, the births, the deaths), welcoming new faces, and ending with a thought for the previous generation, "who came from Italy and gave us our traditions." Salut, we say, and then undertake the hours-long ceremony of what can probably best be described as ethnic stunt-eating, which is all I have ever needed by way of religious observation.

A lot to miss, to be sure. In holiday quarantine with my gracious in-laws, I made some rigatoni, threw together a makeshift antipasto, opened a chianti—small compensations, really, and in truth no more than an echo of the months I'd spent transmuting all my feelings into carbs, the better to eat them. By the winter I'd taken to concluding each meal with a nice little *decáf*, like the eighty-year-old *nana* I seemed determined to transform myself into. *We become what we have lost* is an old psychoanalytic chestnut, which is not less true when it involves pasta fagioli.

And so, at last, as we made the wide turn into the new year, I *did* get around to that comprehensive rewatch of *The Sopranos*, under new if no less charged circumstances. It has found me here in these odd in-between days, in which my parents and uncles and aunts have begun to get their vaccination appointments. My mom, as I write, has had both shots, which is the simplest of facts, but also one of such bewildering immensity I don't begin to know where to put it. What do you even call this feeling, which is something so much more unmanageable, so much queasier and more terrible, than relief? I don't know, but I do know that, this time around, I sailed right through the run of episodes, season after season.

About the merits of the thing itself—about the bravura acting, the tuning of Shakespearean conflict to the rhythms of North Jersey, about the vogue for brutal male antiheros redeemed perhaps too easily through psychological interiorization, about the women, the whiteness, the clothes, the songs, the end—I am honestly the last person who can speak authoritatively. I see it all, even now, through the scrim of my family's responses to it, a distorting influence for which there is no correction.

There is one thing I can say about *The Sopranos*, though, and it is this: It is not possible, in the pinched and broken medium of human speech, to overstate the precision and the detail and the granular fucking *correctness* of its depiction of the textures of that particular ethnic milieu. The food and the talking, sure: words like *gabagool* and *ricot'* (which till I was probably nine I thought was spelled *rigot*) as well as *aspiet', stunod, gagootz, andiam'*—a litany of phrases that lay around the rooms of my childhood like threadbare furniture. Oh, but also: the salutations, the sometimes starchy formality. The infinitely expressive shrugs and smirks, the equivocal half-frowning nods. The Sunday dinners, the funerals, the constant and constantly *physical* intimacy between the men. The décor at the homes of the older characters, dear god! Every least calibration, from the set of Charmaine Bucco's disapproving scowl to the glint of the plastic sheeting that covers Paulie Gaultieri's armchair, faithful out to the last decimal place. There's a moment when Neapolitan bodyman Furio, possibly flirting with Carmela, informs her that he's bought a home nearby—and then, in a voice straight out of my grandfather's mouth, he says, "*I make a party, for the housewarm'.*" You may not be surprised to hear that this moment, after I stopped laughing at it, reduced me once again to hiccupping weepiness.

The Sopranos, I have told my friends, has been the aperture through which I have entered into the cavernous fact of missing my family, and I am piteously grateful for that. Maybe you've made use of something different—a movie about New Orleans, a Joni Mitchell album, or, I don't know, a George Eliot novel. But this, for me, has been the thing. Like nothing else at all, it has allowed me to miss everybody—but in a measured, and semiridiculous, and let's say a *bearable* way. Before it became too much.

And that I suppose is the second thing I can say about *The Sopranos*. If you've seen even just a little of it, you know it is a show that concerns itself with the devious ways we manage to tell ourselves things that, in the ordinary circuits of living, we cannot bear to know. Sometimes we do this with illness, anxiety, depression; sometimes with rage, or lust, or violence. This is how your life conspires to deliver the news it cannot get to you by more straightforward routes: that the mother who "loves" you, for instance, also regards you with murderous resentment; that the worlds of American abundance are *made of brutality*, of a violence being done to others, all the time, elsewhere; that the family is less a noble preserve apart from that violence than one of its principal scenes of condensation. None of this, the show proposes, is easy to know, and this is not even to speak of marriage, parenthood, childhood, aging, money, or sex, where things get really entangled.

I am willing to grant that there is something larger even than irony involved in making use of this show—where the gap between blood-ties and bloodshed is so dismayingly narrow—to come into glancing contact with just how catastrophically I have missed my left-behind East Coast family, with its messiness and misunderstandings, its confusion of generational tongues, its noisiness and intrusiveness and stubborn determination just to keep loving us, my cousins and me, in whatever configurations of life we bring back to it. *The Sopranos* unravels that kind of warming familial sentiment, even as it indulges it, and what it leaves behind is something substantially more unconsoling. Fair enough.

But then I'm not certain this is the whole of it. I don't know that it's only longing and love that have spoken up in those gusts of wrung-out tearfulness that, hour by hour, have come squalling over me as I've sat watching prestige TV from twenty years ago. Even now, even inside these weeks of battered and flinching hopefulness, there is so much else to make a person feel undone. I keep thinking of Tony, with all the menace and massiveness with which Gandolfini plays him, in those iconic panic-attack moments from early on: his face gone heavy-lidded and blank, as he lists, wobbles, and comes toppling enormously to the floor. What does *The Sopranos* tell you, if not that there are things we cannot recognize, not straight on, because if we allowed them into our lives they would short the fuses, blow out all the delicate mazy wiring we need to conduct ourselves from one ailing day into the next? I don't know how to begin taking the measure of a year—*an entire year*—of illness, fear, isolation, and death. I don't know how to begin to reckon with the alternating numbness and panic, or with the long dark months occupied by nothing so much as a clenched paralytic dread. I do know this, though: getting into some companionable relation to it all will be long and roiling work, and it will put to rout even the deftest attempts at evasion. No one will be able to say when it's done with us.

So if, along the way, you find some song or story that helps you in that slow-dose reckoning, or that allows you to address all that's happened with some saving measure of proportion or equability, then with Anthony John Soprano I say unto you: *god'bless.*

Exit Wounds

But seriously, friends:
What do you make of this darkness that surrounds us?

DANIEL BORZUTZKY,
"The Performance of Becoming Human"

Back in my unmoored later thirties, as I groped around in what one of my favorite novelists somewhere calls a "fog of postmarital misjudgment," I made a friend in Brooklyn, about ten years younger than I, who could never, but never, meet up on Saturday mornings.[1] She had, she told me, forever plans, a standing and unbreakable date. She and a couple of friends liked to case the farmers markets—fall was best for this, she confided—grab an organic donut, some upstate eggs. And then, thus fortified, and with an appraising and sniperlike precision of gaze, they'd take turns scoping out the flourishing subspecies of Hot Dad.

"It's like fucking Normandy," she said. "Wave upon wave."

She was great, this friend. She was meanwitted but not cynical, poised in the way of a person who'd only recently discovered gig economy cruelty, art world pretension, the general fact of New York relentlessness—none of it left her overmatched. She wore high-buttoned, collared shirts that gave her an improbable librarianish aspect. And she had a wonderful name: *Mercedes*, she was called. Romance was never going to be our thing. (Unmoored, befogged, even I could tell this.) But she was an excellent companion in idle hangouts. She knew some things.

"You're going to run into a real sneaker avant-garde out there," I told her. "Some world-historical denims."

"Listen, old man," I remember her saying, "those guys may not be your kin. But one day you'll get your shit together. And when you do? My dude, they are going to surround you. They're *all* going to be your neighbors."

Kin to them I was not. But she was right in all the other ways. Get to a certain stage in your middling-bougie city life and you too may find it hard not to live in a neighborhood besieged by reproduction, strollers massing in hectic ranks, the Maclarens and Peg Peregos and for all I know self-navigating micro-Teslas revving up and down the high street in uncoordinated battalions. Moms and dads, dads and dads, moms and moms, the whole bright array. From the wide window of the coffeeshop where I spend most of my studious mornings, you can watch them promenade and process.

And maybe it's just another pandemic effect—the shut-in tedium, each day a Himalaya of hours to surmount—but the ranks of the visibly pregnant seem very much to have, you could say, swelled. I share this space each morning with minimally two, often as many as five, pregnant women, sometimes accompanied, sometimes not, enjoying a midtier scone and an unsolitary hour amid the faux-teak furnishings and neighborly clamor. The other day a woman arranged herself beside me, propped her sneakers on the stool opposite, slouched into a puffer coat zipped open around her convex middle. She had lank dark hair pressed into place by one of those generationally ubiquitous Carharttish watch caps, beneath which she wore an expression of mild relief and half-bored serenity, as of a person slipping at last into a sudsy evening bath. She settled. She became involved with her phone. Some time later she tapped me on the arm, her eyes friendly and inquiring above her mask.

Would I watch her stuff for a minute?

Of course I would.

She balanced herself vertical, deposited her coat, strode around the corner. For the rest of the week I tried to puzzle it out, the sudden rush that visited me then, persisted upon her return, followed me home. It wasn't the bruisy tenderness, envy and heartsickness doing their little dance. Those I knew. Stranger by far was the acidic aftertaste, the rising undercurrent of something sharper, meaner. I guess I just mean the anger. The idiot bloodred surge.

*   *   *

One of the most properly murderable things about our current overclass of billionaire jackals—we're among friends, right?—has to do with a particular combination, a one-two move, that breaks fresh ground in the odiousness sector, which you'd think would have been tapped out by now, but no. It goes like this. First and most importantly, you absent yourself in all material ways from the shared fate of the species, whether by security detail, obscure financial instrument, island redoubt, space travel, what you will. That done, you contrive to address that mass of failing and begrimed humanity as a populace in starving need of your Delphic counsel, those TRUTHS you have mined from deep in the fearful bowels of the world. That said truths are to a one the same shining tokens of witlessness that have beguiled the stupid for ages (what if the wealthy are the truly oppressed? can Woman think? is the Negro a Man?) gives less pause than you might hope. And so we find ourselves in a mediasphere glutted with the peacocking opinionating of megayacht charlatans—"contrarian" is, I believe, the term they self-apply—eager to explain to you why trans people aren't real, Wokeness Is Killing America, socialism is a fine idea but *just doesn't work*, and all the blithering rest of it.

Surely no age is free of overcompensated idiots, yowling their arias of self-exaltation. No part of me doubts that the tubercular, intermarrying magnates and duchesses and gentry of less online centuries were as vociferously fatuous and vile as their inferior media platforms would allow. But the pleasure of not having to encounter so much sour obstreperousness, of not having to know the every thought and contrivance of the planetary über-elite, each one a shouty metonym for catastrophic systemwide rot—honestly, I don't know that it can be gainsaid.

You don't need me to tell you that hate—disproportionate, implacable, self-engorging—is by now the chief national pastime, emotional outlet, maybe even fitness regime. It was Sam Lipsyte who some years back noted how much money there was to be made from the recognition that people really only wanted to sit, supine and alone, "firing off sequences of virulent gibberish at other deliquescing life-forms."[2] It's easy to decry all this, the twisted spasms and darkening mood. But listen: I am saying something else. I am saying that when I think of the current crop of preening pseudo-titans and world-arsonists, their sweaty acolytes and wheel-greasing fixers, I do not rush to regret how much the labor of thwarted despising has poisoned my days, derailed hours that might have been spent at least a little less pointlessly. No. My overpowering sense is rather that *I do not hate them enough*, that they have ascended beyond some event-horizon of actionable loathsomeness, and here I am stranded in the lower atmosphere, not a jet-pack in sight.

They've done a terrible thing to hate, I think. They have

transformed it into that sickliest of things, a virtuous emotion—something, I mean, that by its very nature you are now obliged to mistrust. You could hate them just for that.

Not that the poison isn't real. For a long time I have suffered what a friend once described, with caustic clarity, as the purest case of "middle-class class rage" she had ever seen. She meant I was a person who'd grown up nothing like poor—with enough people around at least for everyone to feel pretty sheltered from the harder edges of want, living inside limits that felt spacious and ordinary—but who somehow managed not to notice this outer world of people who were, by sharp contrast, rich. "Middle-class class rage": I remember the phrase because it landed with the arrow-sunk thud of hard quivering truth. This was the case before I began teaching at an expensive East Coast college, that tranquil scene of old-growth pine and solemnly maturing trusts, though polychromatically more so afterward.

But the toxicity of more recent years has done its corrosive work, effectively rotting out the tanks in which it seems I had been holding still greater quantities of churning vitriol. I started to feel the venomousness seeping into new precincts; prompts for gawping stupefaction flared on every horizon. For instance: it turns out that, if you do what I do, you'll run across a startling number of people who might casually let drop that their families own, say, a vineyard, a seaside compound, or (in one hallucinatory exchange) an island. Or not even that. The number of people who've never metered out a set of student loans, or spent an hour fretting over how to pay for a kid to go to college; who do not check every expenditure against the possibility of a parent's or sibling's or cousin's unforeseen illness; who with a crystalline innocence of irony will explain the environmental design of their oceanfront cottage, or broach the word "summer" as a verb—that number might surprise you! It surprised me. On my bad days I'd grow twitchy with the sense that the academy harbored a whole rank of people in whom there slept the mute conviction that the wrong life of our ruinous modernity *could* be lived rightly (our dour man Adorno notwithstanding), and that they had figured out how to do it. All you needed was an astounding amount of money.

"Maybe get off the socials," a friend wrote from afar, when I told him something of these splenetic interludes. A fair point. Where better to have run together, in confused seamlessness, the colossal hatefulness of bleeding-edge multibillionaire hucksters and the more garden-variety one-percentishness of people who maybe know people who know people you know? "The thing about hate," this friend said, "is it's one of the best things we've got. You don't want to go around wasting it." I had entered, it was true, into a period of profligate expenditure. Perhaps I needed a touch of what the managerial classes like to call right-sizing. Who could argue?

I took Twitter off my phone, stepped away from Facebook. I'd kiss Julie goodbye in the morning, leave her amid the clutter and teetering piles of her desk, feel a steadying inrush of rightness in the world. I'd put in my hours at the coffeeshop.

*   *   *

How do you decide *not* to do something? What are the protocols?

On an afternoon about a half-dozen years ago, under the vaulted lowland skies of a Louisiana winter, we took one of those walks that becomes a milestone, a star marked on the calendar of days. It was during our first real holiday, before we'd moved in, begun the more large-scale merger of life. A mid-December jaunt to New Orleans seemed a fine way to get in a little postsemester replenishment, submit to a lazy regime of dozing and decadence. It seemed a great place, too, to spend a few more days with our hands cupped around the flame of our eager, moony togetherness. In days like that you carry the rooms of your happiness around with you. It's hard not to want to go out touring with it, showing it the sights.

And so, in the great expanse of City Park, and then following a meandering trail through Mid-City and back toward the river, we talked about children. Not the ones I had, in my own some- what weird fashion, already. By then Julie knew, in overarticulated detail, the story of my turbulent stepparenthood, its ruptures and restorations; she knew the girls. We talked rather about the imag- inary children couples newly in love talk about, when they feel all that yearning and fidgety ardor beginning to resolve themselves toward some unspecified solidity, a durable structure that they prefer to call "the future" or "our future." These were the children that we would, or again would not, try to have, together.

A true fact about us, Julie and me, is that we had never felt es- pecially susceptible to the fevers of quasi-biological baby-longing we had watched tear, with malarial decimation, through various friend-groups. We had no special objection to it, really; just the consciousness of its failure to appear. Neither did we live in the kind of social world where kids were, if not a basic requirement to full-fledged belonging, near to it. We were people who liked going out and drinking and setting our days among crowds of friends who mostly did the same. Then, too, we were people who spent bracing amounts of time in more isolating endeavors, like reading and writing and—dear god was this true of Julie—thinking. *Julie, thinking*: even then it was clear to me that I had never known any- one who made so much, such combustive and vibrant delight, out of that ordinary procedure. Each day spent in lived-in proximity to

her mind was like being presented with this sumptuous, overspilling feast. For a long time, especially around the terrible dissolution surrounding my life with the girls, I thought the big discovery
of my middle-age was that sorrow, too, was one of the passions. In
Julie I found vivid demonstration that this unlikeliest quantity—
thinking—was as passionate an undertaking, as roiling and volatile
and luminous, as any you could name.

None of this made us ideal candidates for parenthood. Julie had no rosy misapprehensions about the toll, on women, that
children could take—bodily, psychically, let alone professionally.
For my part I tried to put into words something of my own dim
worry about the prospect of having children as a sort of rearguard
attempt to stitch up the old unclosed wounds of my stepparenthood, redeem those broken-off days at last.

We talked, listened. We walked and walked and walked.

At the end of the day, like a pair of pretend-actuaries of the yet-
to-come, we represented ourselves to one another in mock percentages. I came in around 40–60, against. Julie was around 60–
40 for, give or take. I can't say now if those numbers seem high,
given all the misgivings we had so patiently itemized. But uncertainty, argument, articulated anxiety: these were like the words
you use for the vaulted sky, the dome of chalky blue, rather than
the light itself, the settling radiance.

Mostly I remember the radiance. I remember thinking that, as
much as I liked walking with Julie, and holding her, and waking
up beside her, I liked being near her as she thought. It was like a
pathway into the secret core of who she was, or at least the first
step toward an explanation of one of the great beguiling mysteries
about her. This was simply the mystery of how someone so incan-
descently powerful-minded could at the same time possess such
an offhand talent for *pleasure*, an unfussy openness to all the sus-

taining small-bore joys of being in the world. Just that was before me in every step: the Julieness of Julie, that vaulting abundance of mind, her unrivaled talent for the daily fucking wonder of being happy.

We came to one decision, and one decision only, on that trip. I don't mean the decision to keep talking about it, though we would. I mean that we decided not to pretend there were any griefless paths laid out before us. Every choice, no matter how right, came trailing its sorrows, and no dazzling sequence of moves on the chessboard of living could change this. So it was time, we said, to put away the bright prospect of losslessness. At some unmarked point on the trajectory of our being together, we had moved beyond the need for that particular vector of fantasy, and had arrived, together, in this new place. And what was strange, what made me almost dizzy with the unexpectedness of it, is that this discovery shook through me then as a sort of bodywide thrill of gladness. I remember it made everything—the flushed sky, the flatland park, Julie with the clouds stacked up enormously behind her—shimmer with sudden aliveness. And there we were, the two of us, out in it. A star on the calendar of days.

*   *   *

Then two things happened. We moved in, got married, moved— the usual unfolding. But the world, meanwhile, moved along with us, as it does. And somewhere in the traffic between the two there came a strange reversal.

All the days with Julie nudged my numbers, those half-joked percentages, up and up and up. Whereas Julie, after a compressed season of intense grieving for one of the lives we would not live, saw hers go into a steep, a crashlike decline. The reasons for this were not obscure. At their center was nothing other than the gargantuan fact that, as Julie would sometimes put it, having a baby precisely now, at this exact moment on the long arc of human striving, seemed a favor, a kindness, to *no one at all*, with the sole possible exception of ourselves. Me, I could see myself getting right with those calculations, the New Math of planetary immolation. But Julie, as I say, is a person more scrupulous. And she is also a person more humanly averse to an activity that, under the guise of a giving selflessness, necessarily entails so, so, so much self-centered striving and seizing and repossession, so much of the unending labor of clawing back vanishing resources for *mine*, for *ours*. (Even to say this is to imagine there *are* resources to claw back, and I mean—have you seen the faces of your friends managing life with little children across these seasons of pandemic abandonment? *Have you looked into their eyes?* If so, you'll know: don't bet on it.) Julie wished neither for that seizing to be an exercise woven so entirely into the texture of days, nor, I think, for a fantasist's life, one made up of pretending this was not what we were doing when, with every piano lesson or in-class visit or Mozart-branded toy, it was fucking exactly what we would be doing.

There was a sharp sorrow in all this, Julie said, a life-sized ache she would not pretend away. But it was a slightly lesser quantity, on most days, than the contortions of spirit required to go all in, consign this as-yet purely fictive person to a life stretching into the later twenty-first century, or whatever was left of it.

And my numbers? In some ways, it's simple: the Julieness of Julie is, as I have said, most of the answer—just the ripening vision of doing this extravagant, toilsome thing alongside her, making this semiprivate galaxy, for days without end. But then too, I suppose, there was something maybe murkier, something nearer to my own deep-cut patterns and intractabilities.

Put it like this: I'm a person susceptible to a certain kind of crush, demi-addictions I tend to spiral down into. With few exceptions, these have involved records, bands, books. I dial in on a frequency and, like the lab rat in the dopamine experiment, I'm hooked. Years ago it was Thomas Pynchon, Billie Holiday. More recently, Anna Burns, Sam Lipsyte, second-trio Bill Evans. I once spent an entire New York summer inhaling the stories of Sarah Orne Jewett like they'd been razor-cut, served up on a gleaming hotel mirror. George Eliot says of one aloofish, aspiring character in *Middlemarch* that "she did not readily commit herself by admiration," and in the margins of my copy I can still find my youthful marginalia: *very much not me.*[3]

Criticism, as you know, is littered with sad case studies in over-attachment, doing its delusive work on objects that are maybe only OK, located securely on the level of *meh, sure, fine.* Have you heard people talk about *Folklore?* The latest prestige miniseries? Christopher Nolan? I encounter talk like that and think, *You really need to want it.* But the brutal thing is, I have spent a long, long time brewing up a real regard for precisely that sort of wanting. I've made a life, or a little section of life, out of its sparking magic and weird intensities. Whatever else I am, I know myself to have been a person for whom most every act of appraisal, every focusing turn of critical attention, ripens eventually toward an argument on behalf of whatever's being appraised, its subterranean power or misperceived grace. Give me an intricate thing upon which to expend a healthy quantity of scrutinizing imagination and I will give back to you something you might have reason to love.

That is at least part of what criticism, *the thing I most know how to do,* has been for me. And dear god has it left me emptyhanded— stricken, bewildered, worse—in the face of a want of such categorically different shape.

So, yes, I get it. Having a baby is almost certainly not the right choice for us, for all the reasons I've said—despoiled earth, plutocratic dominion, resource hoarding dressing itself up as saintly care, the world in 2055. I have no abstract hunger for progeny, "fatherhood," whatever. These are true statements. Yet the more I've thought and imagined and appraised, the more I've found myself on the receiving end of these strange communiqués—fevered messages that seem to come blinking in from some swarming and unsecured territory of self, an outerland alive with squabbling factions and insurgent juntas. The news from there is jumbled, confusing. But it's clear. Out there, somebody just goddamn motherfucking wants it.

*   *   *

God, that poor pregnant lady in the coffeeshop, with her puffer coat and dreamy gaze. None of this is her fault. Her watch cap didn't punch a hole in the ozone, storm the Capitol. She did not make the world.

I'll give her this, though. She did make at least a little more clear to me how it is I'd managed to turn myself, over the last few years, into a kind of armed incendiary device, ready to burst grenadelike at the least grazing provocation. Because how exactly am I *supposed* to feel about the people, the class, the whole stupid pharaohish demimonde, who preside over this world—the one whose by now all-but-foregone futurelessness has deposited me precisely here, inside this tangle of irreconcilable wishes, walking through the rooms of my days with Julie, handing back and forth to her this strange, this heavy absence? It is, I know, the tiniest, tiniest, tiniest quantity of sorrow. I think all the time of *Moby-Dick*, that unsurpassed field guide to annihilation, which cheerfully recommends you treat your griefs with a kind of laughing Solomonic judiciousness: "What does that indignity amount," Ishmael asks, "weighed, I mean, in the scales of the New Testament?"⁴ In a world of inconceivable affliction, a vastness of suffering beyond any available term or measure, what could be more preposterously small than this deliberated, chosen loss?

But then I think of Julie, for whom I would after all happily murder a mogul, or even three, and all my sanguineness is gone.

Perhaps your own passages of vengefulness are sourced by waters more unclouded, some clear-flowing brook of conviction and acute analysis. Let it be said that I don't *not* have an analysis, and given the right occasion I'd be happy to bore you with it, because I think it's true, as true as desalination and shelving ice, what the economists call "secular stagnation," and for that matter forced birth and the inexorably unfolding fascist sequence. It is no less true, I'm afraid, that mine is a loathing irreversibly mixed up with something far closer in, no larger than an apartment, a handful of northside rooms.

And you know what? That's not even the worst of it. Because inside it all, at the heart of the real humiliation, there lies a different cravenness, a cringing quite entirely my own. It is the thing that visits me at night, goading and inquisitive, speaking in its everyday voice. It just wants to know how everything might have gone if I'd only been, oh, a different person—more accomplished, more gracious, more persuasive in care, better capable of securing life against calamity. Would Julie have felt differently, wished otherwise? Would I have? Is it all maybe just another reminder of the ways I have made of myself something faltering, obscurely wrong? Something failing at the better disciplines of love?

Deep inside the motherboard, I sometimes think, there's a row of dividing switches: old grief or another cleansing jolt of despising. It's not really a choice.

*   *   *

It would please me very much to tell you these childish reveries haven't wrapped themselves up in the ruin of everything else, are not the mulch and rot out of which the many branching tangles of more legitimate feeling have managed to grow. I'd like to say I know the difference between slow-rolling world-sized cataclysm and the pathetically lesser dramas of private sorrow, and that they are everywhere clear and hard. As a critic, god knows, I'd like very much to tell you that what ghosts between me and the glittering objects of the world is just love, or fascination, or a righteous and clear-minded hate, and not some sad amalgam, a hopeless smutching mire.

Maybe, some other time, I will do just that. Maybe I'll speak to you from inside a different prospect altogether, some new-made scene hovering just over the ridgeline, out beyond the trail of these skittering, schizoid, calamity-drunk days. Until then, I will make my way to the crowded coffeeshop in the morning, kiss Julie goodbye as I go, an easy laugh in my throat, saying, "Promise you'll be here when I get back."

Acknowledgments

Early versions of many of these pieces appeared over the last decade in a range of venues: *Avidly*, the *Los Angeles Review of Books*, *Bullybloggers*, *ASAP Journal*, *Post-45*, the *Boston Review*, *Hyped on Melancholy*, *Elle*, *Public Books*, *Joni Mitchell: New Critical Readings*, *Frieze*, *The Believer*. I'm grateful for the labor and care of all the editors who toiled over first forays, fumbling revisions, misfiring drafts. Special thanks to Nicholas Dames, Dan Fox, Heidi Julavitz, and, dear god, to Sarah Blackwood, peerless interlocutor, ceaseless inspiration, friend to my heart.

This book is among other things the chronicle of several decades of conversation, so I hereby give thanks to the friends who, with grace and love and tremendous forbearance, talked through all of it. Especially saving interventions came from Kathleen Blackburn, Adrienne Brown, Frank Burroughs, Ruth Charnock, Brock Clarke, Brian Connolly, Gio Coviello, Willing Davidson, Andi Diamond, David Diamond, Beth Freeman, Michael Gillespie, Tasha Graff, Daniel Immerwahr, Dana Luciano, John Modern, Nasser Mufti, Emily Ogden, Kim O'Neil, Anne Helen Petersen, Jasbir Puar, Justin Raden, Jordy Rosenberg, Anna Sale, Kyla Schuller, Gus Stadler, Jordan Stein, Pam Thurschwell, Justin Tussing, and Sandy Zipp. For years now Elda Rotor and Chris

Parris-Lamb have provided patient, indispensable counsel. And nothing here is possible without the vision, friendship, and galvanizing acuity of Alan Thomas, whom I am proud to call my editor.

Long ago, when it mattered enormously, Mark Goble and John Dorr gave me detailed instruction in the brighter possibilities of love, and for their pains I've stolen all their best lines. My lifewide thanks to them. Similarly incalculable thanks, too—in respect to hilarity, awesomeness, profound heroisms of care—to Sophie D'Anieri and Eliza D'Anieri: surpassingly, and forever.

Finally, for mornings and for shut-in nights, for kindling brilliance and for everyday joyousness—for all of everything, and love most of all—*Is There God after Prince?* is dedicated to Julie Orlemanski.

Notes

Introduction

1. Jane Austen, *Persuasion* (New York: Penguin, 1998), 158.
2. Vladimir Nabokov, *Lolita* (New York: Vintage, 1997), 283.

Talk, Talk

1. Thomas Pynchon, *Vineland* (New York: Penguin, 1990), 18.
2. Dave Hickey, *Air Guitar* (Los Angeles: Art Issues Press, 1997), 13, 207.
3. Hickey, *Air Guitar*, 101.

Is There God after Prince?

1. Gustavus Stadler, "Case of You," at the "Critical Karaoke" panel, EMP Pop Conference, Seattle, 26 April 2014.
2. John Modern, "Vinyl Prayers: A Curatorial Introduction," in *Reverberations: New Directions in the Study of Prayer*, 19 November 2013, http://forums.ssrc.org/ndsp/2013/11/19/vinyl-prayers-a-curatorial-introduction/.

The Last Psychedelic Band

1. Paul Beatty, *Slumberland* (New York, Bloomsbury, 2008), 113–14.
2. Greg Tate, *Flyboy in the Buttermilk* (New York: Simon & Schuster, 1992), 20.

Notes

Karaoke for the People

1. George Eliot, *Middlemarch* (New York: Books, 1994), 666.

The Everyday Disaster

1. Jennifer Doyle, *Campus Sex Campus Security* (South Pasadena: Semitext(e), 2015), 51.

2. It's worth noting that this was written before Bridgers's account of having been sexually harassed by Ryan Adams came out. That news makes only more resonant the sense of her record as an account of the disasters of heterosexuality, and only more singeing the recurring lines from "Scott Street": "Do you feel ashamed / when you hear my name?"

3. Hortense Spillers, "Interstices: A Small Drama of Words," in *Black, White, and in Color: Essays on American Literature and Culture* (Chicago: University of Chicago Press, 2003), 165.

What We Fight about When We Fight about Doctor Wu

1. Michael Chabon, *Wonder Boys* (New York: Picador, 1995), 284.

2. The phrase is pick-pocketed from Philip Larkin's poem "The Old Fools," the second stanza of which begins:

> At death you break up: the bits that were you
> Start speeding away from each other for ever
> With no one to see. It's only oblivion, true:
> We had it before, but then it was going to end,
> And was all the time merging with a unique endeavour
> To bring to bloom the million-petalled flower
> Of being here.

Philip Larkin, *Collected Poems* (New York: Farrar, Straus and Giroux, 1988), 131.

Love in the Ruins

1. Jonathan Senchyne, "Working Classes" (blog), 28 July 2011, https://jsench.wordpress.com/2011/07/28/working-classes/

Notes

Circumstance

1. Elizabeth Freeman, *The Wedding Complex: Forms of Belonging in Modern American Culture* (Durham, NC: Duke University Press, 2002).

2. Eve Kosofsky Sedgwick, "Queer and Now," in *Tendencies* (Durham, NC: Duke University Press, 1993), 16.

3. Sedgwick, "Is the Rectum Straight?" in *Tendencies*, 78.

4. Michael Warner, "Queer and Then?" *Chronicle Review*, 1 January 2012, https://www.chronicle.com/article/queer-and-then/. See also Jasbir Puar, *Terrorist Assemblages: Homonationalism in Queer Times* (Durham, NC: Duke University Press, 2007).

5. Lauren Berlant, "Lauren Berlant on her book *Cruel Optimism*," interview in *Rorotoko*, 4 June 2012, rorotoko.com/interview/20120605_berlant_lauren_on_cruel_optimism.

6. "The Whitsun Weddings," in Philip Larkin, *Collected Poems* (New York: Farrar, Straus and Giroux, 1988), 94.

Joy Rounds First

1. Tom Scocca, "Derek Jeter Was OK," *Gawker*, 25 September 2014, https://www.gawker.com/derek-jeter-was-ok-1639023597

2. Roger Angell, "The Interior Stadium," in *The Summer Game* (Lincoln: University of Nebraska Press, 1972), 292. "This inner game—baseball in the mind—has no season, but it is best played in the winter, without the distraction of other baseball news. At first, it is a game of recollections, recaputurings, and visions. Figures and occasions return, enormous sounds rise and swell, and the interior stadium fills with light and yields up the sight of a young ballplayer—some hero perfectly memorized—just completing his own unique swing and now racing toward first. See the way he runs? Yes, that's him! Unmistakable, he leans in, following the distant flight of the ball with his eyes, and takes his big turn at the base. Yet this is only the beginning, for baseball in the mind is not a mere returning. . . . By thinking about baseball like this—by playing it over, keeping it warm in a cold season—we begin to make discoveries. With luck, we may even penetrate some of its mysteries" (292).

Notes

Loving John

1. John O'Hara, *Imagine Kissing Pete*, in *Collected Stories of John O'Hara*, ed. Frank McShane (New York: Random House, 1984), 138–39.

2. Laura Kipnis, "Adultery," *Critical Inquiry*, "Intimacy" special issue, 24, no. 2 (1998): 289–327, 322.

3. G. Stanley Hall, *Adolescence: Its Psychology and Its Relations to Physiology, Anthropology, Sociology, Sex, Crime, Religion, and Education* (New York: D. Appleton & Co., 1904), 60. Before these sentences he writes, "They are abandoned to joy, grief, passion, fear, and rage. They are bashful, show off, weep, laugh, desire, are curious, eager, regret, swell with passion, not knowing that these last two are especially outlawed by our guild."

4. John Darnielle, *Last Plane to Jakarta* 6 (2001): 11. This is the last print edition of Darnielle's 'zine; it would relocate to http://www.lastplane tojakarta.com/.

5. From the conclusion to Larkin's poem "Sad Steps":

> One shivers slightly, looking up there.
> The hardness and the brightness and the plain
> Far-reaching singleness of that wide stare
>
> Is a reminder of the strength and pain
> Of being young; that it can't come again,
> But is for others undiminished somewhere.

See Phillip Larkin, *Collected Poems*, ed. Anthony Thwaite (New York: Farrar, Straus, and Giroux, 1988), 144.

6. Darnielle, *Last Plane to Jakarta* 6 (2001): 30–31.

7. Darnielle, *Last Plane to Jakarta* 6 (2001): 15.

Easy

1. Jennifer L. Fleissner, "The Song That Gets Stuck in Your Head," paper presented at the Post45 conference, Cleveland, Ohio, April 2011.

Notes

Our Noise

1. Joshua Clover, "Concern Trolls, Speechbros, and the Free-Speech Fraud," *The Nation*, 17 December 2015, https://www.thenation.com/article /archive/speechbros-concern-trolls-and-the-free-speech-fraud/

Ghost Stories

1. Philip Roth, *The Human Stain* (New York: Vintage, 2000), 209.

Rhapsody for the Crash Years

1. Hortense Spillers, "Interstices: A Small Drama of Words," in *Black, White, and in Color: Essays on American Literature and Culture* (Chicago: University of Chicago Press, 2003), 166, 165.

So-Called Normal People

1. See especially the "Reading Sally Rooney" cluster in *Post-45*, edited by Gloria Fisk, https://post45.org/sections/contemporaries-essays/reading -sally-rooney/.

Say Chi City

1. Liesl Olson, *Chicago Renaissance: Literature and Art in the Midwest Metropolis* (New Haven, CT: Yale University Press, 2017), 29–30.
2. Walton's "Gwendolyn Brooks" first appeared in the *New Yorker*, December 18, 2000.

Our Man in the Fifteenth

1. David Brooks, "How Moderates Failed Black America," *New York Times*, 18 June 2020, A27.
2. Adam Creighton, "Want to study Foucault? Don't expect a cent," *The Australian*, 19 June 2020, https://www.theaustralian.com.au/commentary /uni-fee-shakeup-explosion-of-degrees-has-sapped-their-value/news -story/86cee36cb7a65ddc1e79a4dbf2ceaaff.

Notes

3. Behrooz Ghamari-Tabrizi, *Foucault in Iran: Islamic Revolution after the Enlightenment* (Minneapolis: University of Minnesota Press, 2016), 5.

4. Ghamari-Tabrizi, *Foucault in Iran*, 6, 17.

5. See, for instance, Joshua Clover's sharp rebuke to Latour in *Critical Inquiry*, in "The Rise and Fall of Biopolitics: A Response to Bruno Latour," 29 March 2020, https://critinq.wordpress.com/2020/03/29/the-rise-and -fall-of-biopolitics-a-response-to-bruno-latour/. On Latourian derealizations of political conflict, see also Jordy Rosenberg, "The Molecularization of Sexuality: On Some Primitivisms of the Present," *Theory & Event* 17, no. 2 (2014).

6. Jasbir Puar, *The Right to Maim: Debility, Capacity, Disability* (Durham, NC: Duke University Press, 2017).

Hollow

1. Henry James, *The Portrait of a Lady* (London: Dent, 1983), 281. The phrase, which comes early in chapter 28, appears in the New York Edition, of 1907–1909.

2. See especially John Hollander's 1981 *Rhyme's Reason: A Guide to English Verse* (New Haven, CT: Yale University Press, 2001) and Josephine Miles's 1957 *Eras and Modes in English Poetry* (Westport, CT: Greenwood Press, 1976). On "small and local movements" of style as a register of the distinctiveness of a given writer's disposition, see Mary Kinzie, *The Cure of Poetry in An Age of Prose: Moral Essays on the Poet's Calling* (Chicago: University of Chicago Press, 1993), xii–xiii.

3. Thurschwell writes, "But then, as the verse finishes, he ruins it all by mansplaining enlightenment, and she leaves." See "'Here's a Man and a Woman Sitting on a Rock': Joni Mitchell, Margaret Atwood, and Irritable Feminism," in *Joni Mitchell: New Critical Readings*, ed. Ruth Charnock (London: Bloomsbury, 2019), 167–83, 178. So much of what I have to say about Mitchell, her impatience with the idioms of "freedom" that surround her, and her ties to Paula Fox, is indebted to Thurschwell's bravura reading.

4. This line, "the heart moves roomier," closes A. R. Ammons's poem "The City Limits." See Ammons, *The Selected Poems: Expanded Edition* (New York: Norton, 1986), 89.

5. Paula Fox, *Desperate Characters* (New York: Norton, 1999), 25.

Notes

6. Fox, *Desperate Characters*, 60.

7. Fox, *Desperate Characters*, 85.

8. Fox, *Desperate Characters*, 80.

9. Fox, *Desperate Characters*, 39.

10. Fox, *Desperate Characters*, 185.

11. Quoted in Malka Marom, *Joni Mitchell: In Her Own Words; Conversations with Malka Marom* (Toronto: ECW Press, 2014), 62. It is here, too, that Mitchell narrates her own chronicled experiments in blackface (as on the cover of *Don Juan's Reckless Daughter*, from 1977). See especially 206–12.

My Thoughts Are Murder

1. W. H. Auden, "September 1, 1939," in *Selected Poems*, ed. Edward Mendelson (New York: Vintage, 1989), 86.

2. Henry David Thoreau, "Slavery in Massachusetts," in *Collected Essays & Poems*, ed. Elizabeth Hall Witherell (New York: Library of America, 2001).

Mercy Hours

1. Edward St. Aubyn, *Some Hope*, in *The Patrick Melrose Novels* (New York: Picador, 2012), 366.

2. St. Aubyn, *Some Hope*, 368.

3. St. Aubyn, *Some Hope*, 301.

In the Maze

1. Much of what I think about *The Shining* comes from having had the chance to teach it, over several years, in a course called "The Queer Child." Four students in particular—Luca Cowles, K. B. Kinkel, Linda Kinstler, and Mikel McCavana—shaped my understanding of the film in indelible ways.

2. Michel Foucault, *"Society Must Be Defended": Lectures at the Collége de France, 1975–76*, ed. Mauro Bertani and Alessandro Fontana, trans. David Macey (New York: Picador, 2003), 260.

3. Giovanni Arrighi, *The Long Twentieth Century: Money, Power, and the Origins of Our Times* (1994; London: Verso, 2010), 384.

Notes

4. Quoted in Sam Dean, "Mike Davis Is Still a Damn Good Storyteller," *Los Angeles Times*, 5 July 2022, https://www.latimes.com/lifestyle/image/story/2022-07-25/mike-davis-reflects-on-life-activism-climate-change-bernie-sanders-aoc-los-angeles-politics.

5. Sándor Ferenczi, "Confusion of Tongues between Adults and the Child," trans. Jeffrey M. Masson and Marianne Loring, in Masson, *The Assault on Truth: Freud's Suppression of the Seduction Theory* (New York: Farrar, Straus, and Giroux, 1984), 283–95, 290.

6. Ferenczi, "Confusion of Tongues," 288.

7. Brian Connolly, "A Comet Is Not a Metaphor," *Avidly*, 26 January 2022, https://avidly.lareviewofbooks.org/2022/01/26/a-comet-is-not-a-metaphor/.

Anthony and Carmela Get Vaccinated

1. Robert Pinsky, "The Night Game," in *The Want Bone* (New York: Ecco Press, 1990), 55.

Exit Wounds

1. Thomas Pynchon, *Vineland* (New York: Vintage, 1990), 63.

2. Sam Lipsyte, *The Ask* (New York: Picador, 2010), 28.

3. George Eliot, *Middlemarch* (New York: Penguin, 1994), 271.

4. Herman Melville, *Moby-Dick; or, The Whale* (New York: Penguin, 1992), 6.

Index

Index

Index

Index